Star Pieces

DAVID LINLEY

CHARLES CATOR

HELEN CHISLETT

Star Pieces

The Enduring Beauty
of Spectacular Furniture

The Monacelli Press

Contents

HALF-TITLE PAGE A George III giltwood sofa designed by Robert Adam and made by Thomas Chippendale, c. 1765.

FRONTISPIECE TOP ROW, LEFT TO RIGHT Breakfront bookcase supplied by Thomas Chippendale to the 5th Earl of Dumfries, 1759; Louis XIV ormolu-mounted torchère by André-Charles Boulle; Chinese export lacquered side chair, c. 1730. MIDDLE ROW, LEFT TO RIGHT Anglo-Indian chair in solid ivory, 18th century; solid aluminium table by Zaha Hadid, 2008; burr elm table by Danny Lane, 2005. BOTTOM ROW, LEFT TO RIGHT 'Impression' chair by Julian Mayor, 2002; 'Stingray' surface by Based Upon, 2007; 'L'Armoire' by Tord Boontje for Meta, 2008.

OPPOSITE ABOVE The 'Swoop' low chair by Pottinger & Cole, 2008. CENTRE Two views of a Louis XVI ormolu-mounted Chinese lacquer commode attributed to Pierre Garnier, c. 1760. BOTTOM 'Bowline' table base by Danny Lane, 2006.

First published simultaneously in 2009 in the United Kingdom by Thames & Hudson, Ltd., London and by The Monacelli Press, a division of Random House, Inc., New York.

Library of Congress Cataloging-in-Publication Data
Linley, David, 1961–
Star pieces : the enduring beauty of spectacular furniture / David Linley, Charles Cator, Helen Chislett.

Includes index.
ISBN 978-1-58093-259-2 (hardcover)
1. Furniture. I. Cator, Charles. II. Chislett, Helen. III. Title.
NK2231.L56 S73 2009
749—dc22   2009018842

Printed and bound in China

10 9 8 7 6 5 4 3 2 1

Designed by Niki Medlik

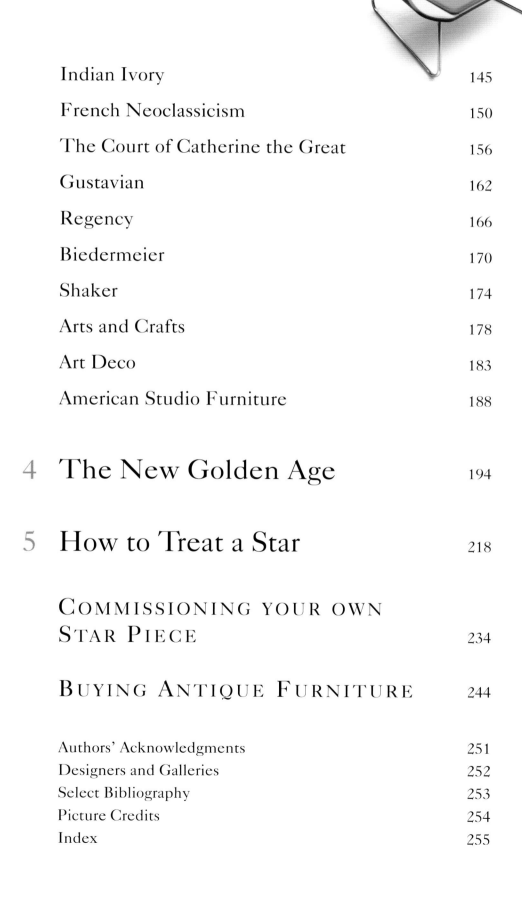

BELOW The humidor that David Linley made for his
grandmother, Queen Elizabeth, when a schoolboy
at Bedales.

A PASSION FOR FURNITURE

David Linley

When someone says to me, could you have chosen
something to do other than furniture, I say no.
Why? Because it is the most difficult world in the
most difficult medium for the lowest amount of
profit – in a nutshell, it appeals to my perverse
nature. My personal motto is Always Do The
Difficult Thing. What else could have given me
so much pleasure by being so difficult?

Furniture also brings together two passions
in my life: mechanics and materials. From the
time when I was very young, I loved taking things
apart – my Go Kart, bicycle, and, when I was older,
my motorbike and MG sports car. Even now, I go
on a motorbiking holiday each year with a group
of friends from Parnham College, and instead of
riding sleek, reliable, modern machines, we use a
motley collection of vintage bikes. The point is that
one at least is bound to break down and part of the
fun is waiting to see which one it will be and then
having the joy of taking it apart and putting it back
together again. Of course this is probably not
everyone's idea of a great holiday, but for us it
becomes part of folklore.

My favourite visits as a boy were to the
Science Museum in London, because everything
from the power of steam locomotives to the fine-
tuning of scientific instruments resonated with me.
Inanimate objects over which you have full control,
can find out how they work, how they were made
and what they were made with, give huge pleasure.

This pleasure is something I share with my father –
a man who is known worldwide for his photography,
but who is also a great maker of buildings, of objects
and of furniture.

At school, Bedales, in Hampshire, there was
no mechanics teacher, but I did have a fantastic form
tutor, Mr Butcher, who was also a furniture designer.
To begin with, I was interested purely in the making
side – in effect taking principles of mechanics into
a different material: wood. It was he who first taught
me complicated joinery techniques, such as secret
mitred dovetails. I was absolutely fascinated by the
precision needed: if one-sixth of a joint is wrong,

RIGHT Two details of the 'Helix'
dining table of 2004 by Linley –
the bespoke furniture company that
David Linley founded in 1985 – in
Santos rosewood and walnut, with
hidden drawers.

BELOW A 'Classic' pedestal desk by
Linley, in sycamore with rosewood
stringing and burr ash inlay, 1990.

it will put out every other joint. The first object
I made there, of which I was really proud, was a
humidor – essentially a box for the storing of cigars –
which had those same secret mitred dovetail joints.
If you looked inside, you could see only plain sides
apparently held together by magic. I gave it to my
grandmother, Queen Elizabeth, knowing she would
appreciate the beauty of something that you cannot
see, but know is there. Every day, that box was used
at Clarence House to offer guests cigars, not because
most people smoke cigars, but because she liked
them to admire the technique. This was the also
the piece I took with me for my interview at
Parnham College (see p. 216). John Makepeace said
to me, 'Why bother to make something that no-one
else will ever see? They don't know how the box is
constructed – they just have to take your word for it.'
There was only one answer I could possibly give:

'Because *I* know it is there.' Thankfully, he seemed
to like that and I was accepted to study at Parnham.

However, my love of furniture did not stop with
the mechanics of it. Mastering those was one thing,
but I also discovered within myself a real love of wood.
It is such a warm material: emotional, characterful and
tactile. I began to want to know more about it – what
the various timbers were, where they came from, and
how they could be engineered into furniture. I had
always been taught to appreciate beautiful objects, but
I took that appreciation to the engineering side of my
brain and began to focus on how to achieve a beautiful
object that has also been beautifully made. Whereas
a love of mechanics is something that unites my father
and me, my obsession with a piece being perfectly
executed is not something I inherited from his side
of the family. Like my great-uncle, the late Oliver
Messel, theatre designer, my father is essentially

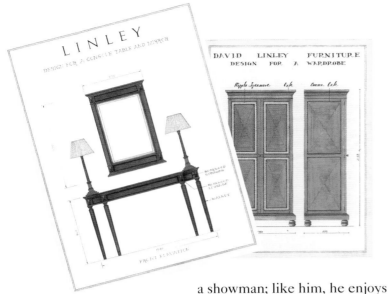

Watercolour sketches showing furniture made on commission by Linley.

a showman; like him, he enjoys creating objects that are beautiful when seen from a distance, but that may in reality be roughly hewn. For the purposes of a stage set, you could create a blue-and-white vase that looks like porcelain but is in fact papier-mâché. Would that matter to my father? No. His way of making things is to listen and to look, and then to create his own interpretation very quickly. Would it matter to me? Yes, passionately. I would want it to be not only porcelain, but also 18th-century, and Japanese. This is not because I am bothered by the monetary value of something: it is simply because I want to know that something is not only beautiful on its surface, but beautiful to its core.

There is a further strand to furniture design, which also enthrals me: ornamentation. Woods combine, for example, into wonderful marquetry, parquetry and banding. But it doesn't end there: you can use gilding, leatherwork, mother-of-pearl, porcelain and other embellishments to add layers of beauty to the surface of a piece of furniture. I love jewelry, so this stage of design offers up all kinds of possibilities that give me deep satisfaction. It is not enough that something is beautifully made out of a wonderful timber: it has to be finished to perfection as well. I remember my grandmother showing me an ebony cabinet, bas-relief carved, which made a deep impression on me. It had allegorical stories all around, which would have been so much easier to inlay in marquetry, but someone had taken the time and trouble not only to carve them, but to carve them in relief. It appealed to me because it was the opposite of taking the easy route. I could see the point of it entirely. There is so much about pleasure which is subtle, and sometimes you only find that pleasure by slowing down a bit.

On one level the challenge of making furniture is finding the best design solution for the brief. The mechanics of how you do that are obviously critical, but first you have to solve it intellectually. However, for me that will never be the whole story. I think of it as a triangle – inspiration, mechanics and materials. It is the fact that you need all three to be successful in creating a piece of fine furniture that keeps me fascinated.

I also have a perverse streak, which has fuelled my professional life. We live in an age where everything is apparently transitory: you buy a car and replace it a year later. The same goes for virtually all electrical appliances. Fashions are over before they begin, not only in clothes but also in interiors. It is the norm to buy a piece of furniture and put it on a skip after five years or so. Few things are now made to last, and apparently we don't want them to anyway. All my working life I have been out of kilter with this feeling. Of course it makes perfect business sense to produce something with a limited shelf life, so that people throw it away and come back to buy something else. However, ever since I began making furniture at school, I have wanted to make things to last. It isn't enough to make a fantastic chair: I want to know what it is about the construction of that chair that will endure. Or a table or a bookcase or a desk . . .

When I was at college, we were always trying to break the rules. We wanted to push the boundaries out, find ways of incorporating new materials, or come up with brave new designs. I remember designing an architect's table that opened in a particularly clever way and thinking I was a total genius. When I discovered that in fact 'my' design had been around two hundred years ago, I began to learn one of the most crucial lessons for any furniture designer: *if you want to move forward, you must first look backwards*. If you don't understand history, you are wasting your time. The roots of great furniture design go down a long way. The trick is in understanding what has gone before and keeping that line going forward.

BELOW A late Louis XV Japanese black lacquer and ebony commode sold to the Marquis de Marigny by Joseph Baumhauer in 1766 and later owned by the Rothschilds.

Charles Cator

The wonderful thing about furniture is that, like us, it is on a journey through life. If you buy something that is one or two hundred years old, you are buying into a piece of human history – not just the people who have used it, but those who made it in the first place. We engage with furniture in a very physical way. Furniture is rooted in natural, earthy things and on some subliminal level it is in touch with our souls. It does not need to have secret meanings explained in the way fine art might. You do not have to have someone else telling you what is good and what is not. You can use your own eyes and trust your own instincts. With pictures, there is a sense of the divine settling down on the artist. With furniture, you sense the hand of man – the craftsman who brought it into being.

Provenance, whereby you can trace the history of a piece of furniture right back to its creation, is always of interest to those who collect furniture, but is not necessarily so important to those who want to use it simply for its decorative qualities. I have always been fascinated by collections and collecting and regard provenance as part of the fun. One of the first pieces of furniture that really inspired me was a superb French commode we sold in 1975, when I had been working at Christie's for less than two years. It was a late Louis XV piece made for the Marquis de Marigny, the brother of Madame de Pompadour. He was a great proponent of Neoclassical taste (see pp. 150–52) and this was a very noble example. It had later belonged to the Rothschilds, so it had further interest because of that. The house a piece of furniture comes from, the family who commissioned it, the individuals who have shared its life – for me, this adds immeasurably to the enjoyment.

On another level, it can be something as simple as the curve of a leg or the figuring of a piece of wood that gives a jolt of pleasure. Furniture does not have to be grand to be admired: plain mid-Georgian furniture endures because of its absolute simplicity. Proportions, line and timber can look as modern today as when a piece was first created.

    I arrived at furniture by accident, not design. Having studied History of Art at Bristol University, I came to Christie's for an interview and to my great surprise was offered a trainee position. It was a baptism of fire. The front desk was the realm of a man called Mr Leadbeater, who ran it like an army sergeant-major. In those days it was not unusual for people to walk in off the street wanting something valued. We juniors were clustered behind Mr Leadbeater, ready to take such items for valuation by an expert – usually some short-tempered, over-worked person trying to write a catalogue. It was our job to translate the verdict of 'This is complete rubbish' into something more palatable, such as 'This is very interesting, but sadly has little commercial value.' The next move from the front desk was the shipping department. It was not my happiest time, and after a few months I began to worry that I would be there for ever. In 1975 the opening of Christie's South Kensington meant some changes at King Street and I was offered a job in the furniture department there, working for Anthony Coleridge, an expert on Chippendale among other cabinetmakers, and Hugh Roberts – now Director of the Royal Collection. It was like taking a crash course in furniture. By accompanying Hugh to houses all over Britain where there was furniture to be valued, I learnt an incredible amount very fast. I became particularly interested in both English and French furniture, and also in the collecting of French furniture in England. I may know a great deal more than I did then, but I never feel I totally know the subject through and through. There is still so much to discover.

A George III mahogany commode attributed to Thomas Chippendale, almost certainly supplied to Sir Rowland Winn, Bt, for his London house in St James's Square *c.* 1766. In the 20th century it belonged to the great collector of English furniture Samuel Messer.

Furniture collecting also appeals to the detective within me. In France, family archives were scattered because of the Revolution. The extraordinary thing about England is that so many archives survive intact. You can often know for sure not only that something was made by Chippendale, for example, but when it was made, for whom and how much it cost originally. In France, furniture is usually stamped, so you know the maker, but you do not necessarily know who it was made for or the details of its history. It is thrilling when something turns up out of the blue and you can fit it into the jigsaw. I love the fact that even in two hundred years' time, a researcher may be burrowing away and make sense of the provenance of a piece. Furniture connects us through the centuries.

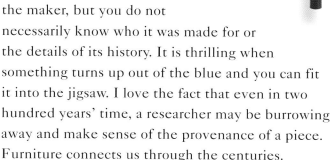

I have a personal interest in both contemporary art and contemporary design, but if I have one complaint about modern furniture en masse it is that it is sometimes so bland. So often it is not designed to have any presence at all. Yet furniture with presence is an important design ingredient within interiors, whether it be the madness of Memphis, the iconic form of the 'Barcelona Chair', or, looking to the past, the wow factor of a maker such as George Bullock [26]: Bullock was active in the early 19th century, but his work has struck a chord with many contemporary architects and designers. It is fascinating to see how designers of boutique hotels, for example, rework what in another context would be considered old-fashioned designs to create interiors that guests read as contemporary, without perhaps understanding the origins of the designs.

I like to think of furniture as an old friend, with whom you share your life in a very intimate way. It brings so much pleasure in the way it looks, the way it feels, the way it engages with our desire for often hand-made objects in an array of pleasing materials. Furniture is a living thing in that sense. It is time to give it the respect and appreciation it deserves.

A George II mahogany Pembroke table, *c.* 1745, from the Simon Sainsbury collection, which exemplifies the restrained quality of the best mid-Georgian furniture: it is neat, deceptively simple, and made of beautifully figured timber.

A George I gilt-gesso open armchair, one of a pair attributed to James Moore, of very sculptural form. It is upholstered in original silk velvet floral damask.

1

Why Furniture Matters

Why Furniture Matters

Furniture is the backdrop against which we live our lives. We sleep on it, sit on it, eat from it and work at it. It may be inanimate, and yet we have an intensely personal relationship with it. In form, it is the man-made object closest to us, boasting arms, legs, feet and backs. In construction it reveals not only the hand of the maker, but gives glimpses of the soul too. Great furniture is an expression of intellect, artisan skill and personal philosophy. It tells us something not only about changing decorative styles, but about what forces lay at the heart of such changes. Furniture is a barometer of social status, not just of the past but of today as well. Once you begin to understand the significance of furniture, it is hard not to agree with the architect Peter Smithson's thought-provoking dictum: 'When we design a chair, we make a society and city in miniature.'

Furniture connects us to history, to iconic men and women, to unsung craftsmen, to departed loved ones, and to far-flung places around the globe. The paradox is that, perhaps because we are so closely linked to it both physically and historically, few of us pay it the regard it deserves. The phrase 'just part of the furniture' is a metaphor for the unimportant, the undervalued, the invisible. It also reflects perhaps how furniture is 'family', something that is always there, always to be relied upon, missed only when suddenly absent through theft, accident, or the unyielding dimensions of a new home.

So why does furniture matter? Because through its design, its craftsmanship, the memories it holds and the way we engage with it on a very personal level, it can add a further dimension of enjoyment to our daily lives. While it is true that not all furniture can claim to be a star piece, the fact is that when it comes to the design of our homes, furniture is the real star of the show.

Furniture and us

The way we respond to furniture is informed by four of our senses. First, we appreciate the way it looks – the curve of a leg, the height of a back.

Touch is the main way we show appreciation of furniture. Often without thinking, we run our fingers over the material of which it is constructed, be it carved wood from several centuries ago or a sculptural piece of glass today. We particularly revel in upholstery, invited to sit down on wonderfully

ABOVE LEFT A fur-clad low armchair by Jean Royère, 1955.

ABOVE 'Peony' in cut cowhide by Helen Amy Murray shown on a contemporary tub chair, 2008.

tactile velvet, silk, linen or leather by restaurants and hotels who understand our need for sensory comfort.

We can even enjoy the sound – or absence of sound – that furniture offers. Makers of top-quality kitchen and bedroom furniture vie with each other to produce the most silent drawer and cupboard openings, challenging customers to listen patiently for the sound of . . . nothing. But for some of us, the click of a much-loved dresser door or the creak of a sofa moulded to our body shape and weight are as comforting as our favourite books and shoes.

Then of course there is smell. Wise owners of antique shops spend considerable time polishing their wares with old-fashioned beeswax, because it is so seductive to the noses of potential customers. This is particularly true if you have memories of a grandparent or parent's home filled with the smell of newly polished furniture. But individual pieces of furniture can themselves have very distinctive smells, which add to our sensory experience. Our relationship with our furniture is in fact a cocktail of sight, touch, sound, and smell.

Furniture is also very close to us because of the way it echoes our bodies. In time, beds, sofas and chairs will all carry an imprint of the people who use them. We talk of 'breaking in' new pieces, because they can never be as comfortable immediately as the things to which we are used. New furniture can need breaking in visually as well: it may look too big and cumbersome for the space at first, and you have to

allow time for it to 'settle'. What this really means is that you have to adapt to having this new companion in your home.

Chairs sustain a far greater physical and psychological relationship with us than any other piece of furniture. They even look rather like us. It is for this reason that the artist Rolf Sachs often uses chairs as a metaphor for human relationships in his work. Since the beginning of civilization, humans have required something to sit upon – but not all chairs, or people, are equal. It is not difficult to imagine that sitting on a throne is an experience quite different from that of sitting on the same mass-produced 'functional' chair that everyone in a particular workplace sits upon. Indeed, as a symbolic object the chair has few equals. Chairs send out clear messages about their occupiers – their status in the family or the workplace, how much that status matters to them, what they expect your reaction to be. Sit in a chair designed to indicate power and it is surprising how powerful you do feel. But chairs can also have negative connotations – the dentist's chair, the hospital waiting-room chair, not to mention the nightmarish electric chair. These are chairs that reflect our darker fears, a far cry from the rocking chair, the child's high chair, or the love seat.

LEFT AND BELOW An old school desk was used by Based Upon in London in 2005 as a focus for childhood memories: coated in liquid metal, it takes on new relevance and beauty.

OPPOSITE For Rolf Sachs, chairs represent an entire vocabulary of community, companionship and conversation. The unprepossessing school chair is reborn in materials such as cast resin, creating an object both familiar and unfamiliar – here 'No rest for the rust' and 'Can't sit still', both of 2006.

Furniture is woven through every aspect of our lives from cradle to grave. It is our constant companion, an intimate expression of our achievements, ambitions and values. No wonder then that people talk of 'loving' particular pieces of furniture: they are the friends in life that demand nothing from us in return.

Furniture and memories

At home, family members often have a chair which they perceive to be 'theirs', and it can be an awkward moment when a new visitor unwittingly takes the seat that is reserved for the most senior member of the family. When the family sit down to dine, each tends to go to 'his' or 'her' place, where they habitually eat. When we go to bed – our most territorial of furniture pieces – there is no question of deciding on a whim that we would prefer someone else's bed to our own or even swapping which side we sleep on. We take all these things for granted, and yet they show how strong and deep our relationships are with our furniture. A cushion, a fork or a pillow

are not going to engender the same feelings of ownership and reassuring comfort as the chair, the table or the bed.

Just as furniture builds up a patina over time, the surface's expression of its life, so it builds up a patina of memories. Occasionally the two become enmeshed together: a school desk, for example, often carries on its scratched and battered surface the messages, jokes, thoughts and longings of those who have occupied it. Indeed, redundant vintage school desks are snapped up quickly when sold, precisely because people want this link back to the past and their own schooldays. It might not be the same desk, but it will fill that nostalgic need.

Nostalgia and familiarity are powerful emotions when it comes to our relationship with furniture. That is why pieces inherited from friends and family are so treasured – not so much for their monetary value, but for what they represent. The table that still carries the impressions of your own childish handwriting, the chair where your grandmother liked to sit and knit, the desk where

your father kept his most important documents – these have an emotional significance that few other people in the world would or could understand. When such things come into your own possession, you are reminded in the best way possible of the person who handed them down to you and of the memories that you shared.

New furniture comes with no such emotional baggage, but it too will build up a patina of memories over time. When you choose a piece of furniture, you should make the decision on more than purely functional questions of dimension and budget. Furniture is not the sort of item you should buy on impulse or as a merely temporary solution. Ideally, you should regard it as a new addition to your life and your home, which should 'speak' to you on some level. There should be something about it that makes you feel comfortable with the fact that it could be with you for a long time, if not for ever. The moment of purchase is no different from buying a piece of art or a bespoke garment: it is not the end, but rather the beginning of an enduring relationship.

It might sound fanciful, but furniture you love does reflect your own personality and soul. Just as inherited pieces link you to previous generations, so the furniture you choose can tie you to the next generation, who may imprint their own memories of you, metaphorically speaking, onto its surface. A few designers today have begun to explore this link between furniture and memory in exciting and creative ways. The young London design atelier Based Upon, for example, produces bespoke 'legacy' pieces, which are made not so much *for* clients as *with* them [*opposite*]. As much emphasis is placed on the emotional value of a piece as on its market value. A table surface, for example, may incorporate actual mementoes of family history, from handprints, souvenirs and letters to photographs, jewelry, and even locks of hair. It is a way of connecting clients creatively to the things that matter most to them.

As for the surface patina, treasure that as well. Furniture is not supposed to stay as pristine and unmarked as the day it was delivered. It is made for people – people are not made for furniture. So do

not be too precious about the things you own. Accept that they will take a few knocks and scratches, spills and stains: each tells a story that relates to your own life, so regard these 'imperfections' with humour and good nature. That does not mean you should be neglectful, but rather that you should take good care of the furniture you have, mindful of the fact that it will probably outlive you, and accept that its history and your own will be very closely entwined.

Furniture and makers

Just as furniture is expressive of the people we are, so it also tells us a great deal about the people who designed or made it. You may be fortunate enough to own a piece of furniture with documentation to show when it was bought, by whom, from whom, and for what price. This connects you to a slice of history in a very direct and personal way. However, you can feel just as closely connected through antique pieces of no particular provenance. You may never know the name of the maker, but if you run your hands over the carving of the wood or take

ABOVE The 'Wooden' chair designed by Marc Newson for Cappellini in 1992. Made of bent natural beech heartwood, it is both comfortable and eye-catching.

RIGHT A Louis XV ormolu-mounted tulipwood, kingwood and bois de bout marquetry table en chiffonnière bearing the stamp of the great *ébéniste* BVRB – Bernard II van Risenburgh (see pp. 129–31).

time to appreciate the fineness of the dovetail joints, you can still feel enormously privileged to own something that so clearly shows the hand of the maker. If it has already lasted for a hundred years or more, then the chances are that the person who made it had worked hard at their craft. The chances are they loved what they did, too – there have always been easier ways to acquire money than through furniture-making – so a little bit of their essence went into creating the piece that now stands in your home. In some way, they live on through the furniture they left behind.

It is no different when it comes to 20th- or 21st-century furniture made by the iconic designers of the day. Furniture for them is often as much about expressing their personal philosophy as fulfilling functional needs. It states clearly the sort of society a designer envisages, without him or her having to say a great deal else. Whether it is the Paimio chair, No. 41, of 1932/33 by Alvar Aalto, with its bent laminated birch frame, or the hand-forged

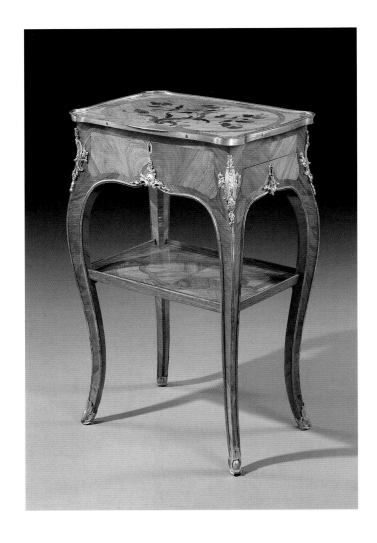

'La Chaise', a Charles and Ray Eames prototype, 1948 (reissued), juxtaposed with a spiral sculpture by British designer Tom Dixon. Even the cast-iron radiator behind becomes part of the tableau.

'Spine' chair of 1988 by André Dubreuil (b. 1951), this is furniture that speaks eloquently of its creators' personalities. As the rage for design-art pieces gathers speed today, this is as true as ever. Big hitters such as Marc Newson (b. 1963), an Australian designer (formerly of jewelry) based in London and Paris [*opposite, 30, 31, 39, 44, 187, 198*], and Tel Aviv-born visionary Ron Arad (b. 1951) [*37, 49, 196–97, 225*] offer a cohesive and seductive vision of the world in which they would like to live, articulated at times in revolutionary forms. The furniture of the Iraqi-born British architect Zaha Hadid (b. 1950), for example, undulates, bends and curves in a way that is unusual, to say the least, for tables and shelves [*21, 46*].

The gap is narrowing between designers and craftsmen, the former increasingly interested in harnessing the technical expertise of the latter to produce limited-edition series or one-off creations. While mass production will always have its market, it seems that we are hankering once more after the unique, the hand-crafted, and the truly individual.

It stands to reason, therefore, that if you are in a position to do so, there is no better way of acquiring a piece of furniture than to have it made for you by a master craftsman whose work you admire (see pp. 234–42). At its best, commissioning is a journey that you and the maker go on together, a fascinating conversation over many months that explores all the different possibilities, but eventually settles on the one perfect solution. Make time to be involved every step of the way: you can even go to see the raw materials being chosen, or drop by the workshop to see the piece taking shape. Don't be vague about what you require: be as exact as you can be, because this is furniture that is made by you as much as the person physically creating it. Not only does the commissioning process allow you to have the furniture you desire, right down to special requests for secret drawers or sumptuous drawer linings, but you can be sure that it is absolutely unique. A bespoke piece of furniture can be as individual as you like, whether through the clever integration of personal mottoes or symbols or through the way it is contoured to fit your own body. But that is not all. This is also a piece of furniture that the maker will love, and you will see his or her hand in every line and joint. It takes years to develop the skill that a great piece of furniture requires, so you can be sure this is someone who has spent a long time learning the craft, not for money but for love. The furniture that you create together will carry a piece of both of your souls – a truly unique collaboration that nobody else could have achieved.

Furniture as an expression of status

In our modern society, we tend to regard the *function* of furniture as the most important of its qualities. Most of it is designed to fulfil a specific purpose within a specific budget. It is easy to forget that for centuries designers and makers of furniture had no such constraints – far from it, in fact. Royalty, nobility and wealthy merchants commissioned furniture less for practical use than as a way to display wealth, prestige, intellect and taste. It was also a means whereby the status of a province or country could be displayed to visiting dignitaries, a powerful tool with which to further commerce by showing the technical expertise, luxurious materials and aesthetic judgment that were available to commission.

Furniture was seen as a form of artistic expression, with the *ébénistes* of Paris being the most highly paid artists of the day. In the last quarter of the 18th century, few paintings would have commanded a price as high as £1,000. Yet when Madame du Barry, last mistress of Louis XV, purchased a commode mounted with Sèvres porcelain plaques [*below*], the cost was in excess of £3,000. Furniture was seen as a standard of the fashionable world, one that was vital to the maintenance of social prestige.

The importance of furniture can also be seen in the mass of documentation that still survives in the great country houses of England. As well as providing an invaluable record for scholars of furniture history, this is also an indication of how highly furniture was prized – often as much as, if not more than, possessions such as paintings, sculpture and fine textiles. It was taken for granted that furniture added immeasurably to the value of the estate in total.

Even in more modest homes, furniture was something that was treated with pride. It may have been made by a local carpenter rather than one of the great cabinetmakers of the day, but it was no less valued for that. Furniture was not taken for granted, but regarded as an asset and a piece of good fortune. It was handed down through generations not so much from nostalgia, but as something of real worth. Brides' dowries often listed furniture that the wife-to-be would provide to her new husband's home – an important bargaining chip, as it could well elevate a family's status.

While fine furniture was still sought-after in the late 19th and early 20th centuries, there was a sea change underway. By the mid-20th century, many designers had focused their attention on how

BELOW A late Louis XV commode mounted with Sèvres porcelain plaques commissioned by the *marchand-mercier* Poirier and attributed to Martin Carlin, supplied to Madame du Barry in 1772 at Versailles.

OPPOSITE A table by Zaha Hadid, commissioned by Hauser and Wirth to display small sculptures, 2008. The newest automative techniques were used to whittle solid blocks of aluminium into legs and tops, which were then hand-polished, welded and polished again to create a single, seamless piece.

to produce 'functional' furniture for the masses, devised to furnish limited spaces as ingeniously as possible, with efficiency of living as the aim. Generally speaking, furniture began to lose its reputation as a status symbol, replaced by art, cars, travel, clothes, and almost every other lifestyle strand.

However, as we write, all that is changing. Furniture is on the cusp of a new golden age, with renewed interest on the part both of makers and designers and of those in a position to commission bespoke pieces, buy from limited-edition ranges or invest in a one-off masterpiece. It seems the world is finally waking up to the fact that buying a well designed, beautifully crafted, eloquent and enduring star piece is still an expression of good taste, excellent judgment and sound intellect.

Furniture as interior decoration

From the mid-17th century, there was a shift in attitude towards the way that houses were furnished and decorated. This was the age when the architect became pre-eminent, taking charge of interior decoration so that a balanced and sumptuous setting was created – a suitably magnificent backdrop for royalty or nobility against which to play out their lives.

In the higher reaches of society, furniture became a vital decorative feature, deployed almost in a military sense to enhance the most carefully planned architectural schemes. Furniture continued to take centre stage in the interiors of the 18th and 19th centuries, although responsibility for its commissioning increasingly lay with the upholsterer or 'upholder'. The late 19th and early 20th century were a springboard for new

technological advances, and the rise of the designer. However, at some point in the last quarter of the last century, many interior designers became less interested in furniture than in the choice of fabric, wallcovering, flooring or lamps. Furniture almost came to seem like something to be added in at the end of the design process. Functionality and

economy were the driving forces. It was no longer the glamorous star of the show.

Great furniture continued to be made and bought, but by an ever declining circle of the discerning and the wealthy. With so much accessible and expendable design increasingly available on the high street, most people preferred to spend their

OPPOSITE 'Gulliver's Chair' of 1987 by Julienne Dolphin-Wildings (b. 1960) plays with the idea of scale and makes a majestic punctuation point at the foot of contemporary floating stairs.

RIGHT Gerrit Rietveld's 'Billet' chair of 1923, one of an edition of five. His radically uncompromising designs are seen as icons of the Modern Movement.

money elsewhere. It seemed as though furniture had become the poor relation of interior design, a necessary but unexciting item that was given scant regard. Happily, in the last few years, all this has begun to change. Decorators have enjoyed mixing in all styles, ages and materials where furniture is concerned, combining high-street mass-produced models with vintage or inherited pieces, placing East next to West, juxtaposing the worn patina of 18th-century timber with contemporary steel. This textural and visual play has encouraged people to view furniture once again as a sculptural shape that can have enormous impact within a room. Indeed, 'texture' is a key word in contemporary interior design, and what else offers such textural possibilities? Furniture can be made of every conceivable type of material, from wood, stone, metal or glass to wicker, plastic, fibreglass or even cardboard. Its surface can be as smooth as lacquer or as rough as granite. It can carry no ornamentation, or a fantastic array of marquetry and inlays. When it comes to upholstery, the possibilities are also enormous, in terms not only of texture but of colour and pattern too.

Designers are enjoying a play with scale, and there is new appreciation for the way that one overscaled piece of furniture can significantly change the look of a room. Large spaces demand large-scale furniture, but small ones also benefit from it, because one enormous object can trick the eye into thinking a room is bigger than it really is. Add form to the equation – from the thinly elegant to the boldly rustic, from the square to the curved, from the traditional to the radical – and it is obvious that furniture offers an immense range of options to the ambitious interior designer or enthusiastic home owner.

While not every piece of furniture can or should have the wow factor, the fact is that every room should have its star piece – an extravagant,

exuberant extrovert around which everything else orbits. It does not matter whether this is an antique, a flea-market find, or a modern iconic collectable: what matters is that it should be assessed for form, colour, texture and character, and have enough of each to hold a scheme together.

This recognition of furniture as the central ingredient of contemporary interior design echoes what has happened in the fashion world, where the stylishly confident enjoy dressing up high-street bargains with designer pieces and vintage treasures. Nobody wants their home to look like everyone else's: the only way to achieve true originality is by embracing this idea, and adding pizzazz through a clever and show-stopping mix of furniture.

The Beauty
of Furniture

PREVIOUS PAGE The 'Crochet' chair by Marcel Wanders, 2006, constructed from individual hand-crocheted flowers.

ABOVE LEFT AND ABOVE A sofa table and centre table by George Bullock, one of the most innovative makers of the Regency, both of brown oak, oak and holly, supplied to Matthew Robinson Boulton at Tew Park in 1817. Bullock's use of strong designs and unusual British woods gives his furniture a timeless appeal.

The star pieces to which this book is dedicated are those furniture creations that transcend pure functionality. The beauty and character inherent in their design combine to produce the show-stopping qualities that guarantee their place as the focal point of a room. Age is not so relevant: a piece by Chippendale [*e.g. 137*] or BVRB [*e.g. 127*] can have just as much visual excitement as one by Arad [*e.g. 225*] or Newson [*e.g. 198*].

If you have never really given furniture much consideration before, you may think of it as being primarily wooden, conservatively upholstered, of a scale in line with our human bodies. While this may be true of the majority of mass-produced furniture, it is not applicable to the stars of the genre. As you will find in the pages of this chapter, furniture is made of wood – but also of glass, metal, stone, horn, wicker and all manner of man-made materials. When it comes to ornamentation, you can add other ingredients and processes into the mix, from marquetry and gilding to extraordinary upholstery techniques. Often overscaled for maximum impact, this is furniture that rightly grabs the attention and the imagination, an expression of the maker's passion and skill.

In fact, once you begin really to look at and notice great furniture, whether antique or contemporary, it is frankly amazing to discover what the possibilities are. Add to this the way that continuing technological breakthroughs are allowing designers to experiment further with form and materials, and it seems obvious that new chapters will soon be added to the already fascinating history of furniture. At its best, furniture offers far more than a practical solution for the way we live – it echoes our preoccupation with our own lives and futures. At a time when the human species is increasingly feeling beleaguered and anxious, it is perhaps no surprise that design should be so very much in the ascendant.

BELOW A late Louis XV grey-painted and parcel-gilt chaise à la reine made by Louis Delanois, one of a set of twenty-one supplied to the Salon du Roi of Madame du Barry's Pavilion at Louveciennes in 1771. The carving, which is extremely rich, includes olive leaves and branches.

Balance, Proportion, Form and Colour

There is a much-used phrase in design circles that refers to 'having an eye'. This centres on the idea that some fortunate people have an innate appreciation and understanding of anything they see. The implication is that it is not a skill that can be learnt. But is that really true? When it comes to furniture, it is questions of balance and proportion that make the first important impression, and these are not so very hard to understand.

If you wish to train your eye to appreciate more fully the beauty of furniture, then there is no better way of doing so than simply by spending more time looking. Attending the viewing days of auction houses, browsing antique shops, studying pieces in museums or country houses: these are all excellent opportunities to look closely at many different styles of antique furniture, some of far better pedigree than others. For contemporary design, visit the websites of leading makers and look out for sale shows in commercial galleries. The fact is that nobody is born with 'an eye', but with a will to do so it is possible to train your eyes to a much greater appreciation of the beauty and skill inherent in furniture.

One of the key points at which furniture differs from art is functionality. Tables have been recognizably tables for centuries, as have chairs, chests-of-drawers, beds and so forth. Fashions may dictate that in form they may be rigidly straight or sensuously *bombé*, gracefully slender or magnificently heavy, but essentially their shapes have changed very little in five thousand years of human civilization. A furniture-maker differs from an artist because he or she must work within the constraints of functionality; the canvas is in that sense not blank at the start. What marks out a great designer or maker from a mediocre one is his or her ability to arrive at an excellent creative solution to the challenges of such function – one that is distinctive visually, but which also works.

It follows therefore that everything else – form, method of construction, materials used – is informed, though not necessarily constrained, by function. But if all this happens without also imbuing a piece with a sense of proportion and balance, then the finished item may look ugly and ungainly. Imagine how awkward a chunky oak table top would look on spindly legs, for example. Or how a tall slender chair back would be at odds with a squat seat and chubby arms. You don't need an 'eye' to recognize such things: they would so obviously be, in a sense, wrong.

What is more difficult perhaps is to understand how very carefully considered matters of balance and proportion are in the design and construction of fine furniture, as opposed to the good, solid, artisan sort. The latter may not make you wince visually, but also may not appear to be quite so perfectly executed as the former. One reason is the use of the golden mean

or golden section. Great makers, such as Chippendale (see pp. 134–39), used mathematical formulae first recorded by the ancient Greeks to guide them in the all-important question of proportion. These formulae were almost certainly inspired by the natural world (the internal spiral of certain seashells can be contained in a set of rectangles proportioned to the golden section, as can the distances that separate leaves on certain trees). This is not the place for a mathematical lecture, but it is worth noting that much of the aesthetic beauty of great furniture is directly related to the mathematics of Euclid, who determined the ideal ratio to be 1:0.618. Much of classical architecture precisely mirrors this mathematical certainty; the façade of the Pantheon in Rome, for example, has a height that is 0.618th its length. Furniture-makers, both past and present, have long used the golden mean to achieve a balance that looks right to the eye.

ABOVE Two illustrations of chairs from the *The Gentleman and Cabinet-Maker's Director* by Thomas Chippendale (third edition, 1762). The one on the left is called a 'Ribband Back' chair.

OPPOSITE The 'Ear-Chair', by Studio Makkink & Bey, 2002. The gargantuan wings both play with the sense of proportion and create a defined space that is akin to a room within a room.

For a long time, form in furniture was something that barely altered over the centuries: tables, chairs, desks, armoires, beds, chest-of-drawers – all followed similar lines. An ancient Egyptian would have no trouble recognizing the function of a table in most homes today, and a Roman would be just as comfortable lying horizontal on a sofa as on a couch. However, owing to increasingly sophisticated technology, designers have been able to experiment with form in the last few years to spectacular effect. Sebastian Brajkovic (b. 1975) [*133*], Demakersvan (see p. 209) [*209*] and Julian Mayor (b. 1976) [*33*]

are among those who are rewriting how furniture should be constructed.

It was the use of plastics in furniture (see pp. 45–47) that first saw bright and punchy colours used. Happily, designers are enjoying a new love affair with colour that is no longer restricted to man-made materials. British architects BarberOsgerby – Edward Barber (b. 1969) and Jay Osgerby (b. 1969) – have produced limited-edition ranges in electrifying colours [*below left*], while Richard Woods (b. 1966) and Sebastian Wrong (b. 1971) have taken a cartoon-inspired palette for their witty collaborations [*49*]. Marc Newson [*below and opposite*], Future Systems, Ron Arad [*196–97*] and Wendell Castle [*opposite*] have also harnessed colour to spectacular effect, while with Squint – founded by sculptor and painter Lisa Whatmough (b. 1968) in 2005 – upholstery has become synonymous with a joyous riot of pattern and colour [*opposite*].

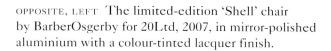

LEFT The 'Embryo' chair by Marc Newson for Cappellini, 1998, reflects his love of curves and space-age forms.

BELOW 'Roxborough' by Squint, 2008, is an electrifying fusion of period furniture and colourful vintage textiles.

OPPOSITE, LEFT The limited-edition 'Shell' chair by BarberOsgerby for 20Ltd, 2007, in mirror-polished aluminium with a colour-tinted lacquer finish.

OPPOSITE, RIGHT The 'Alufelt' chair by Marc Newson, 1993, is the handmade limited-edition interpretation of the 'Felt' chair he created for Cappellini in 1989.

BELOW The limited-edition 'Osborne' coffee table by Wendell Castle, 2008, made in polychromed fibreglass.

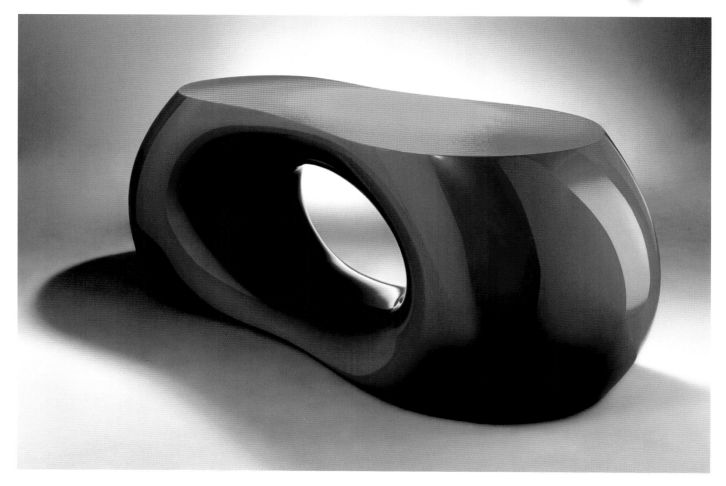

BELOW Pablo Reinoso created the 'Spaghetti Bale' bench from wood and steel in 2008: it takes its inspiration from the universal park bench, then literally twists the familiar with each slat hand-carved to create a sinuous curve.

OPPOSITE, ABOVE 'Impression' in plywood by Julian Mayor, 2002, echoes the outline of the human shape. It was created from the contour of a seated body that was digitized and sectioned onto a computer, and then exactly recreated. The interface between human and technological forms dominates Mayor's work.

Materials

aThe material used to construct a piece of furniture imbues it with immediate character, be it the warmth of wood or leather, or the coolness of glass or metal. Makers combine materials both for practical reasons and for textural contrast, which adds to the visual enjoyment and impact of a piece. Rare, luxurious, or simply unexpected materials may also be used to add further interest and beauty.

Wood

Think of furniture and most people think of wood. It has long been used as the primary material because it is enduring, practical, robust, beautiful, and of course available. It is important, however, to distinguish between wood from which a piece of furniture is constructed and wood used for its ornamentation. The first includes timbers such as oak, walnut, sycamore, cherrywood, mahogany (not often used today because of ethical issues) and ubiquitous pine. When it comes to veneers, there are many to choose from, including burr oak, burr walnut, burr ash, ripple sycamore, rosewood, satinwood, ebony and Macassar ebony. Ebony is a particularly hard and heavy timber, which ranges in colour from black to shades of purple-grey. Because it is so exotic, it was often chosen as a foil to the decoration supplied by precious and semi-precious stones, tortoiseshell and mother-of-pearl. By the beginning of the 18th century, it was widely

imitated, with such methods as staining pearwood. Even in the 17th century, the cabinetmakers of Augsburg were so concerned that imitations would devalue their work in real ebony [40] that they stamped their pieces with the word 'EBEN'. Wood continues to inspire and excite artists today, including the French-Argentinian sculptor Pablo Reinoso (b. 1955) [*opposite*], Julian Mayor [*above, and below left*], German designer Maarten Baas (b. 1978) [*203*], and the Dutch collaboration of Studio Makkink and Jurgen Bey (b. 1965) [*203*].

BELOW The 'Empress' chair by Julian Mayor, 2003, made in San Francisco, was inspired by the gridded streets and tall buildings of American cities. The sticks were cut by hand and then glued together one by one.

BELOW RIGHT A bedroom cabinet by Wales & Wales, 2007, with contrasting colours achieved using a combination of fumed, natural and brown oak.

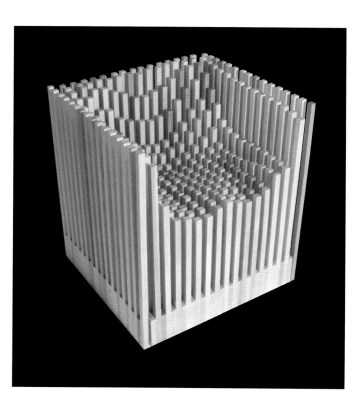

Glass

Glass has been associated with furniture since ancient Egypt; its earliest use was for decoration, as pieces of mosaic. Its development was driven by technology, in particular the clear glass developed around 1450 by glassworkers in Murano, Venice. From the 17th century onwards, it was mainly used for mirrors and candleholders, as well as for some early furniture: Lady Mary Wortley Montagu recorded seeing a set of furniture in Italy in 1756 made entirely of glass.

While the Venetians had established a lead in mirror glass by the early 16th century, its marketable value was not lost on English entrepreneurs. By 1664, the importation of mirror glass was forbidden and the Worshipful Company of Glass Sellers and Looking-Glass Makers had been established. However, mirror glass was often imported in an unfinished state from France or Italy and then finished in England. By the mid-18th century,

techniques had improved so much that it was possible to make mirrors of extraordinary size: Chippendale routinely supplied ones measuring 8 ft × 3 ft 10 in. (2.45 × 1.2 m.) [*cf. 102*].

In the technique of verre églomisé, often used to decorate mirrors, gold leaf is applied to the back of glass and then engraved. Known to the Romans and recorded in Italy during the 14th century, it was later widely employed in Europe and America [*159*].

By the mid-19th century, the British firm of F. & C. Osler was renowned for its crystal glass furniture, including stools, settees, bedheads, cradles, thrones, tables and sideboards. Baccarat in France and Libbey in the United States were also known for their glass furniture. In the 20th century glass remained a popular medium – be it Art Deco furniture produced in France by René Lalique (1860–1945), Modernist interpretations such as a glass chair and table of *c.* 1930 by the British designer Denham MacLaren

BELOW A detail of the glass 'Greenstone' table by Danny Lane, 2005.

OPPOSITE, ABOVE LEFT Shiro Kuramata's 'Glass Chair' of 1976 appears to have floated together as if by magic.

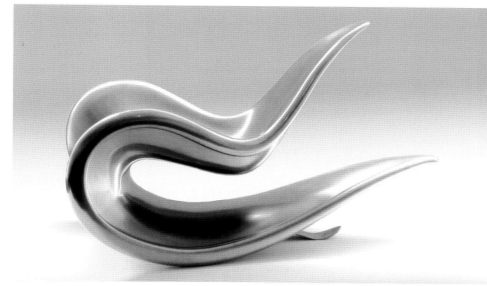

(1903–89), the technical brilliance of Shiro Kuramata (1934–91) [*above*], or the technically groundbreaking designs of the London-based American Danny Lane (b. 1955) [*opposite*].

ABOVE Wendell Castle's limited-edition 'Abilene' stainless steel rocking chair of 2007 shows a masterful balance between metal and light, making it appear weightless.

Metal

Wrought iron was used by the Romans for folding chairs, and iron bedsteads were popular in the 14th century because they were inhospitable to bedbugs and fleas. It was revived as a decorative medium in the 1880s, most notably by the French designer–blacksmith Emile Robert (1880–1948), a close friend and collaborator of Lalique. Metalwork found favour with Art Deco designers: Edgar Brandt (1880–1960), for instance, built on the pioneering activity of Emile Robert: his work in iron of the 1920s and later includes screens [*184*], console tables, mirror

frames and lamp bases. Jean Prouvé (1901–84), the great French engineer and designer, was apprenticed to Emile Robert at the age of fifteen, and later worked for the firm of Szabo. In 1923 he set up his own workshop in Nancy, taking on commissions for ornamental and wrought-iron work. However, keen to embrace the Modern Movement, he began investigating new processes and materials – steel, aluminium and arc welding. In 1931 he founded his own atelier.

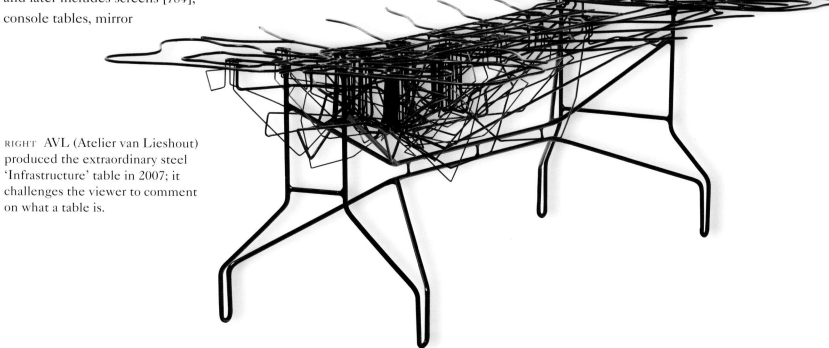

RIGHT AVL (Atelier van Lieshout) produced the extraordinary steel 'Infrastructure' table in 2007; it challenges the viewer to comment on what a table is.

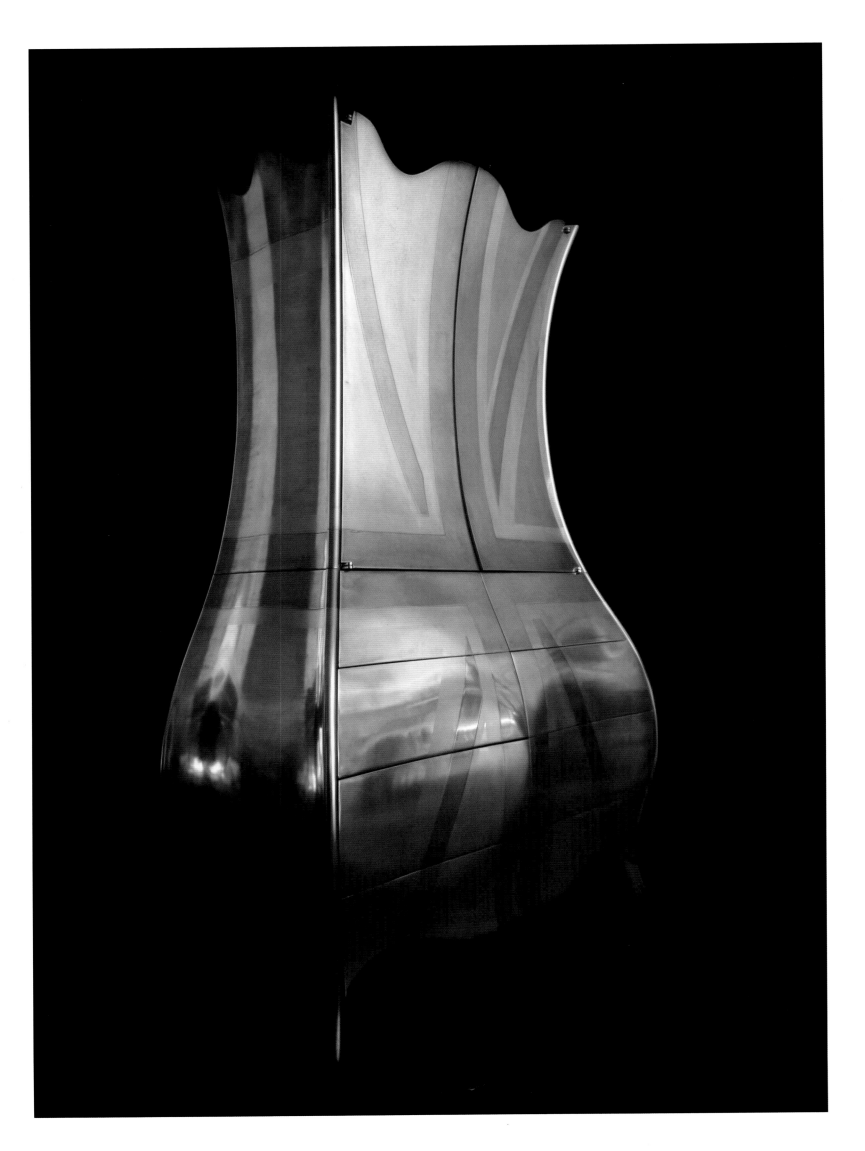

OPPOSITE The magnificent platinum-coated 'Patriotic' armoire was designed by Alastair Graham and executed by the London atelier Based Upon, 2007.

ABOVE The laser-cut, mirror-polished stainless steel 'Cartier' table by Ron Arad, 1994. Against the wall behind it is 'Q-bus' shelving by Rolf Sachs, 1992.

There he began to make metal furniture influenced by the work of architects such as Le Corbusier.

Cast iron was first used for outdoor furniture by the Prussian architect Karl Friedrich Schinkel (1781–1841) between 1820 and 1825. By the 1840s, manufacturers were realizing that it had a wider market. One of the most important names associated with its decorative development is the Coalbrookdale Iron Company in Britain, which produced for the 1851 Great Exhibition items such as chess tables, hall and console tables, armchairs and plant stands.

The use of silver either in solid form or as a veneer dates back to Roman times. It returned to fashion in the 16th century, being a German speciality for inlays and marquetry, and was popular in France at the court of Louis XIV and in Britain at the time of William and Mary (see p. 124). By the 19th century, silver furniture was becoming something of a rarity, viable only for one-off pieces. The American company Gorham & Co. built a dressing table and stool in solid silver for the 1900 Paris Exhibition.

Today, metal and metallic finishes continue to excite artists, such as the design atelier of Based Upon, founded by twins Richard and Ian Abell (b. 1974) [16, 36] and AVL (Atelier van Lieshout), the multidisciplinary art practice founded by Joep van Lieshout (b. 1963) [35]. Tom Dixon (b. 1959) [228], Danny Lane [5] and André Dubreuil [200] are among those who have embraced traditional metalworking techniques, while Ron Arad [37] and BarberOsgerby [30] have polished it to a mirror-like finish.

RIGHT A Dutch silver stand of 1670, thought to have been acquired by Charles II of England.

BELOW A magnificent silver table, part of a suite of silver furniture commissioned by William III for Kensington Palace in 1698 and delivered in 1699. It is struck with the maker's mark of Andrew Moore.

ABOVE David Adjaye's powerful 'Monoforms', here shown in Hassan Green granite, are functional sculpture inspired by time spent in the Siwa quarry in Egypt.

BELOW 'Extruded Table 3' by Marc Newson, 2008, is made from Striato Olimpico marble, a link to the luxurious stone furniture of previous centuries.

Stone

Stone has been used as a material for furniture since its earliest conception. Marble, for example, is available in a wide range of colours and patterns that can be worked in the solid, as a veneer, as mosaic or as inlay. Solid marble was commonly used for table and commode tops, first in Renaissance Italy and, by the 18th century, in England. By 1851, the taste for marble was so widespread that marble imitations were developed, including a paint effect of the same name. Slate was also commonly used for furniture, but it is marble that continues to fascinate designers today – among them Demakersvan [*209*], Marc Quinn (b. 1964) [*55*], Marc Newson [*right*], and David Adjaye (b. 1966) [*above*]. Young designers, such as Max Lamb (b. 1980), are even returning to the idea of quarrying their own stone by hand.

Ivory

Taken from the tusks of elephants, or, in some regions, sea elephants and walruses, ivory has long been used as an ingredient for the ornamentation of

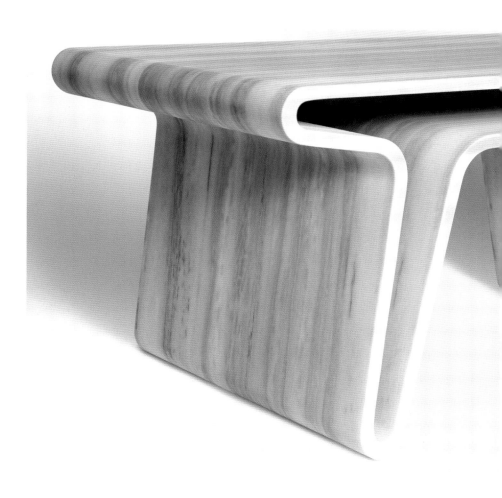

furniture [*above and 50*]. In some regions of India, furniture was made in both ivory veneer and solid ivory, the ultimate in luxury and magnificence for the elite of the land [*145–49*]. Today the trade in ivory is severely restricted, making these antique pieces increasingly rare and precious.

Tortoiseshell

Despite the name, this derives almost invariably from the carapace of the turtle rather than the tortoise. Typical colours are dark brown, amber and red; they were sometimes enhanced with substances such as red lead, lapis lazuli and gold powder. Tortoiseshell is a very versatile material: when exposed to heat it becomes malleable, allowing separate sections to be welded together. The use of tortoiseshell for decoration is ancient. It came back into fashion in Italy and the Low Countries in the 17th century, when it was used as a veneer for cabinets, tables and picture frames. It made a particularly spectacular contrast to black ebony, and has been an essential component of boulle marquetry

ABOVE An Augsburg cabinet of ivory and ebony inset with Florentine *pietra dura* plaques, with gilt-bronze mounts, attributed to Melchior Baumgartner, *c.* 1650.

OPPOSITE, ABOVE LEFT For this 'Stingray' table surface, of 2007, Based Upon created an animal-friendly, contemporary version of shagreen using black resin and a gold finish.

[*53, 112–18*]. French makers such as Jacques-Emile Ruhlmann (see p. 184) and Jules Leleu (1883–1961) revived its use in the Art Deco period.

Shagreen

Shagreen is dried and highly polished fish skin – usually shark or ray – used as a veneer on cabinet work. It was probably introduced into Europe as a decorative material in the 17th century, and was used in Jacobean England for covering items such as small desks. In the second half of the 18th century, specialists established businesses as shagreen case-makers. Shagreen is also associated with the Art Deco period, particularly the furniture of Ruhlmann.

Horn

Hooves, horns and antlers have long been mounted as mementoes of the hunt. Chandeliers adorned with stag horns were popular in Austria and Germany from the Renaissance onwards. Antler furniture was unveiled to the British public in 1851 at the Great Exhibition by the German firm of Rampendahl, feeding the Victorian appetite for baronial splendour and its romantic love of all things Scottish. Prince Albert, the German consort of Queen Victoria, was ahead of the fashion, having ordered a suite of horn furniture for Osborne House on the Isle of Wight in the mid-1840s. In America, too, horns – taken from steer – were regarded as emblems of the pioneering spirit. In Texas, companies such as Wenzel Friedrich made chairs, sofas, tables and hall stands using steer horn; Chicago was another centre for such furniture. By the 1890s horn furniture was widely available, popular both for its novelty and for its romantic representation of the Wild West.

ABOVE RIGHT A pair of armchairs incorporating steer horns, ram's horns and antlers, with back and seat covered in hide. Such pieces were popular in the USA around 1900.

RIGHT A cabinet by Alastair Graham, 2006, has drawer and door fronts of nautilus shell, set in bleached sycamore; the handles are of solid silver.

Mother-of-pearl

The lining of pearl oysters and other shells has a lustrous sheen that has made it perfect for the decoration of furniture for centuries. In the Renaissance, it was used across Europe as an inlay or as part of a marquetry design. It remained popular throughout the 17th and 18th centuries, and in the

19th century was used to contrast with fashionable darker woods in French furniture. While rarity and cost have meant a decrease in shell-ornamented furniture since then, its beauty is still an inspiration to designers today working at the upper reaches of bespoke design, such as Alastair Graham [41].

Leather

Leather has long been used by furniture-makers, for both functional and decorative purposes. It comes in a huge variety of types and finishes. Damask leather was produced in the 17th and 18th centuries by processing leather to imitate the patterns of damask fabric. Gilt leather, or Spanish leather, originated in Islamic Spain, possibly as far back as the 8th century: leather is punched or embossed with a pattern, then painted in colours, and a yellowish varnish added to give the look of gold. Morocco leather is made from goat skin; it was used in the 18th century to line desk and table tops, as well as to cover chair seats and backs. Leather remains the material of choice for fine upholstery today, for reasons of durability and longevity, but in the hands of designers such as Helen Amy Murray (b. 1980) [*15, above, 71*] it takes on new relevance and personality.

OPPOSITE Helen Amy Murray's 'Peacock' design of sculpted Novasuede, 2007, used to cover a Danish tub chair (one of a pair).

LEFT An Arne Jacobsen 'Egg' chair and stool covered by Helen Amy Murray in leather sculpted and embroidered with her 'Peony' design, 2007.

The 'Aston' chair by Linley – moulded to echo the Aston Martin car seat – here covered in alligator, 2005.

ABOVE An armchair of painted beech with chequerboard woven cane seat, designed by Koloman Moser (1868–1918) for the Purkersdorf Sanatorium, Vienna, 1901, manufactured by Prag Rudniker.

BELOW Marc Newson's 'Wicker' chair, 1990, manufactured by Idee. Newson takes a traditional material and gives it new relevance.

OPPOSITE Children's chairs from the 'Transplastic' series by the Campana brothers, 2007. These playful hybrids reflect on the replacement of traditional wicker café furniture by ubiquitous plastic in the Campanas' native Brazil.

Straw, cane and wicker

Straw was traditionally used as a filling for mattresses and seat cushions right up to the 19th century. In the 17th century it was plaited and woven into chair seats. In England, some chairs were also made entirely of straw, using an ancient technique known as lipp work, which involves coils of straw lashed together with bark or other vegetation.

The use of woven cane set into chair frames became established in England during the reign of Charles II, meeting a demand for relatively cheap and comfortable chairs that was stimulated by the Great Fire of London in 1666, which left thousands of people without furniture of any kind. The cane, imported by the East India Company, was split and interlaced to form an open mesh. Canework initially had a large mesh [122]; it became finer by the end of the 17th century and into the 18th century.

Wicker, a form of basketry using willow, rush, reed, rattan or straw produced on a warp of still rods called stake frames, is one of the oldest materials for furniture, known in ancient Egypt from 3000 BC.

Techniques have barely altered in five thousand years. In the 17th century, wicker chairs were popular all over Europe, sometimes with arms or hooded backs. In North America in the 17th century,

settlers brought with them wicker furniture as well as the techniques with which to construct it. In the 18th century it came to be considered an inferior medium, but in the 19th century it experienced a massive revival for both indoor and outdoor use. It lent itself to a wide variety of designs, could be painted or upholstered, and was regarded as an honest wholesome material evocative of country living and good health. Modernist designers, such as the German Ludwig Mies van der Rohe (see p. 205), also adopted wicker, often using it in conjunction with tubular steel, as in his 'Weissenhof Chair No. MR20' of 1927 and 'Chair B32' of 1928. In 1988, Tom Dixon produced his familiar 'S' chair for Cappellini in

woven wicker on a welded steel frame. Other contemporary designers, such as Marc Newson [*opposite*] and the Campana brothers (see p. 201) [*above and 201*], have invested it with new relevance.

Man-made materials

In the period after the Second World War ended in 1945, there was an economic boom, with many architect-designers concentrating their creative energies on the development of low-cost, innovative furniture. Enlightened companies such as New York-based Knoll and Michigan-based Herman Miller were able to offer the general public revolutionary design at an affordable price. In the 1950s, the plastics industry became

increasingly influential, and designers began
exploring the benefits of foam rubber as a suitable
material for upholstery.

In the 1960s, disposable products were
thought to increase productivity and therefore
prosperity, so even furniture was designed to be
ephemeral. Just as dresses appeared that were made
of paper, so designers including the Briton Peter
Murdoch (b. 1940) and the German Peter Raacke
(b. 1928) produced chairs made of cardboard. Aimed
at a youth-orientated market, such furniture was seen
as a lifestyle item, subject to the demands of fashion.
In Italy, Massimo Scolari (b. 1943) , Donato D'Urbino
(b. 1935), Paulo Lomazzi (b. 1936) and Gionatan De
Pas (1932–91) designed the inflatable plastic 'Blow

ABOVE 'Aura' by Zaha Hadid and Patrik Schumacher, 2008,
is a site-specific installation in lacquered fibreglass made
for the Villa Foscari near Venice. Set in the Palladian
interior, it invites the visitor to consider a radical new
form of furniture.

Chair' (1967) in punchy pop art colours, while a
year later the 'Sacco' beanbag made its appearance,
designed by Piero Gatti (b. 1940), Cesare Paolini
(1937–83) and Franco Teodoro (1939–2005).
'Flat-pack' furniture was part of this trend
towards inexpensive, throwaway design that
could be bought off the shelf.

Advances in injection-moulded plastics
during the 1960s meant that a whole new range of

possibilities became available to the furniture designer. The first chair to achieve single-piece construction was the 'Stacking Chair' by the Dane Verner Panton (1926–98), which came into production in 1968 – eight years after he conceived it. In 1962, the Briton Robin Day (b. 1915) launched the 'Polyprop' – to date one of the most successful contract chairs ever produced, with tens of millions sold around the world.

Today designers continue to experiment with materials, from fibreglass, as used by Zaha Hadid [*opposite*] and Wendell Castle [*31*], to carbon resin, radically exploited by Ron Arad, and the spectral Plexiglas shapes of Drift studio founders Ralph Nauta (b. 1978) and Lonneke Gordijn (b. 1980) [*left, below*].

LEFT, ABOVE 'La Marie', by Philippe Starck for Kartell, 1998, is a transparent chair designed to have strength while sacrificing none of its slim elegance.

LEFT The 'Ghost' chair by Ralph Nauta and Lonneke Gordijn of Drift, 2007/8, harnesses laser technology combined with a Plexiglas form to create a chair that appears to contain the ghost of another chair within.

Ornamentation

Carving and turning

Furniture carving has ranged over the centuries from the most elementary scratch marks to full-scale sculptural work. By the 18th century, makers often combined the joint roles of carver and gilder, because of the connections between the two crafts. Expert carvers undertook not only furniture, but also architectural work, internal decoration (such as cornices for windows and beds) and shipwork. Carving requires great artistic skill as well as a steady hand and an unerring eye: the ability to create foliage, fruit, birds, figures and other popular motifs of the day by carving into solid wood was and is highly specialized.

Turning is, in principle, not dissimilar to the creation of ceramics on a potter's wheel: the piece that is to be worked is clamped between two pointed centres and spun; an edged tool, such as a bowstring or sharp-edged wheel, is then used to cut away the surface as it rotates: the design and decoration are created in one process. It is thought that turning was invented around 1000 BC, and it was evidently quite sophisticated by the Middle Ages. One of the most common forms of turned table and chair frames involves the repetition of small ball shapes. Later it was used to produce the barley-twist legs so popular in the 17th and 19th centuries.

This Regency rosewood reading table supplied by Gillows in 1813 to the 2nd Baron Bolton features elaborate carved scrolls and turned stretchers. The solid end-supports are inlaid with brass foliate panels.

Paint effects

Paint has long been associated with giving existing furniture a new lease of life, but designers have taken this further by exploring ways of using faux paint finishes to produce exciting jolts of colour or even a sense of graffiti anarchy. In the hands of artists such as Ron Arad, paint becomes a powerful visual statement.

LEFT The splattered paint effect on Ron Arad's 'New Orleans' chair, 1999, is produced by using pigmented polyester [cf. 196–97].

BELOW A Richard Woods and Sebastian Wrong collaboration, which combines Wrong's utilitarian design with Woods's signature printed laminate.

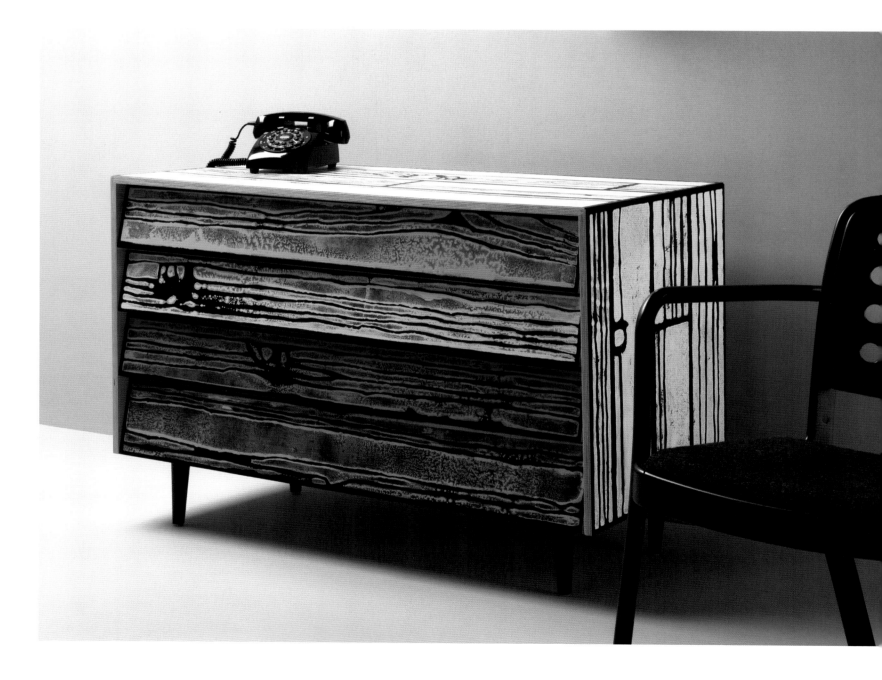

Marquetry and parquetry

Marquetry involves laying a variety of wooden veneers of differing colours and sizes *onto* a solid surface to build up a picture. It is different from inlay, where the material is set *into* the surface. A variety of thin wooden veneers of differing colours and sizes, and occasionally other materials, are combined to build up a picture or pattern. In its purest form, only timbers in their natural state are used – an extremely skilled and time-consuming process. However, timbers were often shaded by burning to increase the effect of contrast. Parquetry is similar in technique, but comprises simple, repeating geometrical shapes [*218*]. Marquetry was known since the ancient world, but the development in the mid-16th century of the fretsaw made more intricate cutting possible.

OPPOSITE A William IV centre table with marquetry of yew, ebony, mother-of-pearl, ivory and green-stained ivory, *c*. 1835–40. Not only the tilt top but the legs are decorated with flowers and foliage.

ABOVE The 'Bavaria' screen by Studio Job, 2008, is made of rosewood and marquetry in seventeen colours. Inspired by 17th- and 18th-century Bavarian painted furniture, it depicts a seemingly happy but severe Calvinistic farm life, including barns, vegetables and livestock, all in a strict, symmetrical order (see also p. 202).

From the 17th century, it was widely used to decorate the surfaces of clock-cases, cabinets, secretaires, chests, tables and mirror frames. Popular forms include seaweed marquetry, with small-scale motifs resembling seaweed or endive; arabesque marquetry, with intricately interwoven flowing lines based on Islamic art; and floral marquetry, where designs of an often complex nature are formed of baskets, sprays or urns of flowers [129]. Marquetry flourished throughout the 18th and 19th centuries, and ways of imitating it were developed. Today, laser cutting techniques have ensured its continued popularity [51, 202].

ABOVE LEFT AND ABOVE A George III satinwood and tulipwood marquetry and gilt console table in the manner of Mayhew and Ince, c. 1775. The serpentine shaped top features a bellflower and crossbanded edge.

BELOW A Louis XVI ormolu-mounted commode of amaranth, sycamore, mahogany, parquetry and marquetry, by Jean-Henri Riesener, from the King's Library at Versailles. With its restrained proportions, and its brilliant marquetry and parquetry panels set off by rich Neoclassical ormolu mounts, Riesener achieved an unrivalled nobility.

LEFT AND BELOW A Louis XIV long-case clock attributed to André-Charles Boulle. Such elaborate surface ornamentation was the signature of this master *ébéniste* and *bronzier*, one of whose skills was the integration of the marquetry with the mounts.

Boulle marquetry

Boulle is a form of marquetry particularly associated with the French cabinetmaker André-Charles Boulle [*112–16*]. In it a spectacular variety of materials, including fine timber veneers, mother-of-pearl, metals such as brass and tin, and precious materials such as ivory, are used to create dramatic contrast and depth. Boulle work is best known for designs with a tortoiseshell background inlaid with brass, known as *première partie* [*116*], and brass inlaid with tortoiseshell, known as *contre partie* [*118*].

Inlay and intarsia

This ancient decorative technique involves cutting shapes in a solid surface and filling them in with a contrasting material. These 'infillers' include timbers such as ash, beech, ebony, fruitwood, holly, pear, poplar, sycamore and yew, and other materials such as bone, ivory, mother-of-pearl, stone and tortoiseshell.

Inlay featured in ancient Egypt, where ebony was often employed as the ground; the back of Tutankhamun's ebony throne is decorated with inlaid faience, carnelians and gold. In Greek literature, Homer recounts that the chair of Odysseus' wife Penelope was inlaid with ivory and silver. In Roman times, inlay was used to demonstrate wealth through the use of precious jewels and metals, although horn, ivory and coloured glass also served to decorative effect. During the 15th, 16th and 17th centuries, inlay was used throughout Europe for the decoration of furniture. From the mid 17th-century marquetry (see pp. 50–52) became the fashionable finish, but inlay was revived in the late 19th century by furniture-makers working in the Arts and Craftstradition.

Intarsia is a particular form of inlay, which involves setting wood into a ground to build up a pictorial design. The designs include *trompe-l'oeil* perspective compositions with humanistic motifs, such as books and globes, and also imaginary buildings, both complete and ruined. It is thought to have originated in Tuscany in the early 14th century, and was initially used for the decoration of religious

ABOVE A Louis XVI ormolu-mounted ebony and *pietra dura* commode à encoignures stamped by Martin Carlin and Adam Weisweiler and then by Martin Carlin. With its immensely rich combination of earlier *pietra dura* – both from the grand-ducal workshops in Florence and from Louis XIV's Gobelins manufactory – with boulle marquetry, it represents the heights of refinement achieved in the 1780s, when the greatest technical skill was combined with a taste for the luxurious propagated by the *marchands-merciers*, such as Dominique Daguerre.

buildings. The process matured in Florence, where at one time it was considered the equal of painting. Brunelleschi, the architect of the dome of the Cathedral (begun in 1420), used intarsia examples to teach perspective to artists. Intarsia came to be sought-after as decoration for cabinets and wall panelling, eventually spreading from Italy to the highly skilled cabinetmakers of South Germany, notably Augsburg and Nuremberg, and from Germany to the Low Countries.

Pietra dura

The use of stone in furniture, as for the solid marble table tops of Baroque Italy and France, is well recognized. However, the use of semi-precious stones was also a feature of court furniture [*above*]. The principle of *pietra dura* – literally 'hard stone' – work is the same as that of inlay, but both ground and infill are of stone rather than timber. The resulting 'jigsaw' is glued to a slate base for stability. The stones typically used include agate, chalcedony, granite, jasper, lapis lazuli, malachite, porphyry and various marbles.

The technique had been known in Italy in Roman times. In Renaissance Florence it was revived for the decoration of furniture and other *objets d'art* first by Cosimo I de' Medici and later by his son Ferdinand I, under whose patronage the Uffizi workshops became famous throughout Europe (see pp. 106–7). Other centres developed in Rome, Spain and Naples, the latter being the home of the Real Laboratorio delle Pietre Dure, founded by the King of Naples in 1737. Although the Italians remained masters of the craft, there are also French and English examples, some of which use locally mined stones such as those of Ashbourne in England.

Mosaic

In mosaic, designs are created through the use of small cubes of marble, stone and glass. The technique originated in the ancient world, was common in the Middle Ages, and was revived in

ABOVE This splendid mosaic top is one of a pair almost certainly commissioned, with the giltwood tables they stand on, by Principe Don Marcantonio Borghese for the Palazzo Borghese in Rome *c.* 1775.

BELOW 'Glacier' from the 'Iceberg' collection by Marc Quinn, 2008. Rough blocks of marble are cut flat and have mosaic images of flowers inlaid into their tops.

the Renaissance. In the 18th century, 'micro-mosaic' was developed in Rome: in this, minute squares of coloured glass are combined to produce the effect of a painting. Such pieces were highly sought after by young noblemen on the Grand Tour, and by the 19th century the micro-mosaic industry was firmly established, It was used as a decorative feature on table tops, for example. Napoleon was a great admirer, as was George IV of England.

Lacquer and japanning

Lacquering (see pp. 93–97) originated in China and from there the skill was exported to Japan. True lacquer is the product of the lac tree and is immensely tough. One of its most surprising characteristics is that contact with moisture hardens, rather than softens, it; bright light, however, will eventually weaken and

A Japanese table screen of the Meiji period, late 19th century, with a black lacquer ground and flowers and cockerels in gold, silver, red and brown lacquer.

destroy it. Lacquer, most frequently black, was also coloured in shades ranging from reds and browns to yellows and greens. The Japanese accentuated its beauty with silver and gold dust and inlays of mother-of-pearl, coloured glass and semi-precious stones.

Lacquered furniture became immensely popular in Europe when trading with China increased in the 17th century. Panelled screens were often imported – many themselves of antique origin – only to be cut up and integrated into Western-style furniture. It was a fashion embraced, for example, by William and Mary of England [*121*], Louis XV of France [*128, 130, 131*], and the nobility of Venice.

Japanning is the name given to the European imitation of Oriental lacquer, based on various recipes using seed-lac, turpentine, resin and gum [*e.g. 100, 101, 109, 123*]. Development of faux lacquers in France was particularly successful: 'vernis Martin' (named after the Martin family who were renowned for this work) is the generic name for French japanning of the mid-18th century. In America as early as the 1690s Boston became the centre for such work: there, because of the density of the wood, it could be applied directly to maple and pine, without the gesso foundation which was usually necessary. Japanning decreased in popularity in the 19th century, but its use was revived in the Art Deco period.

Ormolu or gilt bronze

This expensive technique favoured in France involves casting a mount in brass or bronze and then gilding it with mercury and gold under heat. It was a dangerous process, and it was largely abandoned by English craftsmen in favour of a cheaper version where brass or bronze is covered in lacquer gilding.

Gesso

Gesso was known to the ancient Egyptians. Since the Middle Ages it has been used as a base or primer for painting or gilding on timber. Essentially it is a combination of a powdered form of calcium carbonate and some sort of animal glue, to which other materials, such as linseed oil or sugar, are often added. Recipes vary according to age, location, and the required effect. In the case of furniture, gesso has traditionally been used as a ground or substrate for gilding [*11, 63*], painting and japanning (q.v.). A gesso base is first applied to the underframe. Once dry, it is rubbed down to extreme smoothness. Timber may require as much as six or seven coats of gesso before the surface is smooth enough for the application of gold (less usually for paint). If gesso is used over carving, the sharpness of the sculptural forms needs to be restored before the final finish can be applied.

This elaborately ornamented French ormolu-mounted kingwood and tulipwood marquetry commode is a 19th-century interpretation of the Louis XV style after a model by Charles Cressent.

In the 15th and 16th centuries, gesso was used for the gilding of a particular type of Italian chest known as a *cassone* – a large, richly decorated chest often placed in the bridal suite and containing goods that formed part of the bride's dowry. In the latter part of the 17th century, it was revived for relief work and picture frames. In the early 18th century, some designers specialized in work involving gesso – the English architect and designer William Kent (1685–1748), for example, was well known for his side tables, stands and frames which all employed gilded gesso.

Gilding

Gilding is the application of a thin layer of gold leaf to a prepared surface, which is then burnished to a bright finish. The technique was well known in ancient times. Where wood is to be gilded, a preparatory base is created of gesso (q.v.).

Scagliola

This is a plaster technique used to create the impression of marble. Made from a variety of recipes, it is essentially a mixture of selenite, glue and natural pigments, polished with flax oil for brightness and waxed to protect the surface. It is applied to a rough

plaster surface and worked to produce beautiful effects, akin almost to painting with marble. Of Roman origin, it was revived during the 16th century in Italy, peaking in technique during the 17th and 18th centuries when slabs of scagliola were popular for table tops and commode tops.

ABOVE Thomas Kennedy, a contemporary British master of the art of scagliola, created this exquisite design, copied from work by Paulini, the 16th-century copper engraver, for the tops of a pair of console tables in 2003.

BELOW A late 17th-century table de milieu with a scagliola top signed by Laurent Bonuccelli.

Fur and fabric

Fabric is of course associated with furniture through
upholstery, but some contemporary designers have
also used it to clad or even partly construct furniture.
Its appeal lies in its sensual, tactile qualities, as with
the fur-clad chair of Jean Royère (1902–81) or the
ponyskin-clad chaise longue of 1928 by
Le Corbusier, Pierre Jeanneret
and Charlotte Perriand.

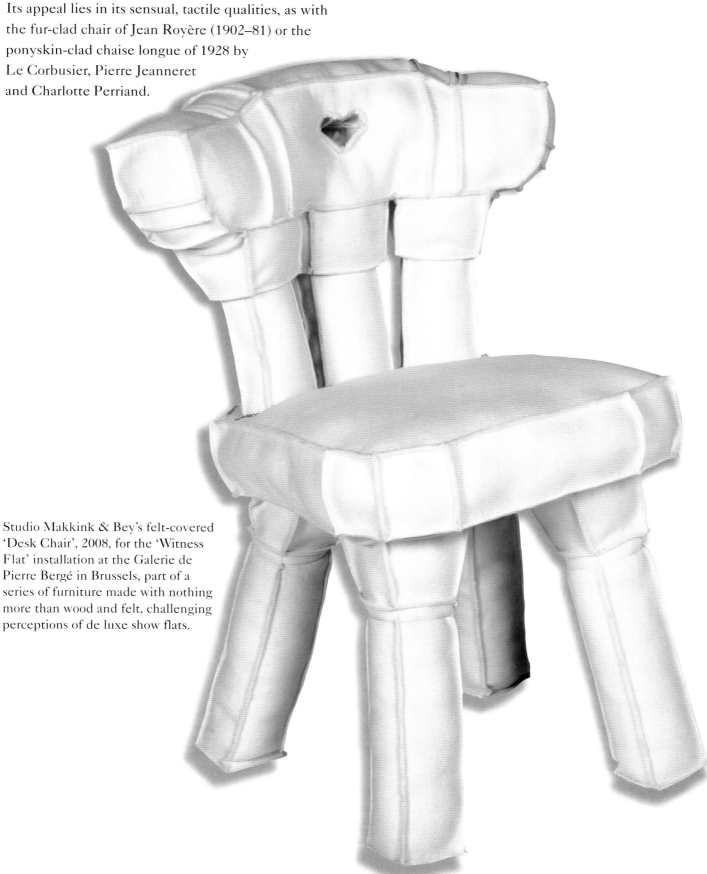

Studio Makkink & Bey's felt-covered
'Desk Chair', 2008, for the 'Witness
Flat' installation at the Galerie de
Pierre Bergé in Brussels, part of a
series of furniture made with nothing
more than wood and felt, challenging
perceptions of de luxe show flats.

RIGHT A pair of early George III mahogany side chairs covered with contemporary needlework.

BELOW Original Genoese velvet covers this William and Mary ebonized beech armchair (see p. 124).

The ornamentation of fabric itself has also played a decorative role in the history of furniture. Hand-embroidered silks and velvets were in high demand since first they were traded. Needlework was once an essential part of a well-bred young lady's education, and needlepoint was often used or decoration. Stumpwork is a form of embroidery where the stitched figures are raised by layers of padding to form a three-dimensional effect. It usually comprised figurative designs using a variety of stitches, highlighted within to accentuate the three-dimensionality. It was too fragile to be functional, but richly coloured panels might be set into the door frames of cabinets and other case furniture.

Grotto ornament

Sculptural and fantastic, grotto furniture was inspired by shells, fish and mythical sea creatures. Shells have a long story as a decorative motif, featuring almost without interruption from antiquity to contemporary design. Scallop shapes were used to embellish both Baroque and Rococo furniture. This fascination with sea creatures took a new form in the 18th century, when grottoes lined with shells were built in the grounds of many of the grand houses of the day (although grottoes existed as early as the 16th century). They were shrines to nature, sites of fabulous beauty. Furniture suitable for such a setting needed to be as imaginative as possible: chairs imitating gnarled tree roots, for example, feature in Chippendale's *Director* (see p. 137). By the 19th century grotto furniture was a speciality of Venice, where a mother-of-pearl effect was achieved by covering the carved wooden base with gesso (q.v.) and then adding layers of silver leaf and lacquer.

Paper filigree

Gold and silver filigree was developed in the 15th century for the ornamentation of religious artefacts. Paper filigree developed as a less expensive alternative, becoming a popular pastime among well-to-do ladies of the 17th century. Tiny strips of coloured paper were rolled up and each applied separately to a surface, in an extremely time-consuming technique, using as many as 135 rolls of paper per square inch

colour of the paper and the way it was rolled. More lavish effects could be achieved by the addition of beads, pearls, prints and painted decorations. Typically paper filigree was used to ornament small objects such as tea caddies, mirror frames and boxes, but some pieces of furniture making use of it do survive: they are often of rudimentary construction, probably made by a local carpenter, and then encrusted with tight rolls of paper and other decorative ingredients on every surface.

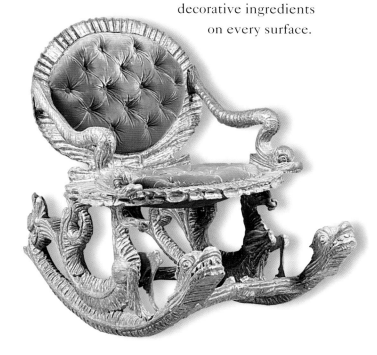

(6.45 sq. cm.). In America, this process is called quilling, because paper was often rolled around a quill or feather. Sets of these strips were available to buy, and filigree patterns were created by varying both the

TOP AND ABOVE Two views of one of a pair of George III console tables decorated in red and green rolled paper, a technique known as filigree or quilling.

ABOVE A Venetian giltwood grotto rocking chair. These fanciful pieces, often incorporating sea creature motifs, were the height of fashion in the 19th century.

BELOW A Louis XV beechwood duchesse brisée, attributed to Jean-Baptiste Tilliard, with carving of foliage and scrolls and cabriole legs. Back, seats, cushions, sides and arms are covered with a (modern) floral damask.

OPPOSITE LEFT A George II gilt-gesso open armchair covered in the original green floral silk, from a set of twelve supplied to Sir Robert Walpole for the Marble Parlour at Houghton.

OPPOSITE RIGHT A George I walnut and parcel-gilt side chair attributed to the Roberts family, from a large set supplied to Sir Robert Walpole. The profile view shows the curve of the original upholstery and the masterful balance between the rake of the back and the splay of the back legs.

Upholstery

We tend to use the term 'upholstery' to mean the coverings of chairs, sofas, bedheads and the like, but in fact it also includes the frame, the support system (usually webbing) and the padding. The techniques of upholstery and the four basic elements were well known by 1588.

To the collector of antique furniture, webbing is particularly important: it should always match with the date given for any upholstered item. If the webbing is later, then the piece concerned either has an original frame which has been reupholstered at a later date, or is a reproduction.

Padding – which until the 1660s commonly comprised hay, wool or straw stitched into tubes of linen – was improved with the introduction of horsehair. By the end of the 17th century, feathers were also used (Chippendale maintained two feather rooms at his London premises).

By the beginning of the 17th century, while the actual upholstery techniques were elementary, effects were often sumptuous due to the richness of the textiles used. Velvet, damask and silk took pride of place. The production of silk and velvet had been established in Lucca, Italy, by the 12th century, spreading through Venice, Genoa, Florence and Milan. Being a heavy fabric, velvet was ideal for embroidery, including that involving metallic thread. Genoese velvets were particularly admired, being unsurpassed in quality [65, 124]. The 17th century saw a surge in French production of cloths

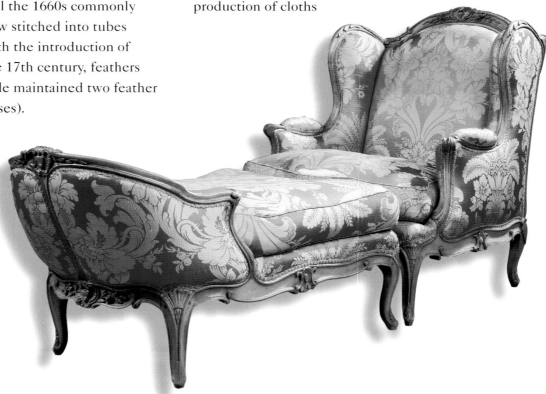

that imitated Genoese velvet, particularly centred around Lyon and Paris.

Historically, however, 'upholstery' denoted all the fine textile furnishings at the centre of sophisticated and costly interior decoration. Inventories and bills that survive from the 18th century in Britain nearly always refer to the work of the upholsterer; indeed, the upholsterer or 'upholder' was considered the 'Chief Agent' in the decorating of a house, his craft being 'to fit up Beds, Window Curtains, Hangings and to cover Chairs that have Stuffed Bottoms' (*London Tradesman*). He was also a contractor, employing men of many skilled trades, including cabinetmakers, glass grinders, carvers, woollen drapers and linen drapers.

The dominance of the upholsterer was based on the French development of upholstered seat furniture and beds in the 17th century. In England, a remarkable series of beds from around 1680 until the 1730s survive which allow the scholar to trace a great deal of upholstery design. The richness of the fabrics and the elaborateness of their working are as amazing as the prices once paid for these magnificent objects. The work was not only inspired by French fashion, but often achieved with the help of French craftsmen – the Huguenots who fled France after Louis XIV had revoked the Edict of Nantes in 1685, an act

which made Protestantism illegal. It is thought that some 40,000–50,000 came to England, including the upholsterer Francis Lapiere (1653–1714), whose name appears in the accounts of the Royal Wardrobe, the Duke of Devonshire, and many other eminent members of the nobility. These skilled Huguenots also enabled England to compete in the production of fine velvets and silks: Spitalfields in London, Norwich and Canterbury were all important centres. The contribution of Daniel Marot (see p. 122) [*124*] is hugely important, as he is recorded as producing complete interior decor schemes that were integrated largely through the use of soft furnishings. Certainly he was the first person in England to produce designs for furniture and upholstery as well as architectural decoration.

During the Regency period, upholstery developed enormously, affecting not only seat furniture and beds, but also cabinet furniture and tables, screens, doors and windows. There was also an expansion in pattern books devoted to the subject by names such as George Smith (1786–1828) and Rudolph Ackermann (1764–1834).

Materials used for the outer surface of upholstery between 1790 and 1840 throughout Europe and the USA included woven, printed and embroidered fabrics. Particularly popular in England were chintzes: these printed and glazed cottons, with colourful often large-scale designs, were as fashionable in middle-class villas and cottages as they were with the aristocracy, including the Prince of Wales, who commissioned a 'rich furniture chintz' for his bedroom at Carlton House in London in 1811.

The 19th century saw the introduction of springs, which had originated in carriage suspension, and the industrial sewing machine aided the sewing of covers. However, unlike other areas of furniture-making, good quality upholstery never really lent itself to the mechanical age, and even today top level manufacturers have factories where much of the work is done by hand.

The bed

Because they were such prominent pieces of furniture, beds were very much the remit of the architect or interior decorator. Designs were published in engraved form as early as the 16th century; as time progressed, beds became more architectural in character, designed specifically for the room in which they stood. In the 17th century, they were usually identified by their hangings: inventories would refer to a 'green velvet' bed, for example.

Some of the finest late 17th-century beds in England were made by French craftsmen, but the form appears to have been an English development – generally speaking, taller and more exaggerated than those found in France. While the frame itself was often roughly finished, the greatest care was taken with the upholstery. A fine bed might feature both inner and outer curtains, the outer ones usually being the more ornate of the two. While the base valances, which hung down over the legs, were usually plain, the head-cloths which hung above the pillow would often constitute a hanging, perhaps with the owner's arms embroidered upon it. Most elaborately decorated were the tester and the counterpane. The tester, which hung over the bed like a ceiling, was usually decorated with needlework or trimmings worked into patterns, although the unseen topside could be considerably simpler. The counterpane, or bed cover, typically featured one central and two side panels and

covered the bed down to the floor, complemented by a matching bolster at the head. Bed curtains were rich and sumptuous – mainly velvets, silks, taffetas, brocades and damasks.

ABOVE A design for a bed, from *The Gentleman and Cabinet-Maker's Director* by Thomas Chippendale (third edition, 1762).

OPPOSITE The Melville Bed was commissioned by George, 1st Earl of Melville, for his new house in Fife in 1700. The sumptuous crimson Genoa velvet hangings are original, and show the immense importance placed at the time on the most elaborate upholstery, especially on beds, which were the focal point of the State Apartment.

One of the most costly fabrics recorded is a seven-colour velvet used for Queen Mary's Bedroom at Kensington Palace in 1688–89, which cost £619. Of the bed made by Francis Lapiere for the Duke of Devonshire at Chatsworth in 1697, the woodwork cost a mere £15 and the upholstery £470. In 1732, Sir Robert Walpole spent £1,200 on the gold lace for the Green Velvet Bed at Houghton.

Embroidered hangings were common. Sometimes they were executed by the women of the household or local needlewomen rather than professional embroiderers working in cities. Ladies' beds are most likely to feature such domestic needlework, not so technically proficient, but often full of charm. Presumably women turned their skill to decorating their own bed curtains and covers. Mens' beds most often feature professional needlework, of great delicacy and beauty, which would have been extremely costly. The expense no doubt enhanced the bed's status.

Very important beds might also feature two sets of hangings, one for summer and one for winter. Every precaution was taken to protect the fragile and highly valuable textiles and trimmings: special

'case curtains' were sometimes provided to protect the upholstery of a great 17th-century bed.

Chairs, covers and cushions

The form of a chair, essentially a stool with a back, is Italian in origin. The 'back stool', popular at the court of Charles I in England, was the simplest form of upholstered chair in the first half of the 17th century. Backs became higher by the end of the century, but it remained the standard chair for both dining and relaxing, with the back and seat usually covered in fabric. The more common type of upholstered armchair evolved from the back stool form, led by the French, who were placing more emphasis on comfortable seating by the last quarter of the 17th century.

In the first quarter of the 18th century, French chair-makers developed a bewildering variety of forms, but upholstery techniques remained fairly standard. Ornamentation is often a by-product of the need to keep stuffing in place, with nails which could either be displayed or hidden by piping or buttoning. Close-nailing, where the lines of the chair are defined by one or two rows of nails, is considered typical of this period. Original nails are hand-made, so are not

Two of a set of six Louis XVI giltwood fauteuils en cabriolet by Henri Jacob, with arched and tapering backs and squab cushions covered in yellow floral cut-velvet.

completely even. In good examples, they do not overlap: rather, there is a slight breathing space between them. The line of a sofa or chair could be accentuated by tailored piping, and combinations of nailing and piping are common from this period.

Buttoning – another both practical and attractive way of keeping stuffing in place – originated in the second half of the 17th century. The deep buttoning so popular in the Victorian era was part of the Rococo revival. Known in France as *capitonné*, it was used to give a voluptuous effect, with threads pulled tight creating a trellis-work of deep pleats between the buttons.

The seat cushions of a chair, usually referred to as squabs, were designed to reflect the line of the frame. They vary considerably in thickness depending on the age and style of the chair, from the thin pancake pad of the rush chair to those made of thick horsehair with a layer of wadding found on 18th-century easy chairs. French chairs of the mid-18th century often featured cushions that could be 5–6 in. (13–15 mm.) thick. The best ones were filled with down, wool or horsehair, covered first in soft

leather and then in silk (the practice of leather lining dates back to the 17th century). Sofas of the late 18th century frequently featured bolsters, very tailored in appearance, with the ends finished in piping and secured by a single button or tassel.

Loose covers, considered a modern invention, were in fact popular in the 17th century, when fine fabrics were so costly that it was necessary to keep wear even and exclude as much light and dust as possible. From the 17th century onwards, fine seat furniture was most usually supplied with one or two sets of covers. For the chairs in the Tapestry Room at Croome Court, Mayhew and Ince supplied calico dust covers and covers of fine crimson, together with chamois stockings to protect the gilt legs.

Passementerie

Trimmings such as fringe, braid, tassels, cord, piping and lace, known collectively as *passementerie*, have long been used to embellish furniture that was already grandly upholstered [*124*]. They were invariably an expensive part of the job: the Duke of Bedford is recorded as having spent over £470 on trimmings for one bed in 1702.

The most interesting and beautiful *passementerie* was made in the late 17th and early 18th century, when not only silk but also a great deal of silver and gold was used in the best work. Orrice, for example, is a gold and silver lace woven on a loom. Trimmings of this period have such variety in colour, texture and form that it can really be seen as the golden age of the *passementerie* trade. Italy and France were particularly notable for the magnificence of the trimmings produced, although skilled craftsmen were also active in England. The finest *passementerie* was made by male professionals, but much work was also done by women – like needlework, such craft was considered a suitable pastime for a lady of the aristocracy or gentry: even Queen Charlotte, the wife of George III, had a frame for making fringe.

OPPOSITE A Louis XVI giltwood bergère à la reine by Jean-Baptiste-Claude Sené, 1789, which belonged to Louis XVI's sister at her country house, the Château de Montreuil. The padded back, arms, seat and squab cushion are upholstered in a modern floral cotton.

Designers today recognize that upholstery is an exciting area in which to explore all kinds of creative possibilities. It is also an easy way with which to inject new life into antique or vintage pieces. Such bespoke and artistic treatments may not be suitable for every piece of furniture you own, but the addition of one fabulous texture, colour or pattern on a chair or sofa can transform a space – like introducing an exclamation mark into a decorative scheme.

Artist Carolyn Quartermaine (b. 1959) works with a mix of antique, vintage and new furniture, covering the pieces in her own fabulous hand-painted silks and linens to create the perfect effect. In 2008, she selected antique chairs for their rich patina and combined them with her own designs for the Epinoy Room of the Château de Beloeil in Belgium and created her 'Giant' hand-painted silk and paper tassel to hang over the magnificent four-poster bed of Genoa velvet in the Amblise Room.

Aiveen Daly (b. 1973) is creating waves by applying many of the rules of dressmaking – smocking, ruching, pleating and so forth – to produce couture upholstery for chairs. Her 'Stiletto Puff' chair, 2006, features super-skinny gloss black legs and delicate knife pleats inspired by a gentleman's ruffle shirt.

LEFT The 'Bonbon Noir' footstool by Spina, 2008, covered in black leather, has an elegant black organza ribbon bow tie, introducing a frou-frou note of fun and femininity.

With her glamorous tailoring for vintage chairs, Aiveen Daly creates furniture that has one foot firmly in the past and the other firmly in today.

ABOVE 'Moneypenny', 2005, here shown in tweed, with a pleated frill and contrasting piping. It is a look reminiscent of tailored women's suits in postwar Britain.

LEFT 'Ming Ming', 2005, is an ottoman-style chaise longue dressed in tightly pleated fabric that recalls the elegant couture clothes of 1930s Hollywood.

RIGHT 'Bloom' of 2006 and 'Damask Floral' of 2005, two of Helen Amy Murray's unique cut leather designs.

BELOW Helen Amy Murray was invited to create a bespoke surface pattern for the 'Gill Wing Chaise' by Linley, 2008, a piece of furniture halfway between a sofa and a day bed: 'Shoal' is cut leather which evokes waves and fish.

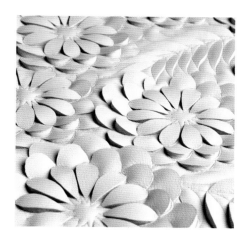

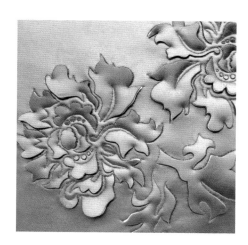

Texture too is providing creative inspiration for many designer–upholsterers. Helen Amy Murray is fast making a name with her talent for bringing chairs, sofas and beds alive with flowers, fishscales and feathers cut from pieces of suede and leather. Everything is bespoke, so colours can be chosen with the client.

Pattern has made a bold comeback – not just in fabric collections, but also in the hands of a new wave of upholsterers such as Lisa Whatmough of Squint. Not only does she cover the parts of furniture that are conventionally upholstered, but also the legs of tables and chairs, bases of lamps, frames of mirrors, and the like. The resulting patchworks look deceptively haphazard, but are in fact carefully thought out to create maximum impact.

ABOVE The 'Press Couch' by Swiss artist Mattia Bonetti, 2006 – a fabulous montage based on Chinese newspaper cuttings.

RIGHT A one-off design by Bokja from the Al-Sabah Art and Design Collection, which promotes the craftsmanship of the Middle East: the 'Mo' chair, covered in a cotton Bukhara *suzani*, 2008.

ABOVE AND RIGHT The 'Hampton' sofa
and the 'Squint Wing Chair', both of
2008, by Lisa Whatmough of Squint,
a knowledgeable and passionate
devotee of antique textiles. Each is
a one-off, priced according to the
final mix of fabrics used – which
cover even the legs.

BELOW This late 18th-century German ormolu-mounted mahogany table by David Roentgen features an oval top, edged by an openwork gallery, which opens like a 'belt'. The drawer at the front slides out to reveal a writing surface of green leather, and there are two further drawers to the side with concealed buttons to open them. The Comtesse de Provence, sister-in-law of Louis XVI, had a table of this model at Versailles, recorded there in 1792.

OPPOSITE A late 18th-century German ormolu-mounted mahogany writing and library table by David Roentgen. The top lifts to form a sloped surface for reading or writing, while the drawer at the front slides forward to reveal another drawer, only one of them being accessible from the outside. Roentgen delivered a table of this model in 1784 to Catherine the Great for the Palace of Pavlovsk.

The Magic of Mechanics

It is not only the external character of furniture that can be appreciated, but the ingenuity and artistry that is often harnessed within the interior. This may involve couture touches, such as secret dovetail joints, mitre finishes, screws drawn up in military precision, or drawers lined with silk, gold leaf or other exotic materials. Mechanical furniture adds a further layer of satisfaction, be it the discovery of secret drawers or the device that causes a concealed plasma screen to rise noiselessly from a cabinet.

Mechanical furniture, long popular with royalty and the aristocracy, has a rich and illustrious history. One of the masters of the art was Jean-François Oeben (see pp. 131, 152). He perfected, for example, a mechanical table which was both a dressing-table and a writing table: the top slides back as the drawer pulls forward, allowing the release of a reading stand and panels. He also conceived an ingenious system of locking all the drawers of a piece with a single turn of the key. He was granted the title of 'Ebéniste-Mécanicien du Roi' in 1760, the same year that he supplied an invalid chair to the Duc de Bourgogne (elder brother of the future Louis XVI) which could be turned, wheeled and regulated in height, with trays for reading and eating. The most important commission of his career, also in 1760, was for a secrétaire à cylindre for Louis XV, completed after Oeben's death by Jean-Henri Riesener (see p. 152),

which included such ingenious touches as a mechanism that allowed servants to refill the ink receptacles without actually opening the desk, full as it was of the king's most confidential papers. Another ingeniously inventive piece by Oeben is the 'table à la Bourgogne': this is in fact a five-drawer chest, from which a concealed bookcase rises at the back when a handle is turned; and not only that, but the fourth drawer can be pulled out and transformed into a

The 'Vortex Credenza' by Linley, 2008, has hidden drawers that reveal further secret drawers, which open in surprising ways. In addition, it plays with the idea of geometry, using op art marquetry to make a traditional rectangular sideboard look both concave and convex.

laptop writing desk, with curved legs that spring out automatically when pressure is applied to the central mechanism.

Other luminaries of furniture mechanics include the German cabinet-maker Abraham Roentgen (1711–93) and his son David (1743–1807). While Abraham established the family name and reputation, it was David who acquired a more international reputation. He made his first commercial trip from Neuwied to Paris in 1774. His first important commission was to provide Prince Charles of Lorraine, an uncle of Marie-Antoinette, with about fifteen pieces of furniture. Following a second visit to Paris, in 1779, his reputation was such that the royal family acquired a number of pieces, including for Louis XVI a large secrétaire à tombeau, identical to one he had made for Charles of Lorraine, purchased for the enormous sum of 96,000 livres. In 1785, the Queen received

'Glissade' by Wales & Wales for Meta, 2008, is a sleek, contemporary interpretation of an 18th-century writing desk in rippled ash. A secret button allows the entire desk to glide silently sideways to reveal a luxurious, leather-lined hiding place.

from David Roentgen an automaton in the form of a female tympanist, and he was rewarded with the title 'Ebéniste-Mécanicien du Roi et de la Reine'. In 1783 Roentgen first visited the court of Catherine the Great of Russia (see pp. 156–58), who was most enamoured of his ingenious designs. While Roentgen's supreme achievement lay in the quality of his marquetry, much royal enthusiasm for his work lay in the astonishing skill of his mechanical furniture, with secret compartments that would spring out at the press of a button to reveal further secret drawers [74–75].

Clever mechanical furniture was also prized for its dual functionality. Metamorphic library steps conjured out of chairs or desks, for example, were a popular addition to the great houses of the 18th century. By around 1800, globe-secretaires – writing desks hidden within the sectors of a globe – were also gaining popularity.

One particularly important development was the design patented in 1835 by Robert Jupe for a method whereby a circular dining table could be mechanically extended. It worked by having the circular top cut into six or eight segments, held on a spoked framework of wooden rails. In the middle was a capstan, a rotating barrel, which appeared to be nothing more than the supporting pedestal. As the top of the table was turned, the capstan pushed the segments out like a flower opening its petals. The gaps between the segments could then be filled with extra leaves. It is a design that has continued to be made in one form or other virtually ever since.

Happily, the age of surprises is not dead: Linley [76] and Meta [77, *right, and opposite*] are just two of the names where it is possible to find furniture that delights internally as much as externally, a testament to the superlative skill and craftsmanship still available today.

ABOVE AND OPPOSITE Tord Boontje's 'L'Armoire' for Meta, 2008, is an extraordinary reinterpretation of an 18th-century veneered cabinet. It is a chamber of secrets, with a central concealed panel which opens to reveal a series of drawers and three additional hidden compartments.

Golden Ages of Furniture

3

Ancient Egypt, Greece and Rome

Ming and Ch'ing

Lacquer

Chinoiserie

Italian Baroque

French Baroque

William and Mary

French Rococo

Thomas Chippendale

Newport and Philadelphia

Indian Ivory

French Neoclassicism

The Court of Catherine the Great

Gustavian

Regency

Biedermeier

Shaker

Arts and Crafts

Art Deco

American Studio Furniture

PREVIOUS OPENING A Louis XV ormolu-mounted kingwood, tulipwood and bois satiné commode attributed to BVRB (see pp. 129–31).

OPPOSITE An international combination of 20th-century fine furniture creates an elegant composition. The cabinet is a 1940s design by Jean Lesage for the Compagnie des Arts Français; the *klismos* chairs are by the London-born American T. H. Robsjohn-Gibbings, *c.* 1965; the 1940s mirror is by the French designer Pierre Pansart; while the light sconces are by the Italian Felix Agostini and date from the 1950s. The terracotta figurine is by the French sculptor Hubert Yencesse.

Furniture is so entwined with our own human history that to appreciate it fully requires some understanding of what was happening in the world when certain forms or decorative styles became popular. It has always been much more than a purely functional item. In the past, designers of furniture served royalty, nobility or rich merchants. That meant furniture had also to be art.

From the 15th century onwards, the skill of the master furniture-maker was highly valued. Fine furniture denoted wealth and status, learning and wisdom, good taste and excellent judgment. This not only applied to the individual who had commissioned it, but to the country, state or family which he represented. Furniture was an important means of attracting commerce, because it embodied the fine materials, technical sophistication and aesthetic expertise that could be found in that place.

Not surprisingly, then, furniture was the centrepiece of an aristocratic residence, part of the remit of the architect who was employed to provide a sumptuous setting to enhance royal splendour or personal grandeur. In time, the role of the upholsterer became more powerful, but the role of furniture was unchanged: to be the sun around which an interior orbited.

Design and technical innovations flowed from country to country, from East to West, sometimes speeded by military conquests or the movement of craftsmen; sometimes through the use of engraved designs and pattern books; at others by the traffic of furniture itself as part of international trade. Despite this, most furniture also has a strong national identity: styles reflected the countries from which they emanated both in terms of materials available and the politics of the day.

This section is intended to give a brief introduction to twenty of the most influential and important developments in the history of furniture. However, this is not simply about looking to the past. In many cases, the influence of these golden ages can be seen in the most cutting-edge interiors and furniture styles of the 21st century. As David Linley said in his introduction, 'If you want to move forward, you must first look backwards.'

BELOW A bronze stool from Pompeii, the town destroyed by the eruption of Vesuvius in AD 79. Stools were a popular form of Roman furniture; some were designed to fold for ease of transport.

OPPOSITE Three views of one of a pair of North European mahogany and parcel-gilt bergères from the second half of the 19th century. The design of these chairs, with their lion-bodied winged supporters, derives in part from the celebrated antique marble throne in the Vatican which was sketched in 1795 by the architect Charles Heathcote Tatham.

Ancient Egypt, Greece and Rome

Classical civilizations have provided inspiration to furniture designers for centuries, so it makes sense to begin this section with an overview of key influences which have endured to this day. Although differing in geography and history, these three ancient civilizations continue to have an impact on our artistic development.

The furniture of pharaonic Egypt achieved a degree of sophistication which is remarkable, considering that five thousand years have passed since the beginning of the First Dynasty. It is known not only from actual examples, which have been preserved intact owing to the dry climate of the Nile valley, but also through reliefs, paintings, statues and funerary models found in excavated tombs. Most preserved furniture dates from the New Kingdom (c. 1539–1150 BC), although furniture shapes are also recorded from both the Old Kingdom (c. 2650–2130 BC) and the Middle Kingdom (c. 1938–1630 BC). These representations, and surviving pieces, reflect the living conditions of the wealthy, for whom furniture was a status symbol. The majority of Egyptians would have sat and slept on mats of reed or rush.

Apart from papyrus, most furniture was constructed from native timbers, particularly acacia, sycamore, cedar and ebony. Poor timber was sometimes gessoed (see p. 57) and painted to imitate more valuable materials, or veneered and inlaid with lapis lazuli, ivory and faience; sheet gold and silver might be applied to luxury furniture. Construction techniques include mortice-and-tenon joints as well as dovetailing, with corners commonly lashed with cords or thongs. Drawers, doors and lids were sometimes incorporated, illustrating the degree of sophistication achieved so early.

Ancient Egyptian furniture has given us many familiar shapes for sofas, chairs and beds, including folding stools, high-backed chairs and curved couches. Legs were often carved in the form of bull's hooves or lion's paws, and seats were of rushwork or leather. Tables were mainly portable and would have served as trays. Possessions were usually stored in chests – from large decorative linen-chests to smaller caskets of ebony and ivory for jewels and other treasured items – or baskets. Beds were a luxury only afforded by the very rich.

Some of the finest surviving examples of furniture were found in the New Kingdom tomb of Tutankhamun. Most notable are a solid ebony bedstead and chair. A beautifully crafted gaming board and stand has lion's paw feet mounted on a sledge. The board is reversible, with ivory facing on both playing surfaces; in the stand was a drawer (now lost) which would have held the playing pieces. Also found in the tomb was a small box on tall legs with ebony and giltwood open-work hieroglyphs, a hinged lid and gilt knobs. Considering how much time has passed between their construction and now, these are truly astonishing designs.

Many of the forms used in Egypt were adopted in Greece. Homer's *Odyssey* evokes the splendours of the early palaces and their formal grandeur. Furniture is known from depictions on painted pottery and reliefs from the mid-5th century BC onwards. One of the most important types of furniture in Greece was the couch, used not only for sleeping at night but also for reclining during the day, particularly at mealtimes. Couches were often decorated with inlays of fine woods and semi-precious materials, featuring feet of silver or ivory, sometimes in the shape of animal legs. Frames were often simply strung with cords or leather thongs, but covers of wool or linen were sometimes woven in multicoloured designs, adding to the air of luxury and glamour.

Individual seats ranged from the throne to the folding stool. Thrones often encompassed startlingly sculptural forms, such as the heads of swans or serpents. Legs could again be in the form of animal legs, but by the 5th century BC rectangular ones were more usual. In the home, by the latter half of that century the favourite piece of furniture was the *klismos* chair [*cf. 82*], a beautifully simple design, curved to achieve ideal proportions, that was light enough to be easily carried. The tapering legs, which sweep in a distinctive concave curve, support a wide backrest and a webbed seat of cording or leather strips, covered with a cushion or animal pelt. (The *klismos* was revived in the Neoclassical period many centuries later: it was first seen widely in Paris in the furniture made by Georges Jacob in 1788 for the painter Jacques-Louis David; in London, Thomas Hope designed *klismos* chairs for his house in Duchess Street.) Also portable was the rectangular stool known as the *diphros*, a design depicted on the Parthenon frieze.

The Greeks used tables rather more than the Egyptians did. They also developed an attractive small type of round table found from the 4th century BC, typically supported on three deer legs terminating in hooves. (Like the *klismos* chair, this was much admired by Neoclassicists.) Chests were used for holding clothing, household equipment and valuables. While wooden examples rarely survive, bronze ones are often beautifully engraved with lively scenes, and frequently have lion's paw feet.

The spread of Roman civilization around the Mediterranean and across Europe ensured the adoption of Roman forms of furniture far beyond the frontiers of what is now Italy. Examples of folding stools in iron and bronze have been recovered from sites in countries including Belgium, the Netherlands and England. Tripod tables – strictly with three, but sometimes with four legs – were favourite items of Roman bronze furniture, typically used to support a tray or a bowl [*opposite*]. Small round tables with animal legs, developed by the Greeks, were also popular: made of bronze, silver, marble or rare imported woods, these were often richly decorated with animal carvings, such as lion or panther heads both on the legs and around the frieze, claw feet, or dogs and hares climbing up the legs. The Romans were also fond of elaborate veneers and inlays in wood, ivory and precious metals. A new fashion resulted in the appearance of wood or marble table tops supported on upright marble slabs, elaborately carved with mythical creatures, flowers and leaves. These were the inspiration for similar marble-topped designs during the Baroque period. Other articles of Roman furniture include chests on low feet, and cupboards with shelves, a new invention.

The characteristic Roman couch or *lectus* signified status within the household. Early designs featured head- and footrests of exquisite workmanship, typically with rich ornamentation of bronze and ivory. By the 1st century AD, however, elaborate headrests were no longer in vogue, and

ABOVE Detail of a Roman 'turned' couch in bronze, with cast ornament and inlaid decoration in silver, from Amiternum, 1st century AD.

a high back and sides were common. Couches often featured decorated rails and mattresses with striped covers, and were complemented by low footstools. Other Roman seats were based on Greek prototypes, such as the *klismos* and *diphros*.

This early furniture enjoyed such sophistication that it has influenced designs over many centuries in different regions around the world, from the splendour of the Italian Baroque to the theatricality of the English Regency.

OPPOSITE Classical references spread their net worldwide. The 'Griffin' table was designed *c.* 1939 by T. H. Robsjohn-Gibbings for the Weber residence in Bel Air, California.

LEFT A Roman circular bronze tripod table from the Temple of Isis in Pompeii, dating from before AD 79.

BELOW One of a pair of 17th-century yokeback armchairs (*guanmaoyi*) of Huanghuali wood. Although nearly four hundred years old, this style blends well into the contemporary design of most Western homes.

OPPOSITE A magnificent imperial twelve-panel zitan and hardwood screen (*weiping*) inlaid with soapstone, from the Kangxi period (1662–1722). Such screens were often used as versatile room dividers.

Ming and Ch'ing

Furniture in China was already well developed in the Han dynasty (206 BC–AD 221): low platforms called *k'ang* were used for sleeping and reclining on, accompanied by low tables and stools. The finest Chinese furniture dates from the Ming dynasty (1368–1644) and the earlier part of the Ch'ing dynasty (1644–1911). The Ming period is remarkable because it produced enduring and recognizable designs that look modern to our eyes even after four or five centuries.

The Chinese revered the idea of elegant living, and furniture was a part of this, along with clothing, gardening and flower arranging. The highest praise offered was *ya*, elegant, while the most condemning was *su*, vulgar. These judgments were not just aesthetic, but moral and social as well – used not simply to describe a situation, but to dictate an ideal. One highly influential cultural arbiter, Wen Zhenheng (1585–1645), included twenty sections on furniture suitable for an elegant interior in his *Zhang wu zhi* (Treatise on Superfluous Things). To him, furniture was more than a necessity of civilized living: it was part of a continuous moral and aesthetic discourse running through Ming culture. The debate centred on *jin*, modern, and *gu* – not so much antique as morally ennobling. A piece of furniture made the previous day could fit with Wen Zhenheng's idea of 'antique' if it lived up to his standards.

It is widely believed that by the 16th century Suzhou, not far from modern Shanghai, was a centre

of fine cabinetmaking. However, it is likely that the craft of furniture-making was diffused through other cities, with results including bamboo chairs from Wujiang, folding beds from Yongjia and Canton, and lacquered furniture from Beijing.

Furniture was made in many different woods according to local taste. The most admired and valued were hardwoods – chiefly rosewood and its varieties, and also a greyish-brown timber that matures to a dark coffee colour, known as 'chicken wing wood', which has been identified with *Cassia siamea* and its varieties. Differences in climate also influenced the use of materials. In the warmer south, bamboo furniture was common, and lacquered furniture was popular, being more resistant to insect attack. In the north, hardwood furniture was the favoured choice.

A unique feature of Chinese furniture is the total absence of nails and dowels (when dowels are present, it generally means a repair has been made). Construction is based on the mortice-and-tenon principle, with a limited use of dovetailing and a minimal use of glue. This was for practical reasons: jointing had to withstand temperature and humidity changes, and it was desired that furniture could be taken apart easily to be transported from one location to another. This intricate interlocking structure was often concealed with the use of bevelling and beading. There was a delight in convex edges, and curved sections were carved from a single block of hardwood where possible. A single piece of furniture often combined different timbers, finely woven cane, and pale brass mounts. Veneer was very uncommon.

In Chinese interiors, most furniture was placed against the walls or at a strict right angle to the wall – never informally grouped in the centre. At mealtimes, a table was brought into the room in which it had been decided to eat, as there was no formal dining room. At meals it was usual to sit on low stools around the table.

Chairs were most finely developed during the Ming period. One type is sometimes described in Ming texts as *chan yi* or 'meditation chairs' and later called 'official hat-shaped chairs' – from the supposed resemblance of their backs to the winged hats of Ming officials. They usually survive in pairs,

OPPOSITE A fine mother-of-pearl, hardwood and glass inlaid tapered cabinet dating from the Ming period. Shape and construction are simple, but embellished with beautiful and lavish surface ornamentation.

BELOW A rare Yuanmingyuan-style three-railing zitan bed from the Qianlong period (1736–95). Such beds were often one of the most important pieces of furniture in a wealthy household of the era.

suggesting something of the symmetry usually aimed for in Chinese room arrangements; Wen Zhenheng says that a set of four such chairs was the most suitable fitting for a gentleman's study. The other highly distinctive chairs of the period are those with round backs, sometimes also called 'horseshoe back' chairs. Chinese paintings show that they were used for dining and signified high status – seats of honour in fact – and in the late Ming period they bore the imposing name of *taishi yi*, 'grand tutor chairs'. They were often converted into sedan chairs with the addition of two carrying poles.

Two other important furniture types were the *ta* or couch and the *chuang* or bed. The former was of particular significance in the Ming period, taking pride of place in private apartments. From these often plain pieces descend the ornate couches of the 18th and early 19th centuries, often lavishly

decorated with lacquer. While the couch dominated the male study, the canopied *chuang*, with its rich silk hangings, was the central piece of furniture for female members of rich families; in it, the textiles rather than the bed frame were the centre of decorative interest. Beds also played an important symbolic role as part of the possessions a woman brought to her husband's family on marriage and one that would be sent back to her family in the event of a divorce.

Tables, used for writing and dining, and set against walls for the display of flowers and ornamental pieces, consist of a mitred frame with a central floating panel, formed of one or more planks, in plain or lacquered wood. In wealthy households small low tables for tea, light meals

and other uses accompanied the *k'ang*, a hollow brick platform, heated by a fire below it, which served as a bed and a space for reading or writing. These *k'ang* tables have particular appeal to Western eyes, resembling as they do our coffee tables.

Coffers and cupboards provided practical storage space in uncluttered, elegant interiors. Multi-drawer cabinets and those with removable shelves were favoured; many have low cupboards where items can be kept out of sight and open upper sections suitable to display prized items such as antique curios, jades and bronzes. Reproductions of such cupboards have become increasingly popular in recent years.

Not a single piece of Chinese furniture of any type or period is signed by its maker, and almost no makers' names are known.

ABOVE A rare standing screen (*zuopinfeng*) of Huanghuali and Tielimu wood inset with marble, dating from the 17th century. The intricate carving reflects the fine workmanship of the period.

LEFT One of a pair of Huanghuali compound wardrobes (*dasijiangui*), dating from the 17th century. Reproductions of such designs have become increasingly popular in the West.

Lacquer

The art of lacquer was given to the world by the Chinese very early in their history. But it was the Japanese, once they had learnt the skill, who raised it to heights of artistry never achieved anywhere else in the world.

True lacquer is the natural juice of *Rhus vernicifera*, the lac tree, which has been recorded in literary work since the 7th century BC. It flourishes today in South China, Korea, Japan and Annam, but almost certainly once had much wider distribution. It should not be confused with the gummy insect deposit left on trees in countries such as India and Burma, known in Hindustani as *lakh*. This was eventually adapted as a decorative substance in Europe, producing techniques such as 'shellac' and 'japanning'.

On exposure to air, raw lacquer turns first yellow-brown and then black. It has remarkable properties, including the fact that contact with moisture hardens it, rather than softening it. When a ship returning the Japanese exhibits of the Vienna Exhibition of 1878 was wrecked, divers recovering the cargo eighteen months later found the lacquer objects unharmed. It also has a high resistance to heat and acids. Only bright light causes it to fade, dry out and eventually decompose.

Lacquered objects are immensely tough, created as they are by the layering process of many coats – as many as thirty on a structure of wood (usually pine). Each layer is ground down with whetstone and finally polished. The result is a substance that an artist can carve, paint, or inlay with materials such as gold, silver or shell.

Chinese lacquer was often coloured by cinnabar, which gives various shades of red. The finest carved specimens come from the Imperial factories at Beijing, set up in about 1680 by the Emperor Kangxi, which reached their peak under Qianlong in the late 18th century. The Chinese have been painting with lacquer (rather than *on* it) since Han times: coloured lacquer in shades of green, turquoise, aubergine, wine red, rose pink, brown, white and yellow is applied to a black, dark brown or red lacquer ground.

One of the glories of Japanese lacquer is the use of gold and silver dust scattered on a usually black ground to create the design. Shell ornamentation, with inlaid mother-of-pearl and other shells, was also popular. Amber, rock crystal, tortoiseshell, ivory, coral, lapis lazuli, turquoise and coloured glass or porcelain were used as inlays on some sumptuous examples from the 15th, 16th and 17th centuries.

Lacquered furniture is of course at the heart of the decorative style known as Chinoiserie (see pp. 98–101). In the 17th century increased trading with the Far East caused an influx of Oriental merchandise in Europe. The Portuguese were the first to establish trading posts, most notably in Japan in 1542 and Macao in 1557. In 1571, Spain set up a

trading post on the Philippine Islands. In 1600, Elizabeth I of England granted a monopoly to the East India Company, which established bases in India and traded with China through the port of Canton. The other great maritime power of the day, the Dutch, reached Canton in 1600 and established the Dutch East India Company in 1602. France was the last great power to reach the Far East, her ships kept out of Chinese waters for many years by the Spanish and Portuguese.

The earliest painted Chinese lacquer to make an impression upon the Western world was the type known as Bantam work or Coromandel [*121*]. Outstanding examples include large screens with many panels of rich decoration [*cf. 89*], which often suffered the ignominious fate in the West of being cut up and made into smaller pieces of furniture, though they were occasionally used to panel entire rooms. Chinese lacquer and Chinese blue-and-white porcelain exerted an enormous influence on the William and Mary style in England (see pp. 120–25), not surprisingly given the links to Cathay through both the English and Dutch

ABOVE One of a pair of George III serpentine commodes sumptuously decorated with ormolu-mounted Chinese black and gilt lacquer, attributed to the London cabinet-maker Pierre Langlois. They were most probably supplied to John, 2rd Earl of Ashburnham, in the early 1760s and remained in the Ashburnham collection until 1953.

OPPOSITE The back of one of a pair of Chinese export black and gold lacquer side chairs, *c.* 1730, formerly at Warwick Castle, home of the Earls of Warwick. ('Chinese export' is the term given to furniture that was made in China especially to please European tastes.)

East India Companies. Venetian Baroque furniture also made use of imported lacquer.

In late 17th-century France, Japanese lacquer was sought after both for integrating into furniture and for the panelling of rooms. It was considered superior to the Chinese type, not just in terms of technical expertise but because the designs were so spare, with beautifully placed motifs of birds and flowers, or romantic landscapes of trees, pagodas and hills. Lacquered furniture was the result of an initiative by three *marchands-merciers* (see p. 126) in particular, Hébert, Darnault and Poirier, who were

among the few to be able to afford Oriental lacquer wares: Japanese chests, screens and cabinets were cut up to form the main panels on commodes [*9*], the remaining surface being filled up by French imitation lacquer – a technique known as japanning, which became popular as a way of imitating the costly and covetable real material throughout Europe (see p. 57). The *ébénistes* who made this furniture on commission for the *marchands-merciers* include BVRB [*130, 131*], who is thought to have produced most of the pieces in Japanese lacquer that were delivered to the Garde-Meuble Royal between 1737 and 1745.

Lacquered furniture enjoyed a revival during the Art Deco period, when there was a taste for all things Oriental and exotic once more.

OPPOSITE A Queen Anne black and gilt lacquered double-domed bureau-cabinet, early 18th century. The flower-trellised panels feature foliage, exotic birds, and figures – including the character of Harlequin.

ABOVE A pair of George III ormolu-mounted Chinese black and gold lacquer and japanned serpentine commodes, supplied to the 4th Earl of Shaftesbury for St Giles's House at Wimborne St Giles in Dorset *c.* 1765.

BELOW One of a pair of late George II giltwood girandoles supplied by Thomas Chippendale to the 5th Earl of Dumfries for Dumfries House in 1759, in the Chinese style so popular in the day. Such designs are included in Chippendale's *Director*.

OPPOSITE An ebonized display-cabinet with Chinoiserie pagoda-style top in the Breakfast Room at Castle Coole in Ireland – a bizarre mixture of French, Chinese and Classical styles which is typically Regency.

Chinoiserie

For centuries, Cathay – the old name for China – fascinated the imagination of the West. The few merchants who penetrated its shores returned with rich cargoes of silk, porcelain, lacquer and tea. They talked of a land of palaces and pagodas, fiery dragons and exotic birds, a landscape of tranquil waters, pointy mountains, delicate pavilions and fantastic flowers. Then there were the people themselves – men with wispy beards and peculiar hats, women richly clad in patterned robes. No wonder China cast such a spell upon the West: it seemed to be out of the pages of a fable.

China's goods, in particular silk, had been imported to the West as far back as Roman times, carried along the caravan trails of Central Asia. However, the Silk Route became increasingly insecure, and in AD 878 China closed its doors to all foreigners. In the 13th century it was invaded by Genghis Khan and his Tartar army. Pisa, Genoa and Venice, which had been trading with Islam since the 7th century, then took advantage of this sweeping political move to return to dealing direct with China, in particular for silk. Other European powers awoke to the possibility, and successive Chinese dynasties sanctioned a limited trade with the West while discouraging any other contact with the outside world. Trading posts were established by the Portuguese and the Spanish, followed by the English and the Dutch (see pp. 93–94). The English East India Company limited its official purchases mainly to tea, raw silk and porcelain, but its employees were allowed to deal privately. It was this private commerce – in furnishing textiles, dress fabrics, wallpapers, ceramics, lacquerware, fans, silver, gold and ivory – that first brought Chinese objects to Britain. By the second half of the 17th century, the *beau monde* of Europe was gripped by a craze for all things Chinese – in particular embroidered silk, lacquer screens and blue-and-white porcelain.

'The East' was viewed as a single entity, with many people uncertain about the actual geography of China, Japan, Siam (Thailand) or India. What mattered was the romance and opulence that such names conjured up, with even the King of France, Louis XIV, appearing at a ball 'dressed in the Chinese manner'.

The fashionable style of the day in Europe was the Baroque (see pp. 104–18), which with its overall sense of grandeur could easily accommodate magnificent Chinese imports. As demand for Oriental wares grew, prices rose, and that in turn prompted European craftsmen to attempt to imitate

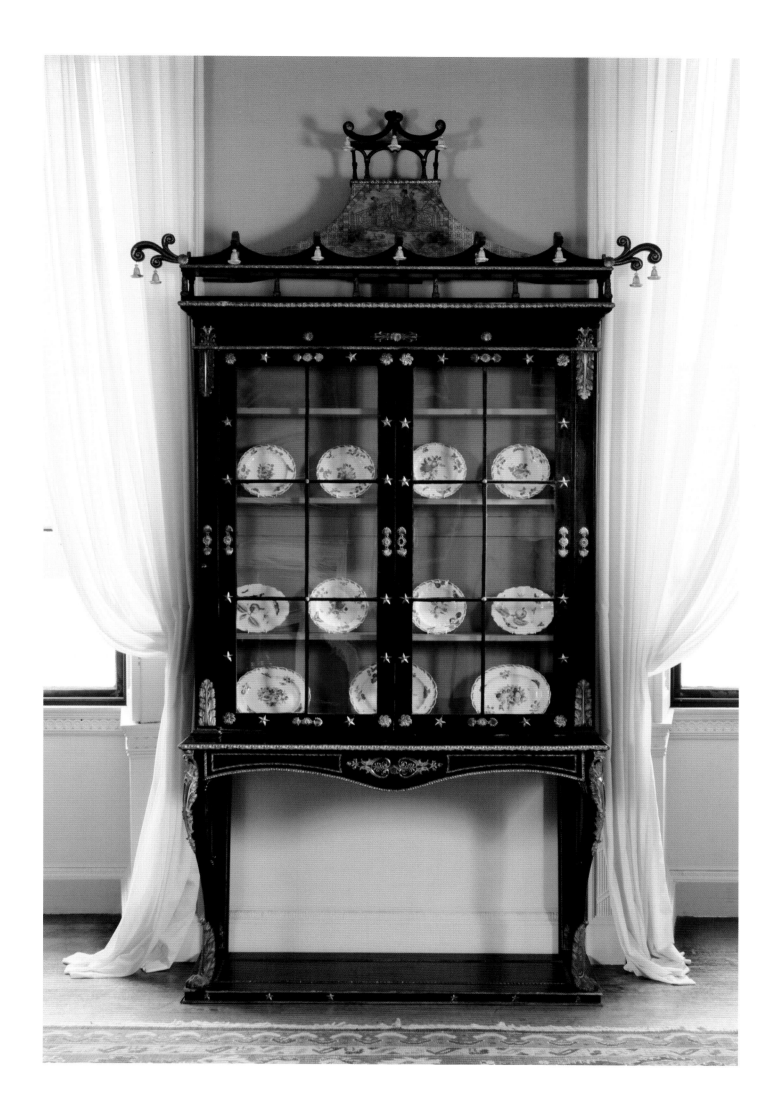

them for less affluent collectors, with quaint scenes of long-tailed birds, angular trees and rickety buildings. In China, this was mirrored by furniture and goods produced for the export market only [95]. By the middle of the 17th century, the exotic picture of Cathay had been firmly stamped on the European imagination. Considerable quantities of genuine lacquer were by then flooding the markets of Paris, London and Amsterdam, along with porcelain and textiles. It is important to distinguish, however, between the vogue for Chinoiserie, a hybrid design style that draws on both Oriental and European influences, and the connoisseur's appreciation of original lacquer, particularly that from Japan.

The George I scarlet japanned bureau cabinet in the State Bedroom of Erddig, in Wales, was probably bought from John Belchier by the house's owner, John Meller, in the 1720s. The green japanned chairs on either side were acquired in 1726, most probably also from John Belchier.

Designs for 'Chinese' furniture were sent out to the East to be manufactured there, but the result was sometimes criticized for being badly made, so a certain amount of furniture was made in Europe, transported to the East for lacquering, and then reimported. The result was European furniture influenced by the Orient, which would have looked distinctly out of place in the home of a true Chinaman.

The disciplined French took to Chinoiserie with discretion, and *ébénistes* in the 17th and 18th centuries often incorporated genuine lacquer panels in their creations [*e.g. 9, 128, 130, 131*]. With lacquer so much in demand, cabinetmakers set about replicating it through the process known as japanning (see p. 57). In England, japanned work of the 17th century [*122*] often features bold pictorial decoration which bears no relation to true Oriental compositions. Designs may comprise a haphazard medley of buildings set in strange, rocky landscapes with flocks of exotic birds and large-petalled flowers, and there are unwittingly comic touches, with figures looking as though they were wearing dressing gowns and tea cosies, rather than Chinese robes.

English needleworkers succumbed to the Orient with the same passion: figures crossing rickety bridges, drinking tea, or entering pagodas were embroidered on silken panels, while lavish displays of peonies, lotus flowers and chrysanthemums were worked in chain-stitch and satin-stitch. A particularly popular motif was the Indian Tree of Life, a single tree twisting its way upwards. English Chinoiserie of this period is often naive, but it is this very innocence that makes it so charming and easily recognizable.

While the fashion for Chinoiserie began in the age of the Baroque, it was the exuberance and romance of the Rococo that gave it full flight. Rococo celebrated all that was amusing and fantastic, and Chinoiserie was tailor-made for it [*98, 102*]. Asymmetry, a key element in Rococo design, is naturally present in Oriental taste. Ornament proliferated – shells, garlands, fruit, foliage, flowers, C-scrolls and S-scrolls, long-legged birds, well-dressed monkeys, and, of course, Chinamen strolling in magical landscapes.

A George III green and gold japanned clothes press supplied by Thomas Chippendale in 1771 for the closet adjoining the State Bedchamber at Nostell Priory.

A Chinoiserie pier glass above a green and gold japanned
commode, both supplied by Thomas Chippendale in
1771 for the Chinese Ante-Room of the State Bedchamber
at Nostell Priory, at a cost of £68 for the pier glass and
£15 10s for the commode.

CHINOISERIE: THE GOLDEN THREAD

For hundreds of years, there has been cross-fertilization
between East and West, but nowhere is this better
expressed today than in the Contrasts galleries of
Pearl Lam, in Shanghai and Beijing, where Lam
both invites Western artists to interpret China
and introduces home-grown Chinese art to
the West.

'Fake' by XYZ Designs, an artistic
consortium led by Pearl Lam. This
chair, of 2007, comments on the
relationship between East and West,
exaggerating the two-way design
traffic which threatens both cultures.

BELOW A giltwood side chair, made in Venice in the third quarter of the 18th century, when the Baroque style still flowered in the city, and supplied to Paolo Renier, the penultimate doge. It features a moulded shield-shaped back flanked by cherubs, and a serpentine seat covered in red flowered silk.

OPPOSITE The Badminton Cabinet: this magnificent *pietra dura*, ebony and gilt bronze cabinet was commissioned from the grand-ducal workshops in Florence by the 3rd Duke of Beaufort in 1726 and completed in 1732, when it was shipped to England. Two of the *pietra dura* panels are signed on the reverse by Baccio Capelli and are dated 1720, while the gilt-bronze figures emblematic of the Four Seasons are by Girolamo Ticciati.

Italian Baroque

The Italian word *barocco* began as a term of abuse, applied to the grotesque and the exaggerated; but in fact, while Italian Baroque is indeed exciting, extraordinary and exuberant, there is still an element of control which prevents it from being unwieldy. Its virtues lie in boldness and elaboration, in the use of precious materials, and in the sculptural excellence of the figures it so often incorporates.

'Italian Baroque' is a slightly misleading term, because what we regard as Italy was a number of individual states until the latter half of the 19th century, and the style took different signatures from region to region. An important development in Italian social history, however, was the emergence in the 16th century of wealthy new families, vying with one another to display their status and influence in as ostentatious a way as possible.

In the late 16th century, Rome was the seat of a powerful papacy, which in turn created around it a strong aristocracy. The city entered a period of enormous prosperity, and many *palazzi* were rebuilt. The private apartments of these great houses were furnished with utilitarian furniture, made by local carpenters and joiners. However, in the state apartments, which invariably included the all-important gallery, it was a different story. The disposition of furniture in Baroque rooms was invariably formal, following the same pattern all over Europe. Chairs stood very close to each other in straight lines against the walls. Furniture was almost completely absent from the centre of the room and eating-tables were set up as required, then removed and the room returned to its balanced architectural state.

By the 17th century, great Roman families displayed their wealth, prestige and ambition in fabulous pieces of furniture, such as enormous console tables with thick tops of jasper or marble supported by near lifesize figures, or magnificent cabinets of ebony, rare woods, semi-precious stones and gilt bronze. These were often made by the same leading sculptors who carved statues for churches. Baroque was a powerful expression of religious might, and they made no professional distinction between carving a Crucifixion or a piece of furniture. The great throne by Gianlorenzo Bernini in St Peter's in Rome (1657–66) was the model for the huge gilded Baroque thrones

105

A lavishly ornamented gilt-bronze-mounted ebony and *pietra dura* casket made in the grand-ducal workshops in Florence, *c.* 1720.

which proved so popular with princely families such as the Borghese and the Barberini. These magnificent thrones were not the only innovation. The Baroque period saw several new types of furniture come into use. The wardrobe, for example, superseded the *cassone* (a chest traditionally made to store a bride's trousseau); it was often architectural in form, with pilasters at the corners and a pediment on top. Ornamented built-in bookcases were commissioned for the great libraries of private houses, rooms which often featured a pair of celestial and terrestrial globes, supported by carved figures of allegorical significance. And the purely ornamental side table or console was also a 17th-century innovation, its marble top resting on extravagant foliage, shells, dolphins, eagles, mermaids, slaves and other figures.

Florence lies slightly outside the mainstream of Italian Baroque, but it is associated with one important technique: that of *pietra dura* inlay (see pp. 54–55). The Galleria dei Lavori in the Uffizi, first organized by Cosimo I de' Medici (1519–74) and renamed Opificio delle Pietre Dure in 1588 by

his son, Ferdinand I (1549–1609), who had become Grand Duke of Tuscany in 1587, was the centre of this craft, an immensely time-consuming form of inlay using pieces of highly coloured marble and semi-precious stones such as agate, lapis lazuli and malachite to create decorative panels featuring birds, flowers and landscapes [*54, 105, above and opposite*]. It was often the result of cooperative effort from a range of different craftsmen, many of them skilled foreigners, all paid by the Grand Duke. The Uffizi craftsmen also produced furniture of silver in some quantity. In overall charge was a renowned artist, architect or sculptor, under whose eye every piece of furniture was produced. Below him were the *capomaestri* (heads of workshops) and under them the *cottimanti* – junior cabinetmakers, goldsmiths, casters, carvers and weavers. A later 17th-century development, which originated outside the grand-

A mid-17th-century *pietra dura* table top. Such work was admired internationally, and this splendid composition of flowers, birds and fruit was taken to France and placed on a slightly later Louis XIV giltwood base.

ducal workshops but was adopted there, was the technique of scagliola, powdered marble painted on fine wet plaster, which when dry is polished to look like solid marble (see p. 58).

The *stippone*, or great cabinet, is the most characteristic piece of the Florentine Baroque, but in fact it is of German derivation. Augsburg and Nuremberg were the centres for the production of these truly awe-inspiring pieces [40]. Several Augsburg cabinets originally given to Cosimo I were almost certainly the inspiration for the designs produced in the Uffizi workshops. During the time of Ferdinand II (ruled 1621–70), fabulous combinations of ivory, ebony, tortoiseshell, lacquer, silver, gilt bronze (ormolu) and *pietra dura* were used to create furniture every bit as grand and exotic as the materials imply. These cabinets became

increasingly complex mechanically, frequently taking the form of miniature palaces, which opened to reveal sumptuous interiors. Sometimes commissioned as a safe place for valuables and jewels, they would often conceal secret drawers and compartments – all part of the theatrical illusion which is very much their signature. Such pieces were still being made by the workshops well into the 18th century. One of the most remarkable examples is the Badminton Cabinet [105], commissioned by the English aristocrat Henry Somerset, 3rd Duke of Beaufort, in 1726 – an astonishing creation of ebony, gilt bronze and *pietra dura* (including amethyst and lapis lazuli) – which it is estimated took five years and thirty craftsmen to make. Another masterpiece is the cabinet made by Giambattista Foggini (1652–1725) between 1707 and 1709 for the then Elector Palatine, Johann Wilhelm II of Neuberg, which featured ebony, *pietra dura* and ormolu mounts.

In 17th-century Venice, as in Rome, state room furniture was almost entirely the province of the sculptor. Again the division was wide between

the simple functional pieces of the family apartments and the massive, ornamented designs created for the vast rooms of the *piano nobile* looking over the Grand Canal. The greatest Venetian furniture-maker of the period was Andrea Brustolon (1662–1732): he had been an assistant to the Genoese sculptor Filippo Parodi, who had in turn worked in Bernini's studio from 1655 to 1661. One of Brustolon's most famous suites of furniture, made for Pietro Venier and now housed in the Ca' Rezzonico, has elaborately carved figures in boxwood, walnut and ebony (the use of natural woods in strong, contrasting colours was

appealing in Venice, where wood of any kind was rare and therefore costly). His most extravagant piece for the Venier home is a large vase-stand and side table of box and ebony, designed as a single piece to display rare imported Japanese vases, and featuring the allegorical figures of Hercules, Cerberus and Classical river gods.

Brustolon's successor as leading furniture-maker was the sculptor Antonio Corradini (1668–1752), famed for his carving of veiled statues. He favoured gilding (the more usual Baroque method), which was quicker and easier for the

ABOVE AND RIGHT Two views of one of a pair of Venetian walnut side tables, the tops elaborately inlaid with stained horn, brass, ebony, rosewood, fruitwood, and boxwood, *c.* 1686, signed in the marquetry Lucio de Lucci.

OPPOSITE An exuberantly carved Venetian polychrome-japanned mother-of-pearl inlaid and giltwood mirror, late 17th–early 18th century. It is one of a pair.

carver since it enabled softwoods such as pear and lime to be used. In his hands, bold curves and scrolls of wood looked as malleable as plaster. A giltwood throne by Corradini, one of the most sumptuous and expensive pieces of furniture from this fertile period, can also be seen today in the Ca' Rezzonico.

In the second half of the 17th century, Venice became renowned for its lacquer furniture, most of it decorated with raised gilt Chinoiserie figures; the technique of japanning – an imitation of true lacquer

(see p. 57) – had been learnt early on through Venice's trading contacts with the East. Green and gold lacquer became something of a Venetian speciality, and remained popular in the later Rococo period. Ebony candlestands in the form of blackamoors echoed the Venetians' love of carnival and fancy dress. It was for glass that Venice was most famous internationally – the islands of Murano and Torcello in the lagoon had been centres of glassmaking since the Middle Ages – and it was the Venetians who produced elaborate glass sconces and enormous chandeliers featuring multicoloured flowers.

The development of Baroque furniture in Genoa followed a path parallel to that in Venice, despite their geographical distance. The Strada Nuova (now Via Garibaldi) in Genoa was, like the Grand Canal in Venice, lined with palaces. Forbidding exteriors concealed an explosion of gilding, mirrors and rich textiles within. Genoa was famous for its rich furnishing materials, such as cut velvets in reds, greens and yellows, damasks woven in several colours, and silks, which were exported to countries as far away as Scotland and Sweden [*e.g. 65, 124*]. Used for covering chairs, these fabrics added greatly to the impression of luxurious opulence. They also heralded an important change in interiors: soft furnishings were to take precedence over case furniture, and in turn upholsterers were to replace architects as the eminent style-setters of the day. Genoese furniture was heavily influenced by Rome. For example, the sculptor Domenico Parodi (1668–1740), son of the sculptor Filippo Parodi who had worked with Bernini in Rome, was the maker of an extraordinary combined pier-glass and table now in the Palazzo Rosso. The sculptor Anton Maria Maragliano (1664–1739) was also adept at monumental furniture of this kind.

Turin was the capital of Sardinia and Savoy, a handsome city popular with Grand Tourists. Its Baroque furniture is clearly influenced by the work of Brustolon and Domenico Parodi, with carved figures, for instance, supporting gargantuan tables, but there is a slightly tighter architectural control – perhaps influenced by French furniture of the same period. The city's development as an artistic centre in its own right came later, with the arrival in 1715 from Rome of the Sicilian architect Filippo Juvarra (1678–1736). For the royal palace of Stupinigi outside the city, Juvarra produced pier-tables on piles of military trophies, enormous clocks flanked by winged sphinxes, and extravagant tripod stands. While the Roman inspiration is clear, Juvarra imbued his designs with a discipline that is not always apparent in furniture made by sculptors steeped in religious imagery. For the Palazzo Reale

in the city, Juvarra collaborated with the sculptor Pietro Piffetti (1701–77), who had returned to Turin after an apprenticeship in Rome and was appointed cabinetmaker to King Carlo Emanuele III in 1731. He specialized in the emerging Rococo style, with designs of dazzling complexity and lavish curved forms, typically inlaid with rich woods, ivory and tortoiseshell; for the Palazzo Reale, he produced wonderfully outlandish designs encrusted with exotic inlays and intricate gilt mounts.

The Baroque in Italy did not disappear from view with the advent of Rococo. It was a style that continued to flower and prosper into the 18th century: both the Badminton Cabinet [*105*] and the carved giltwood chair made for the penultimate doge of Venice [*104*] are of this later period, but they are fully Baroque in attitude, form and splendour.

The influence of Italian Baroque spread widely, in part because of the popularity of the Grand Tour. Wealthy young aristocrats sent home sumptuous Baroque pieces as permanent mementos of their travels.

Baroque encapsulates the idea of furniture with attitude. Often large-scale, sumptuous, uncompromising and magnificent, this is design that is both extravagant and extrovert. Place a Baroque piece in a room and it immediately takes centre stage.

OPPOSITE, LEFT The overscaled 'Bergere' chair by Fredrikson Stallard is a fabulous reinvention of the Baroque throne in stainless steel and white rubber.

OPPOSITE, RIGHT 'Madame Liaisons' folding screen designed by Carlo dal Bianco for Bisazza in glass chip mosaic and white gold leaf – a radical new interpretation of *pietra dura*.

ITALIAN BAROQUE: THE GOLDEN THREAD

Baroque today is still very much a demonstration of status, wealth and taste. The great Italian architect–designers Giò Ponti (1891–1979) and Ettore Sottsass (1917–2007) – founder of the Memphis group – owed much of their flamboyant style to the radically adventurous age of the Baroque. The *pietra dura* process continues to fascinate the Italian company Bisazza, which creates fabulously ornamented surfaces, art installations and furniture through the expert application of thousands of mosaic tiles in a rich variety of colours and textures. It has also more recently informed the work of artist Marc Quinn.

BELOW A Louis XIV ormolu-mounted brass-inlaid brown tortoiseshell, ebony and boulle marquetry petite armoire, *c.* 1700–1710, attributed to André-Charles Boulle. It featured in the celebrated sale at Wanstead House in 1822.

OPPOSITE AND BELOW The Louis XIV ormolu-mounted ebony, cut-brass, tortoiseshell, blue-stained horn and pewter marquetry 'Armoire de l'Histoire d'Apollon' by André-Charles Boulle. The detail shows the ormolu mount top centre. Boulle was a master *bronzier* as well as an *ébéniste*.

French Baroque

Under the long reign of Louis XIV, who came to the throne in 1643 at the age of four, assumed power in 1661 and ruled until 1715, France increased her influence and wealth through strategic military victories. She was also the leader of design and style in Europe, as typified by the Sun King's transformation of the palace of Versailles into the epicentre of artistic taste and achievement. The position of France as a serious, powerful, masculine and unassailable state is reflected in the furniture

and furnishings of the time. Baroque, which was in part fuelled by the powerful, newly aristocratic families of Italy, was an aesthetic that demanded attention – a means to display a nation or individual's wealth, sophistication and prestige through extraordinary and opulent pieces of furniture. The style was adopted but refined to meet French taste, where discipline and control have always been important factors, part of a carefully contrived totality. French Baroque is still essentially a communication of power and influence, but it has none of the wilder fantasies so evident in its Italian forerunner.

The guild system that operated through France in the 17th and 18th centuries was designed to protect the interests of an established group of craftsmen; it did not welcome free competition or the establishment of newcomers (although a good many guild members were themselves first- or second-generation immigrants, mainly from Germany and the Netherlands). Because each guild had its specialization, the technical skill achieved was immense. French 17th- and 18th-century furniture is often and rightly described as the pinnacle of the furniture-making tradition, and this is largely due to the rigid guild system. Originally, craftsmen in wood were grouped together in one guild, the *menuisiers*; of these, the *ébénistes* (literally 'workers in ebony')

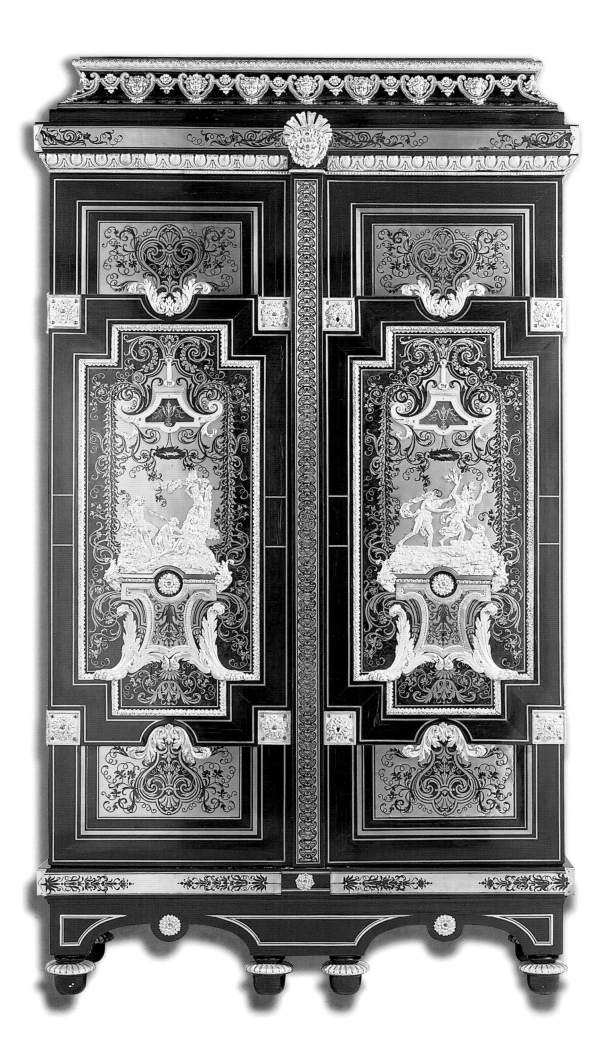

eventually broke away to form their own guild. They specialized in veneered wood or marquetry, embellished with rich metal mounts (originally devised to protect the precious surface of such furniture from knocks). The *menuisiers* then typically made furniture that was to be carved by a *sculpteur* rather than veneered or inlaid by an *ébéniste:* chiefly chairs, but also pieces such as console tables.

The work of André-Charles Boulle (1642–1732) exemplifies French Baroque furniture [*53, 112–16*]. Boulle trained as a cabinetmaker, architect, bronze worker and engraver. The structure of the guild system prevented makers from simultaneously practising two professions, yet Boulle infringed the rules by holding the titles of both *ébéniste* and *bronzier.* The fact that he was 'Ebéniste du Roi' no doubt shielded him from prosecution. In fact he supplied very little furniture to Louis XIV, his main

employment at Versailles being the making of marquetry and parquet floors or decorative details in ormolu. Over a period of forty-two years, between 1672 and 1714, he supplied fewer than twenty pieces of furniture to the court, the first being for the Queen and the Grand Dauphin. He had to wait until 1700 to supply his first piece to the King himself – a large armoire in purplewood for the Garde-Robe du Roi at

BELOW A centre table by André-Charles Boulle, *c.* 1685. The central panel has exceptionally rich marquetry on a lustrous tortoiseshell ground. This too was in the Wanstead sale in 1822.

OPPOSITE Details of a set of Louis XIV ebonized, ormolu-mounted torchères by André-Charles Boulle, with marquetry of brown tortoiseshell, tin, brass and blue-stained horn, from Warwick Castle, where there was a remarkable collection of Boulle furniture.

OPPOSITE One of a pair of Louis XIV ebony and tortoiseshell coffres de la toilette (mariage) by André-Charles Boulle. Boulle's skill at integrating the marquetry and the mounts into a whole is brilliantly illustrated in this coffre. It has *première partie* ornament, with the pattern in brass against a tortoiseshell background; on its fellow, the ornament is *contre partie*, tortoiseshell against brass.

RIGHT A Louis XIV ormolu-mounted ivory, tortoiseshell, ebony and floral marquetry cabinet-on-stand attributed to Pierre Gole.

Marly. Most of his commissions were for noblemen and Parisian financiers.

A typically lavish design by Boulle might well feature elaborate figurative scenes, ebony, tortoiseshell and brass marquetry, inlays of mother-of-pearl, pewter or exotic woods, marble tops, handles and mounts of gilt bronze, intricate scrolls, floral patterns and ornamental mouldings. His skill at combining wood veneers with semi-precious materials led to the development of a genre known as boulle marquetry: although he did not invent the technique himself, it was his name that lived on through this decorative art. Among Boulle's most celebrated signature pieces are two commodes that he supplied to Louis XIV for Versailles in 1708. Commodes were a relatively new form of furniture at the beginning of the 18th century, derived from bureaux. So well received were the Versailles pair that Boulle repeated them, and similar models can be found in other important 18th-century collections. Who could fail to be impressed by the grandeur, might and wealth that such furniture represented?

It would be misleading, however, to suggest that Boulle's grandiose style was the only French interpretation of the Baroque. The work of Pierre Gole (1620–84), who was also much favoured by Louis XIV, is altogether different in feeling: rather than ormolu mounts and ebonized wood, a typical piece might feature intricate marquetry designs of flowers or birds on an ivory ground (Gole had made a speciality of marquetry on ivory) [*right*]. He also produced pieces in the Chinese manner, a restrained development of the taste for Chinoiserie in France. Tables designed around 1670 for the Trianon de Porcelaine at Versailles were decorated with blue-stained horn on an ivory ground in imitation of Chinese porcelain.

Dominique Cucci (before 1640–1705) was an Italian *ébéniste*, one of several persuaded to leave Florence by Louis XIV with the aim of encouraging the decorative arts and crafts in France, and in particular the inlay technique of *pietra dura* (see pp. 54–55). Like Boulle, he was renowned both as an *ébéniste* and as a *bronzier*; but he is also credited with perfecting the art of imitation lapis lazuli. A description in a general inventory of the period of two cabinets made by Cucci for the King between 1667 and 1673 sums up French Baroque: 'Two very large cabinets in ebony outlined in pewter, enriched with various swags, festoons, ciphers and other ornamentation in gilt-bronze, four large twisted columns, grounds of false lapis, overlaid with vine tendrils in gilt bronze, and eight fluted pilasters of tortoiseshell, all with gilt bases and Ionic capitals, supported on six lion-claw feet.'

Antoine-Robert Gaudreaus (1682–1746) supplied an astonishing 850 pieces of furniture to the court, the majority made in walnut or cherry but also in olivewood, kingwood, palisander and tulipwood. These rich timbers, ornamented with lavish ormolu mounts but notable for their lack of marquetry (other than for geometric effects), typify the furniture produced during the Régence – the period from 1715 to 1723, when France was ruled

by the Duc d'Orléans as regent for Louis XV, Louis XIV's great-grandson. Gaudreaus' masterpieces, such as a commode for the King's Bedchamber and a medal cabinet for the King's Cabinet Intérieur at Versailles, are among the greatest examples of French furniture. They also mark a shift from the more overbearing examples of the Baroque towards Rococo.

A Louis XIV ormolu-mounted, brass inlaid, brown tortoiseshell, ebony and ebonized table en bureau. Boulle developed this distinctive model of six-legged console in the first years of the 18th century (there is a related drawing by him of *c*. 1705). Much favoured by later 18th-century collectors, these tables were often sold as pairs by *marchands-merciers*: this *contre-partie* example (with a tortoiseshell pattern inlaid in brass) is stamped by both Jean-François Leleu and Joseph Baumhauer, who acted as repairers in the 1770s.

FRENCH BAROQUE: THE GOLDEN THREAD

The Baroque period has continued to excite and inspire contemporary furniture designers, for example the Dutch/Belgian duo Studio Job (see pp. 207–8). Conceived in 2006, their 'Robber Baron' series comprises a suite of five cast-bronze furnishings, which are magnificent in scale, finely modelled and cast, with precision mechanical movements where required. The master craftsmanship evident in the work is guild-like in its perfection. These highly expressive pieces of limited-edition furniture are narrative works which address power, corruption, industry and art.

ABOVE A restrained interpretation of Baroque grandeur is the triple-bow-fronted cabinet with distressed gold on white gold finish and onyx top by Alastair Graham, 2006.

LEFT Studio Job's 'Robber Baron' cabinet is made of polished bronze with gilded reliefs. In its centre is a black patinated 'bomb crater', a stark reference to the conflict between art and industry.

William and Mary

William III (1650–1702) was the hereditary ruler of the Dutch principality of Orange, and leader of the seven United Provinces that made up the Dutch Republic. He married Protestant Mary (1662–94), eldest daughter of the Catholic Duke of York (later James II), in 1677, and the relationship between the two countries was cemented by the Anglo-Dutch Treaty of the following year. The question of religion was of fundamental importance in 17th-century Europe. The fact that both Holland and England were Protestant countries inevitably gave them common interest against the great Catholic powers of France and Spain. Many in England feared the restoration of the Catholic religion and this led to the so-called Glorious Revolution in 1688, followed in 1689 by William being invited to assume the crown in James's place. He and Queen Mary II were joint sovereigns until her death. William then reigned alone for eight more years.

The Baroque style that bears their name signalled great changes in architecture and the decorative arts. The monarchs were jointly responsible for its promotion: William initiated a renewed spate of building and furnishing at Hampton Court Palace, almost wholly French in its inspiration, while Mary introduced the Dutch fashion for devoting entire rooms to blue-and-white ware – both Oriental blue-and-white porcelain and Dutch Delftware. The monarchs were also enthusiasts for lacquered furniture from China and Japan [*opposite*].

One feature that marks the William and Mary period as a turning point of interior design in England is the introduction of unified schemes of interior decoration created by a single designer. Furniture was richly gilded and inlaid, designed as an integral part of a total effect which included brilliantly coloured fabrics, sculptural silverware and of course blue-and-white ceramics. This comprehensive approach required a team of specialists, such as gilders, carvers and painters, all producing work that fitted the new ornamental style. Motifs such as flutes, shells, ornamental masks and scrolls that had been popularized by cabinetmakers in France now spread rapidly through Britain and the Netherlands and eventually out to the colonies in North America.

This was also the age that first celebrated the art of the upholsterer or 'upholder' (see p. 63), to such an extent that by the end of the 17th century this craftsman had supplanted the carver as the most important figure in furniture-making. Achieving unity of decoration required wall hangings, bed curtains, window drapes, chair covers and settee covers that complemented one other. Upholstery

OPPOSITE A William III Coromandel lacquer and polychrome japanned cabinet-on-stand. With its 'Bantam-work' decoration and its stand with sinuous double-scrolled legs, showing strong Dutch influence, it is stylistically datable to 1680–90.

BELOW   Three of a set of four William and Mary red and gilt japanned caned open armchairs with loose cushions of red velvet. The panelled backs are decorated with Chinoiserie vignettes.

OPPOSITE   A William and Mary simulated tortoiseshell and gilt japanned cabinet on a lacquered silver-gilt stand. The stand, of *c.* 1695, is possibly associated with the Huguenot craftsman Jean Pelletier [*cf. 125*].

was time-consuming and therefore expensive, so it was an indication of both wealth and fashionable taste. It is no coincidence that the greatest status symbol of all was the state bed, replete with hangings, a piece of furniture kept permanently on show to display a family's wealth and power, and used only rarely for an honoured guest.

Many of the craftsmen producing this work were Huguenots, Protestant refugees from France (see p. 63). Although many arrived destitute, they were hardworking and technically highly skilled, and soon the French court style was spreading throughout their adopted lands. The most influential of these French immigrants was

Daniel Marot (1661–1752) [*124*]. He had fled to Holland in 1686, and there was employed by the future William III as an architect and designer at the palace of Het Loo. After 1689, he spent time in both England and Holland. He is often cited as the man who played the greatest part in introducing the French Baroque style to Britain. Certainly his published designs are impressive, with over 230 engravings of subjects including buildings, interiors, fireplaces, furniture and clocks. His greatest contribution to the English interior was the idea of each room being a complete decorative unit, with the same vocabulary of ornamentation found on anything from a state bed to a doorknob.

The most important cabinetmaker of the day was Gerrit Jensen (active 1680–1715), who is thought to have been born in the Netherlands, but is often described as 'the English Boulle' (for Boulle, see pp. 114–17). His work is well documented and a number of pieces survive in the Royal Collection. As well as producing designs in boulle technique, Jensen is closely linked to the technique of arabesque marquetry, so much so that any competently executed example of the day is attributed to him. The forms of many of his pieces are French – undoubtedly he had French craftsmen working for him – or an interesting marriage of English and French styles.

The French were thus a driving force in a style that came to be admired as a pinnacle of English fashion and taste. The other major influence was the Far East, with imports of porcelain and

A William and Mary ebonized beech side chair, armchair and stool, covered in original Genoa velvet. They are thought to have been designed by Daniel Marot, and were supplied to the State Bedroom at Cleveland House, St James's, in London, c. 1690. The growing fashion for sumptuously upholstered furniture was a feature of the period, with many fine cloths imported from the Continent.

lacquer through the Dutch and English East India Companies reaching new heights (see p. 94). Genuine lacquer was in great demand [121], but japanned imitations were also produced in quantity [123]. Delft pottery, inspired by Chinese blue-and-white, was much admired. Lavish silver furniture was highly prized [38], and with the advent of casting – one of the greatest innovations of the Huguenots – solid silver pieces became commoner. A notable example is the great table and mirror-frame at Windsor Castle presented to William III.

While the William and Mary style embraced the French Baroque decorative art of the court of Louis XIV at Versailles, the two sovereigns made it their own. It became less masculine and less severe: Mary loved flowers, for example, and many pieces commissioned by her include exuberant floral marquetry. In time its influence widened, through the aristocratic houses of Britain whose owners wanted to emulate the fashion of the court, through the powerful merchant class of Holland, and eventually to the colonial governors of North America and to provincial towns in Britain, where it came to symbolize domestic harmony and unity.

This magnificent giltwood console table with marble top was made by Jean Pelletier in 1700 and acquired by William III.

BELOW AND OPPOSITE Two views of a Louis XV ormolu-mounted tulipwood, kingwood, amaranth and bois de bout marquetry secrétaire à abattant by BVRB (Bernard II van Risenburgh), *c.* 1760. BVRB is considered the greatest *ébéniste* of the reign of Louis XV. The perfectly controlled balance between the end-cut marquetry panels and the curvaceous outline, emphasized by the mounts, shows the influence of early Neoclassical furniture 'à la grecque'. A secretaire of the same model was bought by the 6th Earl of Coventry from the *marchand-mercier* Simon-Philippe Poirier in 1763 for 1,000 *livres*.

French Rococo

From the time when Louis XV (1710–74) took over government in 1723, a current of change began to be felt right through France. For one thing, there were longer periods of peace during his reign, which in turn meant greater prosperity. It was also an era when women wielded more influence, in particular the King's most eminent mistress, Madame de Pompadour. Coupled with this was the growing role of the dealers known as *marchands-merciers*.

The *marchands-merciers* were distinct from the *marchands-artisans* (dealer–craftsmen), being allowed by statute to sell everything, including imported goods, but forbidden to make anything themselves. It was the *marchands-merciers*, the commercial tastemakers of the day, who commissioned increasingly opulent furniture from the *ébénistes*, in a bid to satisfy an affluent and burgeoning clientèle, many of them women, who were avid for fashionable and luxurious goods. They handled a wide range of merchandise, including provisions, metalwork, fabrics, carpets, stationery, haberdashery, leather goods and jewelry. Most important to the *ébénistes* were the *marchands d'objets d'art*, who sold everything from candelabra to clocks, paintings to prints, cabinets to coffers. The role of the *marchands-merciers* was fundamental to the creation of the fine furniture of 18th-century France. It was they who came up with the ideas, one of which was to marry marquetry to precious materials, such as Chinese or Japanese lacquer, Wedgwood ceramics or Sèvres porcelain, *pietra dura* or silver.

Perhaps not surprisingly in an era when women's taste was increasingly valued, furniture became softer, rounder and less imposing. Think of Rococo and you think of serpentine curves, rather than straight lines; pale woods rather than dark; romance rather than military might. It was a luxurious, aristocratic, sensuous style that spoke of an agreeable, intimate way of living. 'Rococo' was first used as a term of abuse (as 'Baroque' had been), meaning 'immoderately elaborate and complicated'.

For students of the Neoclassical painter Jacques-Louis David in Paris at the end of the 18th century, it stood for everything that they disliked about the Louis XV period. Rococo celebrated natural forms, such as shells, roses and palms, and at its best it has a sense of vitality and movement. The furniture is of far lighter construction than that of the Baroque and of greater elegance; the delicacy of chairs was enhanced by upholstery of silk brocades and pastel-coloured damasks; ormolu mounts were used to outline panels of marquetry, porcelain or lacquer.

Two things have to be stressed about French Rococo, as opposed to the imitations of the style that appeared around Europe. One is the immense technical skill that the *marchands-merciers* could call upon, in part because of the specialization

engendered by the guilds. The second is that
the fashion was always subject to control, balance
and a strong sense of design. In France there was
an intrinsic understanding of where to draw the
line, even in the most magnificent pieces.
This is gracious, elegant furniture with a touch
of feminine wit. It does not over satiate the appetite.

The greatest *ébéniste* of the reign of Louis XV
is considered to be Bernard II van Risenburgh
(after 1696–*c.* 1766), who is identified by the initials
BVRB [*18, 81, 126–28, 130, 131*]. His father, Bernard I
(d. 1738), specialized in the production of bracket-,
mantel- and long-case clocks in boulle marquetry,
while his son, Bernard III (1731–1800), was a creator

OPPOSITE, ABOVE A pair of Louis XV giltwood pliants
stamped 'N.Q. Foliot', one of the renowned Foliot
dynasty of *menuisiers*. The pliant or folding stool had
a particular function in court etiquette, and this pair
was probably ordered by Adolf Fredrik, King of Sweden,
c. 1750–55.

OPPOSITE A Louis XV ormolu, Chinese black, polychrome
and gilt lacquer and japanned commode by BVRB, *c.* 1740.

ABOVE A Louis XV ormolu-mounted tulipwood,
amaranth, sycamore and floral commode, *c.* 1757,
attributed to Jean-François Oeben and Jean-Pierre Latz,
supplied for the Chambre de la Dauphine at the Château
of Choisy-le-Roi. The floral marquetry is exceptional: the
basket of summer flowers fills the space with a controlled
abandon, so that one of the tulip leaves illusionistically
overlaps the boxwood-edged ebony border, itself framed
by the sumptuous mounts.

ABOVE The star piece in the centre is a Louis XV Japanese black lacquer commode by BVRB. Dating from the early 1750s, it shows his development since the example on p. 128. The tripartite arrangement has evolved so that the central panel of Japanese lacquer, highly prized for its quality and spareness, almost fills the whole front. It was bought by Jean-Baptiste de Machaut d'Arnouville, probably for his Château of Arnouville.

of models for gilt-bronze mounts. BVRB began to use his stamp in about 1737, when he supplied a lacquer commode for the Queen at Fontainebleau. His great speciality was lacquered furniture [128], particularly furniture decorated with panels of Japanese lacquer [above and opposite], which was commissioned by certain marchands-merciers keen to find something new and lavish with which to tickle the palette of their wealthy clients. Precious chests, screens and cabinets from Japan were cut up for this purpose, remaining surfaces being filled with French japanning (see p. 57) imitating Japanese lacquer. It was also BVRB who revived the art of floral marquetry, which had fallen out of fashion in France by 1700. Most was composed of flowers in kingwood against light-coloured satinwood or tulipwood [*126–27*]. Later in his career, BVRB was also commissioned by the *marchand-mercier* Poirier to apply Sèvres porcelain plaques to furniture, mainly small tables called 'chiffonnières'. Most sumptuous of all his porcelain-mounted furniture is a commode decorated with ninety such plaques, made for Mademoiselle de Sens and dated 1758 (now in a private collection).

Another important name of the period is Jean-Pierre Latz (1691–1754), whose work is in the

full Rococo style. The production of clock-cases was the mainstay of his business, but he also created commodes that are bombé on all sides, featuring highly stylized marquetry designs and sprays of realistic flowers [*129, 132*].

Jean-François Oeben (1721–63) [*129, 218*], who enjoyed the patronage of Madame de Pompadour among others, is best known for detailed floral marquetry, which typically consists of sprays of carnations or baskets of flowers set against a contrasting striped or geometric ground. However, he offered something more than the decorative: he was also a specialist in mechanical furniture (see p. 74), including a table for Madame de Pompadour (believed to be the one that can be seen in her famous portrait by François Guérin). He even perfected a design which was both writing-table and dressing-table, with a sliding top which allowed the release of a reading stand.

ABOVE A Louis XV ormolu-mounted Japanese lacquer bureau en pente attributed to BVRB, dating from the early 1750s.

LEFT One of a pair of Louis XV giltwood fauteuils attributed to Nicolas Heurtaut. He was both a *maître menuisier* and a *maître sculpteur*.

A Louis XV ormolu-mounted bois satiné, kingwood and bois de bout marquetry commode with the stamp of Jean-Pierre Latz, *c.* 1750. This commode relates closely to the one from the Château of Choisy-le Roi (p. 129).

Eminent *menuisiers* of the period include Nicolas-Quinibert Foliot (1706–76), of the renowned Foliot dynasty, who succeeded his father, Nicolas (1675–1740), as 'Menuisier du Garde-Meuble du Roi'. He often worked alongside his brother, the sculptor Toussaint Foliot (1715–98), producing beautifully carved pieces typically featuring shells and flowers, which were then gilded or painted, before being upholstered by a skilled *tapissier* [*128*]. Nicolas Heurtaut (1720–71) [*131*] was a *maître menuisier* and also a *maître sculpteur*. Other noted *ébénistes* are Gilles Joubert (1689–1775) and Joseph Baumhauer (d. 1772) [*cf. 9, 118*].

Rococo flourished in France from about 1730 to 1750, when a reaction to luxury on such a scale began to set in. In the work of many of the figures of the period, such as Oeben, Nicolas-Quinibert Foliot, Heurtaut, Joubert and Baumhauer, it is possible to trace the passage from exuberant Rococo designs through to more understated examples of the style – a return to symmetry and simpler sculptural forms which marked the beginnings of Neoclassicism, a movement that was already well established by the death of Louis XV (see pp. 150–54).

ROCOCO: THE GOLDEN THREAD

It is time for a reassessment of Rococo, a term that has come to mean largely superfluous applied decoration. In its day it signified much more than that – a celebration of playfulness, sensual feminine curves and romance. Natural forms, such as shells and roses, were popular motifs, with rich gilded surfaces and luxurious silk fabrics.

'Lathe VIII' by Sebastian Brajkovic is part of a series of designs which embrace computer technology, exquisite craftsmanship and traditional techniques. Brajkovic deconstructs historical pieces of furniture and then reconstructs them to his own vision. The witty and fanciful results are a direct path to the exuberant spirit of Rococo.

FOOT OF PAGE One of a set of fourteen George III mahogany dining chairs supplied by Thomas Chippendale in the early 1770s to Daniel Lascelles for Goldsborough Hall, Yorkshire.

BELOW AND OPPOSITE A late George II parcel-gilt padouk and gilded limewood breakfront bookcase supplied by Thomas Chippendale in 1759 to the 5th Earl of Dumfries for Dumfries House.

Thomas Chippendale

In a chapter devoted to golden *ages* of furniture, it may seem perverse to devote an entire section to the work of one man, Thomas Chippendale (1718–79). It certainly raises the question 'Why?' In answer, it is not just because he is the most famous of the English furniture elite, but more because his reputation is absolutely justified. If you look at a piece by Chippendale, whether it is grand or simple, made for a country mansion or a town house, it is without flaw. People who know and love Chippendale's work can take one look at a piece of his furniture and recognize the signature of the man who created it immediately. That is not true of other cabinetmakers. There is an extraordinary confidence in his work, which encompasses everything from the choice of timber – always exceptional – to the technical skill with which it is handled. His mastery is unrivalled. Only Chippendale manages at all times to be grand without once being vulgar, to be sumptuous while retaining perfect balance. In that he is a very English designer – aptly described by the great Chippendale scholar, Christopher Gilbert, as 'the Shakespeare of English cabinetmakers'.

Chippendale was commissioned to furnish many of the grandest houses of the day. He was a successful and innovating designer who, like most 18th-century cabinetmakers, provided a complete house furnishing and decorating business, including wallpaper, carpets, metalware and room schemes when required. He supplied clients with a vast range

135

A George III mahogany breakfront bookcase supplied by Thomas Chippendale in 1764 to Sir Lawrence Dundas, Bt, for the Library at 19 Arlington Street, London.

of furniture, from the fine focal points of the state rooms to 'backstairs' examples. At all times he retained strong control over his workshop, so every piece, whether grand or modest, was subjected to the same rigorous quality control. Chippendale did not enjoy the lavish royal and court patronage of some of his European peers, such as David Roentgen (see pp. 77, 156–58) or BVRB (see pp. 129–31): his own stage was the domestic setting of the British house rather than the opulent palaces of Versailles or St Petersburg – but the technical mastery apparent in his work is always awe-inspiring.

Chippendale was born at Otley in Yorkshire, both his father and grandfather being carpenters. In around 1740 he seems to have worked in the city of York, which was a regional centre of craftsmanship during the reign of George II. It is here that he most likely received a basic training in draughtsmanship and ornament, before moving south to London.

The earliest reference to him in London is the record of his marriage in 1748.

By 1753, he was affluent enough to acquire three houses in St Martin's Lane – a fashionable street with grand houses on one side and tradesmen on the other – which his firm occupied for sixty years. Chippendale lived at no. 60, the shop was at no. 61, and his business partner, the Scot James Rannie (d. 1766), lived at no. 62. Chippendale called his establishment 'The Cabinet and Upholstery Warehouse', and adopted a chair for his sign. The scale of his business is astonishing. As well as a three-storey cabinetmaker's shop, the firm maintained an upholsterer's shop, glass room, feather rooms, veneering shop, carpet room, forge, various warerooms, sheds, stores and four timber stacks. It is likely that there was also a saw pit and premises for turning and japanning, as well as a department for carving and gilding.

In his rise to elite status Chippendale used newspaper advertisements to stimulate trade – a practice frowned upon by the more established London cabinetmakers. Most significantly, in 1754 he published *The Gentleman and Cabinet-Maker's Director*, a pattern book of fashionable furniture intended to attract lucrative commissions and establish his reputation. The *Director* was to have a huge influence on mid-18th-century furniture styles. Bringing together 'Designs of Household Furniture in the Gothic, Chinese and Modern Taste', it contained 161 copper-plate engravings showing chairs, cabinets and upholstery work. Four hundred people were invited to subscribe, and about three hundred initially did so – the majority tradesmen, including cabinetmakers, upholsterers, joiners, carvers, plasterers and carpenters. A second edition followed in 1755. The *Director* is often cited as a guide to 'genteel taste' in London during the 1750s. It includes designs in the English vernacular tradition, such as a severely plain library bookcase, reflecting Palladian proportions but entirely free of modish influences, while at the other end of the scale are designs celebrating the fashions of the day, including Rococo, Chinoiserie and Gothic [139].

A George III commode in finely grained satinwood and neatly finished marquetry set off by sumptuous ormolu mounts, by Thomas Chippendale. The long frieze-drawer is inlaid with flowerhead ovals, above doors with raised centres inlaid with a vase of flowers. This splendid commode is of the same outline as the one probably supplied by Chippendale to Sir Rowland Winn, Bt [10], but was executed in the early 1770s.

The popular success of the *Director* inspired others to follow suit. In July 1759, William Ince (1738–1804) and John Mayhew (1736–1811), who had established their partnership as cabinetmakers and upholsterers only six months previously, announced their own version: *A General System of Useful and Ornamental Furniture*, to be released in weekly parts, with 160 plates. Chippendale responded by announcing the third edition of the *Director*. In the event, when Ince and Mayhew's work appeared in its final form in 1762, as *A Universal System of Household Furniture*, it had fewer than 100 plates. The new edition of the *Director*, also published in 1762 [*28, 64, opposite*], included designs in the Neoclassical style.

In 1759 Chippendale received an order without parallel: over fifty pieces of furniture for the new house of the 5th Earl of Dumfries in Scotland [*98, 135, above left*]. A mixture of specifically commissioned pieces and ready-made pieces available from Chippendale's stock, as Lord Dumfries must have visited him in London, they are generally in the Rococo style, and of those some are Chinoiserie in inspiration. They confirm Chippendale's reputation as a skilful and imaginative interpreter of the Rococo. One reason why the pieces at Dumfries House are of central importance to the history of furniture in Britain is that it is the only completely surviving documented commission

from Chippendale's celebrated *Director* period, on which so much of his fame rests.

In Britain the Rococo style was more usually celebrated by silversmiths, porcelain modellers and engravers of book illustrations. Furniture, because of its links with architecture, was one of the last areas of craft to assimilate Rococo ornamentation; and then the style was mainly adopted for mirrors, wall brackets and stands. Chippendale, however, applied the Rococo idiom to case furniture and chairs as well as carved and gilded wood borders (used to edge damask-covered walls, framing windows, doors, ceiling and dado rail junctions), chimneypieces, clock cases and silverware. It was not an easy style to master, but in his hands it resulted in delightful motifs of waves, reeds, rocks, shells and waterfalls, with many naturalistic plant and animal details.

Dumfries House has Chippendale's most glamorous Chinoiserie furniture, which includes

ABOVE LEFT A late George II mahogany library armchair supplied by Thomas Chippendale in 1759 to the 5th Earl of Dumfries for Dumfries House.

ABOVE CENTRE AND RIGHT A pair of George III giltwood armchairs designed by Robert Adam and made by Thomas Chippendale, supplied in 1765 to Sir Lawrence Dundas, Bt, for the Great Room at 19 Arlington Street, London.

a spectacular pair of gilt girandoles featuring a ho-ho bird and a Chinaman posed over a balustrade [*98*]. Chinoiserie was not a new fashion, but before the advent of Rococo in Britain it was usually expressed only through florid japanned surfaces, typically executed in gold and silver on a scarlet or black ground. Chippendale's Chinoiserie designs were more varied, accomplished and wide-ranging.

If Dumfries House represents the apogee of Chippendale's *Director* phase in the late 1750s, his work at Nostell Priory in the late 1760s and early 1770s represents the summit of his achievement in Neoclassical carved mahogany, and also includes wonderful examples of Chinoiserie [*101, 102*]. His Harewood House commission (1767–78), including seat furniture, beds and mirrors as well as case furniture, one example being the celebrated Harewood House commode, demonstrates his

immense technical brilliance and supreme confidence in handling both complex marquetry and lavish painted and gilded carving.

Chippendale was an extraordinarily adventurous and commercially minded designer, who not only produced work of great quality, but was at the cutting edge of fashion. He enjoyed a relatively long career, producing work for England and Scotland's finest country houses [*101, 102, 134, 248*] as well as a galaxy of London houses [*10, 136*], sometimes in conjunction with Robert Adam [*1, opposite centre and right*] He also had a global impact, with copies of the *Director* circulating as far as North America, Jamaica, India, and other British colonies.

A Gothic 'Library Bookcase' from *The Gentleman and Cabinet-Maker's Director* by Thomas Chippendale (third edition, 1762).

Newport and Philadelphia

Both before and after Independence in 1783, there was no one city in North America to set a single stylistic standard as London did in England. Instead there were a number of regional networks of cabinetmakers, many with distinctive styles. At any given time, the richest and most innovative city developed the newest and most fashionable furniture – influenced also by individual immigrant cabinetmakers, imported pieces of furniture from Europe, and, later, illustrated pattern books. British mercantile policy discouraged the manufacturing of any goods within its colonies; but with so much timber available closer to hand it was inevitable that some sort of furniture-making industry would be established in parallel with furniture imports.

Mahogany, shipped in huge logs from Honduras and the islands of the Caribbean, was the preferred primary wood (that which is visible) in both Britain and America during the second half of the 18th century. As well as its beauty and the ease with which it could be worked, it was also chosen for its strength and imperviousness to rot and insect infestation. Most of the other wood used was native to North America. In New England, the local primary woods were maple or cherry, both almost too hard to carve. The favourite secondary wood (not exposed to view) was northeastern white pine, because of its lightness, strength and carvability.

Boston was the dominant city of New England in the 17th and early 18th centuries, a leader in trade, wealth and population. It was inevitable that it would also become a leader of taste. Most furniture made here, by a thriving industry of about 150 cabinetmakers, was in the William and Mary style (see pp. 120–25). A traditional Boston feature is the block-front, with three vertical sections – two convex ones flanking a concave centre.

By reason of its proximity to Boston, Newport came within that city's orbit. However, Rhode Island had charted a very independent course from the Puritan leadership of the Massachusetts Bay Colony, so it is not surprising perhaps that it should have evolved a distinctive style of furniture. The most famous of the Newport cabinetmakers were the interrelated Quaker Townsend and Goddard families: twenty-one family members dominated the craft – notable among them John Townsend (1733–1809) – and made some of the finest of all American furniture [*opposite, 142, 144*]. The Newport cabinetmakers favoured solid mahogany rather than veneers, because it stood up better to the New England climate. Their signature is the way they combined the traditional Boston block-front form with magnificent lobed shells of their own devising, producing a form known as 'block-and-shell'. By adding the signature shell, the Newport makers transformed blocking into something rich and memorable. The most common showpiece was the two-part cabinet, raised on moulded or claw-and-ball feet.

A 'Chippendale' mahogany block-and-shell bureau
table attributed to John Townsend of Newport,
Rhode Island, *c.* 1790.

By 1750 Philadelphia had replaced Boston as the most eminent colonial city, and was in fact the second city of the English-speaking world. It was now that Rococo became the fashion of the day. The ambitious cabinetmakers and carvers who flourished there acquired Thomas Chippendale's highly influential pattern book, *The Gentleman and Cabinet-Maker's Director* (see p. 137), and other pattern books, by rival firms such as Manwaring and Mayhew and Ince, were also imported. This was the moment when terms such as 'American Chippendale' and 'New French Style' were coined. During the 1760s and 1770s, the furniture produced in Philadelphia could equal that seen in the finest London residences [*right, opposite, 144*].

Rather than copy Chippendale outright, Philadelphia makers tended to take elements from more than one design and combine them in new ways. In part, this is probably because there was typically a time lag, caused by America's remoteness from Europe, of about thirty years between a style's popularity in Britain and across the Atlantic: in America, Queen Anne is the style of *c*. 1730, and Chippendale that of *c*. 1780. This distance both of time and geography had the benefit of engendering a sense of inventiveness and freedom that is unusual in English furniture of the same period. From a

technical point of view, the carving is marvellous, but there is also an appealing independence of spirit.

Philadelphia was the great centre to which furniture was exported from England. New forms were introduced in this way, including the upholstered settee and sofa and the Windsor chair, and imported designs provided further inspiration for the Philadelphia makers. 'Chippendale' chairs were plentiful, as were card-tables, tea-tables and Pembroke tables. Showpieces were chests, high or low, and bureau-cabinets. High chests or highboys have long been a symbol of the Rococo in Philadelphia.

Many of the makers working in Philadelphia were craftsmen from England, enticed to the colony with specific promises of employment. Thomas Affleck (1740–95) [*144*], for instance, is said to have

LEFT A 'Chippendale' carved mahogany block-and-shell tall-case clock attributed to the Townsend-Goddard school, Newport, 1745–65.

ABOVE The General John Cadwalader 'Chippendale' carved mahogany hairy-paw-foot side chair, attributed to Benjamin Randolph, Philadelphia, *c*. 1770.

OPPOSITE The Biddle-Drinker family 'Chippendale' carved and figured mahogany high chest-of-drawers, with carving attributed to Nicholas Bernard, Philadelphia, *c*. 1760.

143

arrived in America in 1763 with a copy of Chippendale's *Director* under his arm; the Philadelphia building boom saw him emerge as the wealthiest of cabinetmakers. Specialist carvers from England include Nicholas Bernard and Martin Jugiez (d. 1815), whose partnership lasted from 1762 to 1783 and was highly influential [*143 and right*], and Benjamin Randolph (1721–91) [*142*] and James Reynolds (*c.* 1736–94), whose technical skill won them fame and fortune. All these craftsmen were involved in remodelling and furnishing the town houses of two rich, young and influential men, John Cadwalader and Samuel Powel, in the most elaborate Rococo fashion. The two houses became the stylistic benchmarks of their day. General Cadwalader (1742–86) was a Revolutionary war hero and his wife, Elizabeth, a Maryland heiress. Their patronage of the leading craftsmen and designers is particularly important from a historical point of view because so much documentation about what they commissioned survives.

The Stevenson family 'Chippendale' mahogany scalloped-top tea table, attributed to Thomas Affleck, with carving attributed to Nicholas Bernard and Martin Jugiez, Philadelphia, *c.* 1770.

BELOW A 'Chippendale' mahogany drop-leaf dining table attributed to the shop of John Goddard, Newport, Rhode Island, 1760–80.

BELOW A pair of Anglo-Indian ivory-inlaid padouk open armchairs made in Vizagapatam, mid-18th century.

Indian Ivory

Furniture in the Western sense did not traditionally exist in Indian interiors, where most people ate and socialized seated cross-legged on the ground. The Portuguese – who arrived in India in the late 15th century – and later the Dutch, British and French fulfilled their desire for more familiar furniture by commissioning Western-style pieces from Indian artisans, who became renowned for their skill as copyists. Europeans were astonished by their facility to reproduce objects often from nothing more than an illustration in an advertisement; pattern-books and fashionable periodicals also played an important role when commissioning such work – not only major works such as Chippendale's *Director* (see p. 137) but also journals such as *The Gentleman's Magazine* and Ackermann's *Repository of Arts*.

Local craftsmen had little understanding of the foreign forms they were being asked to make, and a characteristic of much 'Anglo-Indian' furniture is the disparity between surface ornament and construction. Indian carpenters had no cultural references for the designs, and often disregarded the European desire for a well-figured grain, excellent proportions, or discreet joints (they were unfamiliar with Western joints, and relied instead on dowels and adhesives). Traditional Indian furniture, made for the indigenous wealthy elite, was judged on an entirely different set of aesthetic standards – not for precise joinery, but for rich carving and ornament. Thus furniture made in India for Europeans was exotic in the eyes both of those who produced it and of those who

commissioned it. It was a hybrid, linking two entirely different histories, cultures and craft traditions.

The objects produced for the foreign market ranged from hardwood copies of basic furniture forms to pieces worked with precious materials at specialist centres of craftsmanship. Vizagapatam [*above, 147*], Travancore and Murshidabad [*149*] were particularly noted for ivory work.

Vizagapatam, a port on the northern Coromandel coast in South India, was the finest harbour between Calcutta and Madras (now Kolkata and Chennai), frequented both by local craft and by larger trading vessels. The region to which it belonged yielded extremely fine timbers, among them teak, ebony and various types of rosewood. Other raw materials, such as ivory from Pegu, were also readily available. Technical expertise for the production of furniture existed locally, because

ABOVE A pair of Anglo-Indian polychrome decorated, carved ivory open armchairs, late 18th/early 19th century, acquired in India by the Viceroy, the 1st Marquess Curzon, for Kedleston. They are traditionally thought to have belonged to Tipu Sultan (1750–99), ruler of Mysore.

OPPOSITE A side chair from the set of Anglo-Indian ivory-inlaid padouk chairs from Vizagapatam, mid-18th century [145].

settlements along this coastline had been developed as shipbuilding centres. It was here in the late 17th century that a cabinetmaking industry developed, marrying the skills of ivory inlay known to the Kamsali caste with Western furniture forms.

Prior to the mid-18th century, ivory was used mainly in the form of floral patterns inlaid in wood – chiefly ebony, rosewood and padouk – highlighted with the application of lac. After that, it came increasingly to be used as a veneer covering the entire surface of a piece of furniture. Floral designs were now engraved on the ivory, and new designs, including human figures and architectural scenes, were introduced. This use of veneer affected the carcass timber chosen, with sandalwood being particularly favoured for its scent. Other precious materials, such as tortoiseshell, were used less frequently. Towards the end of the 18th century,

a new technique was introduced which involved setting ivory against a black ground composed of lac. This inspired the fashion in Britain for penwork, an inexpensive way of imitating ivory ornamentation.

Inventories belonging to the British in India from the second half of the 18th century regularly list ivory and ivory-inlaid articles, principally bureaux and dressing cases. These are often described as 'Vizagapatam'. Suites of ivory chairs, dressing tables and bureaux-cabinets were brought back to Britain by eminent people such as Robert Clive, Governor of Bengal in the mid-18th century. The Indian elite also patronized Vizagapatam artisans, commissioning solid ivory objects such as combs and figures of deities. G. N. Gajapathi Rao, Maharaja of Vizianagram, was a great patron of ivory furniture, commissioning examples both for himself and as presents – including the ivory chairs that he gave to Prince Albert, displayed at the Great Exhibition of 1851.

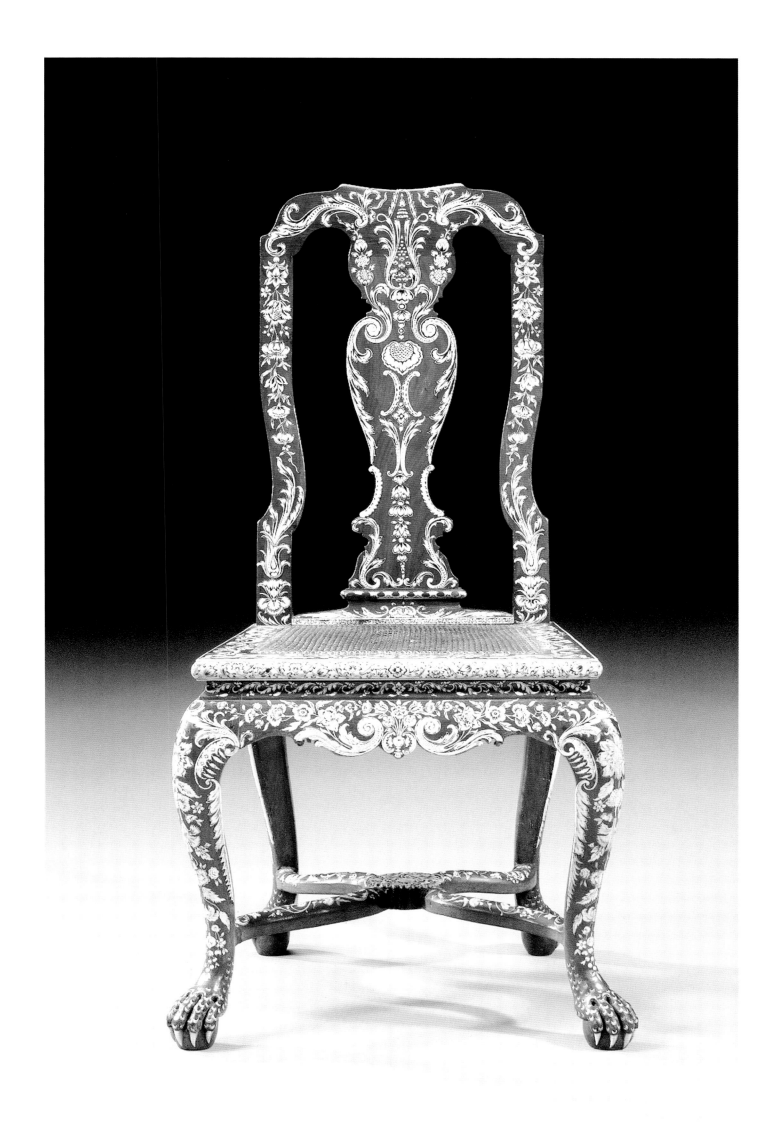

LEFT A detail of an Anglo-Indian carved and polychrome ivory armchair similar to those seen on p. 146.

Travancore, also located in the South, owed much of the success of its ivory carving to the patronage of Maharaja Swathi Thirunal, who ruled the state from 1829 to 1847. According to tradition, Brahmins presented him with images of Hindu deities carved out of ivory using a single knife, and the fine quality of the work inspired him to bring together craftsmen from his domain and encourage them to work together to perfect the art. One of the most spectacular examples is the ivory-veneered throne presented to Queen Victoria by Maharaja Martanda Varma in 1851, which was also shown at the Great Exhibition. Most of the plaques are carved with lions, birds and cherub-like figures, while the cresting shows a pair of mythic lions with elephant trunks. Travancore ivory prospered in the second half of the 19th century, and in response to demand a department of ivory carving was established as a branch of government in 1872–73, with carvers drawn from the Asari and Viswakarma castes. This later merged with the Trivandrum School of Arts, chiefly producing naturalistic depictions of animals, plants and people. By the late 1880s, Travancore ivory work

was being exported worldwide. Rather than coming under Western influence, craftsmen produced objects decorated in the traditional style, something that distinguishes it from other centres of ivory carving.

Murshidabad in eastern India, strategically situated on the main artery of communication between North India and the European settlements along the Hooghly, became a centre of political power and patronage in the early 18th century. Ivory carving may have begun here then, with carvers migrating from Sylhet – itself noted as a centre of the craft from as early as the 11th century. Murshidabad work comprises mainly small objects such as chessmen and caskets, but from the second half of the 18th century Western-style furniture in solid ivory was also commissioned, featuring delicately carved decoration and gilding [*opposite*]. Warren Hastings, who became the first British Governor-General in 1773, was a notable recipient of a large suite of solid ivory furniture from the region. These elaborate pieces borrowed elements from English, French and Chinese furniture – a fusion of tastes popular in Indian courts at the time. From the 1790s on, Murshidabad furniture followed Western models more closely, suggesting that craftsmen were executing designs from British prototypes as well as from pattern-books. By the early 19th century, Murshidabad ivory workers were specializing in figures, including animals, processional scenes and deities from the Hindu pantheon.

Today the trade in ivory is carefully regulated, but ivory-style objects, mainly of acrylic, are still produced, particularly in Vizagapatam. The time required to complete one box is said to be about three days. The magnificence of true ivory furniture is never likely to be repeated, both because of the rarity of the material and because of the skills needed to carve it.

OPPOSITE An Anglo-Indian solid ivory armchair decorated in green, gold and red, from Murshidabad, third quarter of the 18th century. It was probably commissioned by Mani Begum, widow of Nawab Mir Jafar, and possibly presented to Warren Hastings, the first Governor-General of India.

French Neoclassicism

It is misleading to refer to Rococo as the Louis XV style, because at least twenty years before the King's death in 1774 another hugely influential design movement was coming into existence: Neoclassicism. This was marked by a return to straight lines rather than curves, the masculine rather than the feminine, the severe rather than the frivolous. It was inspired by the architectural style of the same period, which in turn had emerged from a wave of philosophical and intellectual interest in and enthusiasm for Classical civilization.

Louis XV was succeeded by his ill-fated grandson Louis XVI (1754–92), who was married to Marie-Antoinette of Austria. Neoclassicism found favour with the young Queen; gradually it became rather less disciplined, and evolved into an accessible and comfortable decorative style.

Just as Rococo had been a reaction to the serious, weighty and masculine Baroque, so Neoclassicism kicked back against the feminine frivolity of Rococo. By the 1760s the terms 'le goût grec' or 'à la grecque' (ancient Greeks had long been considered more venerable than the Romans) came to mean 'Classical' in a wider sense.

Furniture decorated with boulle marquetry had continued to be admired. The chief characteristic of such furniture is its rich, rather sombre look, resulting from the use of ebony veneers coupled with marquetry in brass, dark tortoiseshell and other semi-precious materials, the whole embellished with gilt-bronze mounts. Pieces made by André-Charles Boulle himself [*53, 112–16*] remained collectable throughout the 18th century, regarded both as works of art and as objects of luxury: auction catalogues often included a section on 'Meubles curieux' or 'Meubles de Boulle', and by the end of the 18th century the antique furniture collector had been born.

One of the first enthusiasts for the Neoclassical style was the collector Ange-Laurent Lalive de Jully, who asked the Neoclassical painter Louis-Joseph Le Lorrain (1715–59) – who had himself lived in Rome – to design a suite of furniture for him in the Boulle tradition. This was finished in the mid-1750s and is regarded as the earliest furniture of the 'goût grec' type. It was of course considered ultra-modern.

In the late 1760s, Madame du Barry, the last mistress of Louis XV, ordered 208 Neoclassical pieces for her apartments at Versailles and her Pavilion at Louveciennes [*27*]. Another eminent patron of the new style was the Marquis de Marigny, brother of Madame de Pompadour. He was a principal client of the *ébéniste* Pierre Garnier (1720–1800) [*5*], who was one of the pioneers of Neoclassicism, producing furniture after designs by the architect Charles de Wailly. In 1779, Marigny ordered a complete series of furniture for his house in the Place des Victoires in Paris, including an ebony table with a stand supporting an architectural model of the Louvre Colonnade, a great Classical building of the age of the Sun King. Marigny asserted that furniture

decorated with ebony and gilt bronze was far more 'noble' than that made of mahogany [9]. The Duc de Choiseul, France's first minister, also ordered pieces in what later came to be known – again misleadingly – as the Louis XVI style.

Jean-François Oeben (see p. 131) is an important figure in the transition from Rococo to Neoclassical [218]. His most important commission was the Bureau du Roi, ordered for Louis XV in 1760 (see p. 74). This secrétaire à cylindre – a desk with a sliding cylinder top – was so rich in decoration and mechanically so complex that it took eight years to make: Oeben died in 1763, and the desk was completed by Jean-Henri Riesener (see below) in 1769. Although in form it is Rococo, much of the decoration is purely Neoclassical, showing that the new style had already gained a hold.

Oeben's brother-in-law, Martin Carlin (1730–85) [54], was renowned in particular for the porcelain-mounted furniture he made for the *marchand-mercier* Simon-Philippe Poirier [20]. He also produced sumptuous lacquer pieces which

BELOW LEFT AND ABOVE Two views of a Louis XVI table en chiffonnière stamped by Jean-Henri Riesener, who took over Oeben's workshop after his death. It illustrates on a smaller scale Riesener's immense technical and artistic skill.

incorporated immensely valuable Japanese panels. Among veneers, he favoured tulipwood most highly, sometimes used in signature sunburst motifs of particular refinement. Generally speaking, Carlin dealt directly with *marchands-merciers* rather than private clients.

Another great *ébéniste* of the period was Jean-François Leleu (1729–1807) [151, *opposite*, 154]. He was a strict Neoclassicist, and in his imposing designs architectural elements are often emphasized by fluted pilasters at the corners and robust feet. His speciality was marquetry – not only pictures, such as baskets of flowers, but also geometric patterns.

Adam Weisweiler (1744–1820), like Carlin, dealt with *marchand-merciers* rather than private clients, and it seems the *marchand-mercier* Dominique Daguerre had a quasi-monopoly over his luxurious furniture. It was Daguerre who supplied Weisweiler's charming lacquer table to Marie-Antoinette at Versailles and a lacquer secretaire by him for Louis XVI's Cabinet Intérieur at Versailles. There are similarities of style between Carlin and Weisweiler [54], and the likelihood is that Daguerre supplied both men with designs for the furniture and models of bronze mounts, porcelain plaques and panels of lacquer and *pietra dura*. Weisweiler made many sumptuous pieces in these materials for clients who included the royal family, French nobility, and foreign aristocracy.

Jean-Baptiste-Claude Sené (1748–1803) was a *maître menuisier* by the age of twenty-one, continuing in the tradition set by his father and grandfather. He created much furniture for the royal family [*66*], including a magnificent bed for Marie-Antoinette. After the Revolution, he worked as an administrator

for the Republic, a role which allowed him to continue his business. Georges Jacob (1739–1814), member of another highly skilled *menuisier* dynasty,

BELOW A Louis XVI ormolu-mounted amaranth, tulipwood, bois satiné, sycamore and marquetry commode by Jean-François Leleu, exceptional for its distinctive shape, its marquetry decoration, and the jewel-like quality of the mounts.

became known as the royal chair-maker, so popular were his designs with the court at Versailles. He too managed to keep his business in the new Republic.

The name that was to become synonymous with this period is that of Jean-Henri Riesener (1734–1806). He not only secured Oeben's workshop after his death, but also married his widow, so becoming a member of one of the principal dynasties of *ébénistes* in Paris at the time. He enjoyed his greatest success and prosperity between 1774 and 1784, a period considered the zenith of technical skill and craftsmanship in France. To Marie-Antoinette he supplied furniture of immense luxury and ingenuity, combining materials such as Japanese lacquer, mother-of-pearl and marquetry with the richest of chased and gilded mounts. His pieces have a jewel-like quality, with their use of fabulous timbers and rich marquetry decoration [*52, 152*]. He also, as Oeben had before him, made a speciality of mechanical tables.

Neoclassicism was a pan-European movement, based on intellectual thought as much as aesthetics, that influenced many other Western countries as well as France. It did not disappear immediately after the Revolution, perhaps because it was not associated solely with the royal household. However, the Revolution did mark the end of the demand for luxury goods in France, causing the demise of many of the *ébénistes*. The *marchands-merciers*, however, were inventive at finding new markets, particularly in England, Russia and Spain.

A Louis XVI ormolu-mounted bureau à cylindre by Jean-François Leleu, *c.* 1770. Leleu often emphasized the architectural elements in his designs, such as the fluted legs here. The harmonious proportions are integral to the ideals as well as the aesthetics of the style.

NEOCLASSICISM:
THE GOLDEN THREAD

Neoclassicism remains not just a particular aesthetic, but a continuation of an intellectual movement, a belief that Classical styles and thought are still relevant today. Weighty, serious and masculine, it ignores the passing whims of fashion, continuing largely unchanged through successive generations.

ABOVE Linley 'Classic' bedside tables in walnut and in sycamore (the paler wood) with rosewood stringing, burr inlay and banding, 1990. The central drawer has a pull handle.

RIGHT A 'Collector's Cabinet' made by the British designer Andrew Varah in amboyna, lacewood, satinwood, holly and Indian rosewood, 1998. Classical references abound both internally and externally.

The Court of Catherine the Great

It is Peter I, or Peter the Great (1672–1725), who is credited with transforming Russia from a medieval country into a modern state. He overhauled not only the administrative system but also industry and commerce. St Petersburg, the new capital that he founded in 1703, became a 'window on to Europe', a centre of foreign trade. Between 1715 and 1717, Peter sent thirteen cabinetmakers to England and the Netherlands to perfect their technique, and on their return some of them began working and teaching in the court workshops. Not surprisingly, the style of this early furniture remained derivative, and it is sometimes referred to as 'English' Russian furniture.

Catherine II (1729–96) – also known as Catherine the Great – was a German princess, married to Peter III, grandson of Peter the Great. From 1762 she ruled as Empress in her own right. Catherine had a marked taste for Western European decorative art, and of all the late 18th-century sovereigns, she gave the largest orders to French and English craftsmen. Commissions included the celebrated 800-piece porcelain service decorated with cameos – something of which she was particularly fond – from Sèvres in 1778, the largest order they ever undertook. From Britain came the 900-plus-piece creamware 'Frog' service delivered by Wedgwood in 1774. However, the Empress was also a commissioner of buildings: in no other country were so many palaces built as in Russia in the second half of the 18th century. And these many new magnificent buildings needed furniture of appropriate status and luxury. Catherine was determined to bestow on the court of St Petersburg an elegance and splendour that would reflect her vast empire. She was also determined to show that Russia could hold its own as a sophisticated and influential power in relation to Europe.

The *marchands-merciers* of Paris (see p. 126) were understandably eager to supply demand. Hébert and Darnault are among those known to have supplied pieces, with furniture bearing the marks of BVRB (see pp. 129–31) and Joseph Baumhauer (see p. 132) gracing Catherine's study at Oranienbaum. Another beneficiary was Henri Jacob (1753–1824): although no relation to the highly regarded Georges Jacob (see pp. 153–54), he not only set up business close to his namesake's workshop in Paris, but also copied his designs with great success, and earned many orders from Catherine's court, including a set of chairs for the Marble Palace.

However, it was David Roentgen (see pp. 77–78) who found the greatest favour with Catherine. Already a highly successful entrepreneur with flourishing cabinetmaking workshops in

OPPOSITE AND BELOW One of a pair of Russian gilt-bronze,
Revna jasper and serpentina moschinata console tables,
c. 1800. The rectangular marble top is of green serpentine;
the panelled frieze is inset with Revna jasper panels
centered by a female mask.

Overall view and detail of an ormolu-and-silver-mounted cut-steel centre table from Tula with scrolled dolphin feet, *c*. 1785–90. During the reign of Catherine the Great a new technique was perfected in which metal was cut and polished in facets like diamonds, often combined, as here, with silver inlays and ormolu mounts. This table, one of the finest examples of 'Tula ware', was probably given by the Empress to Grand Duke Peter of Oldenburg, whose inventory brand it bears.

Germany and France, he arrived in St Petersburg in 1783. With him he carried a letter of introduction from Baron Grimm (who had served as a representative of Catherine in Paris, buying works of art and carrying out commissions), describing him as 'without exception the best cabinetmaker of our century' and asking that he be allowed to present the Empress with a piece of furniture, of which 'the world will probably never see its like again'. This irresistible recommendation secured for Roentgen – renowned in particular for his mechanical furniture [*74, 75*] – an audience with the Empress, who not only admired the pieces displayed but bought them, at a suitably high price. In the group was an intricately made desk, which also played music – two flutes with a clavichord accompaniment. So charmed was Catherine that she paid the 20,000 roubles asked and in addition offered Roentgen a further 5,000 roubles and a gold snuffbox. It is estimated that between 1783 and 1791 Roentgen spent half his time in St Petersburg, supplying whole cargoes of furniture to the Empress. His designs were not only suitably grandiose, but full of unexpected hidden features, which charmed and intrigued the Russians. Among

them were two large cabinets, each with one hundred drawers, designed for Catherine to store her large collection of cameos.

However, not all fine furniture had to be imported. Much of it was produced in Russia itself, where the work of cabinetmakers had flourished owing to the huge increase in palaces. Cabinetmakers there organized a guild, dividing members into three categories: masters, joiners and apprentices. The Russian guild system was not as regimented as that in France, so craftsmen were not limited to one area, and the absence of strict demarcations gave a freshness to the work produced.

The role of serfs cannot be overlooked in the structure of society in imperial Russia. Every estate had its own carpentry workshop, where serfs produced any utilitarian furniture needed. Some, however, not only perfected their techniques, but were drawn to skills such as marquetry and carving. As the property of their estate, serfs could not 'sign'

OPPOSITE Overall view and detail of one of a pair of 'Retour d'Egypte' ormolu-mounted verre églomisé and mahogany commodes, *c*. 1800. The corners are decorated with imitation hieroglyphics.

their work with an individual mark or seal, so only a few fine pieces can be attributed to them; but among these is a marquetry gaming table featuring trumpeting angels and an Oriental landscape which carries an inscription identifying its maker as the 'servant workman Matvei Iakovlevich Veretennikov' – a serf of Count Alexander Vasilievich Soltikov.

It is not possible to write about Russian furniture of this period without making reference to the remarkable steel furniture of Tula [*opposite*]. The town, some 125 miles (200 kilometres) south of Moscow, had been of strategic military importance from the 15th century, so it was supplied with a large number of blacksmiths who made helmets, armour and other military equipment. A permanent imperial armoury was established there in 1712. Gradually, the armourers at Tula expanded their skills into useful

everyday objects, perfecting their elaborate wrought work to such a degree that by the 1730s they were making folding furniture of steel inspired by traditional wooden shapes. Decoration of Tula work became increasingly elaborate, rich with garlands, rosettes and bows. A single piece could include decoration in six types of metal: steel, copper, brass, bronze, silver and gold.

Owing to the natural supply and fine quality of semi-precious stones, stonecutting also evolved into a Russian art form. When St Petersburg was built at the beginning of the 18th century, stonecutters contributed their skills alongside artists

and craftsmen, producing rich and elaborate objects and furniture, such as table and console tops suitable for the sumptuous decor. Coloured stones had rarely been used for decoration before that point, but the resulting increase in demand encouraged prospecting for fresh deposits of recognized stones as well as the discovery of new types. Varieties found included porphyry and jaspers of many colours, marbles, quartz and breccia. Imperial stonecutting factories were established at Peterhof, Ekaterinburg and Kolyvan, where master cutters established new skills in polishing and cutting. Many of these craftsmen came from Italy, in particular Florence, where there had been a strong stonecutting tradition for centuries (see p. 106). Not surprisingly, much Russian furniture of this period became a vehicle for displaying such stones to best advantage [157].

In addition to the generous use of brilliantly coloured stones, Russian cabinetmakers also produced furniture that was extravagantly carved, gilded and painted, often with an audacious medley of references borrowed from France, England, Germany and Italy. Rather than following rules, these craftsmen apparently enjoyed an exhilarating freedom of expression and ornamentation, celebrating bright colour and lavish decoration. To the sophisticated Western European eye, such furniture may have bordered on the vulgar, but at the imperial court it was, apparently, a case of anything goes. It is no surprise then that in the mid-19th century, the Marquis de Custine was so overwhelmed by what he found in the Moscow Kremlin that he wrote of 'a rich and rare display that dazzled my sight. Imagine the palaces of the *Thousand and One Nights*: nothing less will do justice to such enchantments.'

THE COURT OF CATHERINE THE GREAT: THE GOLDEN THREAD

The court of Catherine the Great encapsulated the idea of lavish opulence, no-expense-spared magnificence and the commissioning of pieces that were superlative both in the materials used and in the craftsmanship required. Interestingly, there is still work being produced that would have won Catherine's approval.

The 'Kawakubo' chest of drawers by Elisabeth Garouste and Mattia Bonetti, 1996, in wood with white-gold gilding and silver-plated bronze feet.

BELOW One of a set of four Gustaf III white-painted and parcel-gilt tabourets by Johan Lindgren, each with a drop-in seat upholstered in yellow cut velvet.

OPPOSITE A Gustaf III ormolu-mounted amaranth, birch marquetry and parquetry secretaire à abattant by Georg Haupt, one of the greatest cabinetmakers of the day.

Gustavian

The term 'Gustavian' refers to the period that began with the rule of King Gustaf III of Sweden (1746–92), who came to the throne in 1771. His reign introduced a new classicism in architecture and art, which dominated his country's cultural development. Among Gustaf III's many achievements were the creation of the Royal Swedish Opera and the Swedish Academy. It was thanks to his passion for architecture that the late 18th century was such an artistic golden age in Sweden, and it was because of his personal involvement and patronage that the Neoclassical style flowered so richly in a country far north of Paris.

Sweden's transformation into a power to be reckoned with had begun over a hundred years earlier under the reign of Gustaf II, who had led the Protestant Alliance combating the Roman Catholic forces of the Holy Roman Empire in the Thirty Years' War. In 1648, with the Peace of Westphalia, Sweden emerged as one of Europe's strongest military states, with an empire which included Finland, the Baltic area and parts of northern Germany. In keeping with its increased status, noble families started to build their own grand palaces – until then the province of kings – in Stockholm and on their estates. The Swedish court was considered one of the most splendid in Europe.

The Royal Palace in Stockholm, a magnificent expression of the country's ambitions, was begun in 1697, in the Baroque period, but work was held up

for over twenty years owing to lack of funds, spent on war. With the death in battle of Karl XII in 1718 Sweden ceased to be a great power. The palace was completed in 1727 by the young architect Carl Hårleman (1700–1753), who had studied in Paris during the time when France was evolving from the heavy Baroque style of Louis XIV into the playful and graceful Rococo. It was Hårleman who introduced the French Rococo (see pp. 126–32) to Sweden, both in architecture and in the decorative arts.

This was the backdrop to Gustaf III's reign. Completely international in his outlook, he was the nephew of Frederick the Great of Prussia and had made several foreign trips, most importantly to France and Italy. It was while he was on a study trip to Paris that he heard of the death of his father. When he returned to Sweden as king, he brought with him

drawings, models and *objets d'art*, reflecting the degree to which he had been impressed by the new French Neoclassical style (see pp. 150–54). Patriotic, ambitious, intelligent and cultivated, Gustaf III sought to re-establish the greatness of Sweden. Patronage of the arts was an important aspect of this ambition.

Early Neoclassicism in Sweden, as in France, looked back to the 'Grand Siècle' of Louis XIV: it proclaimed a reaction against the excesses of Rococo, and a return to the symmetry of Greco-Roman classicism, which was thought to represent higher moral values and the ideals of the Enlightenment. Columns, pilasters, Greek-key patterns, medallions and other antique motifs replaced exuberant swags and fancies. Interest in Roman antiquities was also growing in Europe as a result of excavations in Herculaneum and Pompeii, the two cities entombed

by the eruption of Vesuvius in AD 79. The king's own interest in Roman decoration can be seen in the suite of rooms in the Haga Pavilion just outside Stockholm (completed in 1790), where wall-paintings, reliefs and furniture are all in the Pompeian style.

Eminent Swedish architects, such as Carl Fredrik Adelcrantz (1717–96) and Jean Eric Rehn (1717–93), had visited France on study trips and sought to recreate the 'goût grec' so revered there, with the result that furniture of the Gustavian period is very similar in style to that known as Louis XVI. One man's name dominates: Georg Haupt (1741–84), a cabinetmaker considered to rank in stature with Jean-Henri Riesener in France, David Roentgen in Germany and Thomas Chippendale in England.

On completing his apprenticeship, Haupt travelled to Amsterdam, Paris and London, returning to Stockholm in 1769 to take up the post of 'Ebéniste du Roi' to Gustaf's father, Adolf Fredrik. During his travels, Haupt worked in the *atelier* of Simon Oeben, brother of the late Jean-François Oeben. During his stay in England, in late 1767 or early 1768, he worked with the cabinetmaker John Linnell on the furnishing of the library at Osterley Park; several pieces there are attributed to him, including a medal cabinet and marquetry pedestal desk.

ABOVE A Gustaf III ormolu-mounted birch, rosewood, tulipwood and marquetry commode by Georg Haupt, inscribed with his name and the title 'Ebéniste Du Roy Stockholm'.

OPPOSITE A Gustaf III ormolu-mounted sycamore, tulipwood, amaranth and marquetry side table by Gustaf Adolf Ditzinger, 1791.

As court cabinetmaker Haupt produced superb pieces, including commodes, cabinets, writing desks, library tables and English-inspired tea tables – an entire repertoire of palatial furniture. Breakfront, cabriole-legged commodes featuring intricate marquetry work and gilt mounts seem directly influenced by his time at the Oeben workshop [*above*]. He also showed a love of French-influenced scrolls, urns, swags and other Classical motifs. Gustaf III after his accession commissioned numerous pieces from Haupt, who was recognized as successfully marrying the severity of Neoclassical lines with the sumptuousness and delicacy of marquetry [*163*]. In doing so, he achieved a uniquely Swedish interpretation of the style.

While case furniture and tables were often richly inlaid with Classical ornament, Gustavian chairs followed French models closely with upholstered seats and backs. The popular 'bathtub' sofa made its appearance in Sweden during the Rococo period, but survived into Neoclassicism with straight turned legs. Such pieces were usually gilded and upholstered in fine silk damask. (Simpler grey-painted furniture was produced for more modest homes.) Rectangular mirrors in giltwood, crowned by urns and other Classical motifs, were also a signature component of the Gustavian style.

Georg Haupt's achievements dominated and guided Swedish furniture development throughout the Gustavian period. His apprentice Gustaf Adolf Ditzinger (1760–1800) not only took over his workshop on Haupt's early death, but also married his widow. While Ditzinger produced pieces still rich in marquetry [*below*], the Late Gustavian period

saw a demand for much simpler pieces, with brass mouldings around the drawers and plain ring handles – a purer and stricter interpretation of the earlier form. It was Ditzinger who, with the designer Louis Masreliez (1748–1810), supplied the furniture for the Haga Pavilion.

Haga was also where Gustaf III planned to create a royal museum to house his important collection of Roman statues, bought while travelling in Italy. However, he was assassinated at the Opera House in Stockholm, the very one he had founded, and after his murder the Swedish National Museum was established in his memory. Since 1794, his collection of antiquities has been on view at the Royal Palace in Stockholm.

Regency

The political regency of George, Prince of Wales, later King George IV (1762–1830), lasted only from 1811 to 1820, but the Regency period is generally accepted as running from around 1800 to 1830. It is a significant length of time, in which a distinctive style in gardens, buildings, interior decoration and furniture evolved. It was also an era when the concepts of 'taste' and 'fashion' dominated. The word 'taste', implying the freedom to choose on aesthetic grounds, had been well established as early as the 1730s, but the growing influence of women was now significant, as was that of the increasingly powerful commercial class. Regency design reflected a mixture of social and economic factors. And with increased informality and a sudden proliferation of exotic modes, the Regency style was more adventurous than that of any previous age in England.

The most characteristic feature of a Regency interior is the disposition of its furniture. Until then, pieces had been placed against the walls when not in use; now, furniture was arranged in a free, easy and asymmetrical fashion. This was so radically different that those with a conservative mind found it quite shocking. When the American Louis Simond visited Osterley Park in 1811, he was horrified to find that 'tables, sofas and chairs were studiously *dérangés* about the fireplaces and in the middle of the room, as if the family had just left them. Such is the modern fashion of placing furniture carried to an extreme, as fashions are always, that make the

apartments of a fashionable house look like an upholsterer's or cabinet-maker's shop.'

This was an age when the theatre, organized spectacles and *fêtes* enjoyed huge popularity, providing an inexpensive way of presenting different styles of interior decoration to an audience largely obsessed with rapidly changing fashions. There was a distinction between people who wanted an 'architectural' interior and those who favoured a 'decorative' one. The former was the province of an architect, while the latter was more likely to be within the remit of an upholsterer (see p. 63). The Prince Regent's exuberant taste was firmly in the domain of the latter.

This theatrical and decorative approach came together in the many exotic styles that make the Regency such an artistically diverse and exciting era. Styles derived from antiquity include arabesque, Etruscan and Pompeian. In addition, there was a bewildering repertory of exotic modes. The gentleman-designer Thomas Hope (1769–1831) introduced the Greco-Egyptian in his *Household Furniture and Interior Decoration* (1807): his use of animal and mythological elements to decorate furniture resulted in spectacles such as a lion's head

OPPOSITE One of a pair of Regency giltwood console tables on winged dolphin supports. Such opulent carving is a signature of the Regency period, and takes its inspiration from furniture of the 1730s in the style of William Kent.

to crown the pediment of a sofa or a griffin to support a dressing table [*cf. 169*]. Some considered the result monstrous, but the more modest pattern-book of the architect George Smith (1782–1869), of 1808, brought such innovations into the grasp of a mass audience on both sides of the Atlantic. Thomas Sheraton (1751–1806) had by then done much to popularize the new trend of 'Grecian' forms in furniture, with his *Cabinet Dictionary*

of 1803, which enjoyed popular success not only in Britain but also in Federalist America.

Gradually, a craze for 'historic' styles emerged, including – in Britain – 'Elizabethan', 'Norman Revival' and 'Saxon'. Also added to the mix were 'Gothic', 'Turkish', 'Hindu', and of course Chinoiserie [*99*] pieces, made newly fashionable thanks to the furnishings of the Indian-style Royal Pavilion that the Prince Regent commissioned John

ABOVE A pair of Regency ebony-inlaid bergeres. New shapes of chair and methods of upholstery were a feature of the style: these are inspired by the antique *klismos* chair.

BELOW A Regency ormolu-mounted rosewood Carlton House desk, attributed to John McLean. The galleried superstructure includes six panelled central drawers flanked by curved panelled doors, framing a leather-lined slide with hinged reading-slope.

Nash to build in Brighton, then a sleepy village on England's south coast.

The Regency was also marked by the emergence of certain key pieces of furniture, often making use of technological innovations. One of the most characteristic is the oval, circular or octagonal table with a single central support on cast-iron pillars with animal-claw feet. Another Regency innovation was the four-legged D-ended table, which could be expanded by the insertion of extra sections. The 'Grecian' sofa featured two scrolled ends of equal height, with tasselled bolsters. Accompanying the sofa was the sofa table, the ideal item for the industrious lady of the house to use for writing, sewing or reading. New forms of chairs proliferated, including the 'Trafalgar chair' and the arc-backed 'curule chair', inspired by Greek and Roman models. A variety of new designs for beds also appeared, including interpretations of four-posters and half-testers; canopy or tent beds; sofa-beds and camp beds. Mirrors also took on different forms, including freestanding cheval glasses and convex circular designs.

The grandest Regency interiors were rich
in gilt, including the furniture [*167*], with mirror and
picture frames inevitably gilded. Even fabrics were
usually provided with gold borders or tassels of
gold-coloured silk. Other exotic finishes included
verre églomisé (see p. 34), boulle marquetry (see
p. 53), and japanning (see p. 57), all of which were
much admired by the Prince Regent. However,
these glittering effects were ill-suited to the sober
Victorian age, and by the 1840s they had become
largely redundant.

RIGHT Napoleon's expedition to Egypt, and the resulting
scholarship of Vivant Denon who accompanied him,
inspired new forms in French and then Regency furniture.
This ormolu-mounted and brass-inlaid mahogany armchair
is one of a pair designed by Denon and made by Georges
and François-Honoré-Georges Jacob, supplied *c.* 1819
to Thomas Hope for the Egyptian Room at his country
house, The Deepdene in Surrey.

BELOW A Regency ormolu-mounted and brass-inlaid
rosewood, ebony and parcel-gilt writing table, almost
certainly designed by Thomas Hope.

Biedermeier

The emergence of the style we recognize as Biedermeier coincided with a time of profound political and social upheaval. It began as the Napoleonic Wars drew to an end, around 1814–15, in the wake of French occupation of Continental Europe. Patriotism had become a force to be reckoned with, and everywhere people had begun to question the systems under which they lived. Under considerable political pressure, the German princes granted their subjects' demand for education, constitutional changes and freedom of trade.

Biedermeier originated in Austria, and took its name from the German words 'Bieder', meaning simple but honest, and 'Meier', a common family name. It kicked back against the French Empire style, a look considered too pompous and aristocratic in an age driven forward by a confident middle class. The country to be emulated was England, because it was there that technical and industrial innovations were flourishing. By 1830–35, this spirit of rebellion and renewal had been largely snuffed out by government action against all liberal movements, and the Biedermeier period effectively came to an end, although the style itself survived. In its heyday, it was a bourgeois Neoclassical look that prevailed throughout the German-speaking countries – Germany, Austria and Switzerland – and also spread its influence through Scandinavia and as far east as Hungary and Russia.

Biedermeier was an aesthetic and an attitude that applied to architecture, painting, sculpture and fashion. It was also the leading furniture style of its day. Functionality and truth to materials were its most important principles. Whereas Empire style furniture involved luxurious materials and a high level of technical skill, this was primarily artisan-

A typically simple and functional South German Biedermeier walnut side cabinet, early 19th century. The pair of doors below the frieze drawer open to reveal a plain interior with a single shelf.

A pair of ebonized and ash cabinets with stepped tops
and glazed and panelled doors on tapering square legs.

designed furniture that reflected both craft skills and the available industrial processes of the day.

Doing justice to the materials used was the primary aim of Biedermeier furniture. The foremost of these was wood, and timber was valued for its qualities as never before. Its grain was emphasized to greatest possible effect, with sheets of veneer taken from a single tree trunk, so within the piece it was possible to see the growth pattern of the tree. Typical light-coloured timbers used included pale fruitwoods, such as cherry and pear. Not only was wood the source of ornament, but the flat boards used determined the form of furniture. Surfaces were plain, with bases, cornices and pediments reduced to simple battens and strips – a far cry from the elaborate sculptural elements that had been the norm in previous decorative styles. Rather than concealing the technical processes used to construct such furniture, the Biedermeier craftsmen consciously

emphasized them. This was also furniture designed to have a very definite display side, rather than being admired from all angles, designed to be placed against walls in modest-sized rooms. This strictly frontal approach applied not only to chests and cabinets, but also to couches and chairs. Curved shapes do exist in Biedermeier furniture, but the effect is more like that of simplified, geometric solids which have been skilfully cut. Ideally, a Biedermeier piece could do entirely without ornamentation and fittings, but in practice this was rarely the case. Motifs such as drapery, vases, bouquets and cornucopias were developed, with thin sheet-brass drawer handles and escutcheons replacing the heavier bronze typical of the Empire period.

Another important difference was the way such furniture was used within the home. Up to and including the Empire period, every piece had its appointed place within a room. In contrast, Biedermeier furniture was truly mobile, as flexible as the inhabitants. The typically round Biedermeier table, for example, was used for dining, of course, but might also serve for sitting and talking, knitting

used to store household items, sheet music or books), the sewing table, and the jardiniere for displaying flowers. This was furniture with clear function at the heart of its design.

In its earliest period, Biedermeier is so light and simple that some of its designs look as though they could have been conceived a hundred years later. The work of Josef Danhauser (1780–1829), who ran his own establishment in Vienna from 1814, is worth particular mention because some of the designs he produced are so startlingly modern. In its early years, it was a style that was light and feminine; as its influence spread geographically, it became heavier, occasionally darker, and less finely proportioned. It enjoyed a major revival at the end of the 19th century, with architects and designers of the day making a link back to this unpretentious, middle-class style that had flowered and died within a couple of decades.

or reading. It could be placed impressively in the middle of the room, but was just as likely to be located in a comfortable corner. Indeed, comfort is the word that separates this style of furniture from the more elaborate ones that preceded it. Biedermeier furniture is nearly always in scale with the humans who used it, with tops of chests, cabinets and even wardrobes either at or only slightly above eye level. This was furniture designed not for palaces – although many pieces found their way there as the fashionable look of the day – but for middle-class homes. That is turn led to some ingenious multipurpose designs, such as small cabinet-bureaus that could double as fire-screens.

The burgeoning middle-class client base also had an influence on the types of furniture produced. Characteristic examples are the vitrine (a glass-fronted cabinet used to display treasured objects, such as fine glassware or presentation pieces of silver), the etagere (a set of unpretentious shelves

ABOVE LEFT A Biedermeier birch and ebonized cylinder bureau cabinet, early 19th century.

RIGHT One of a pair of South German Biedermeier side chairs with lyre splat backs, early 19th century.

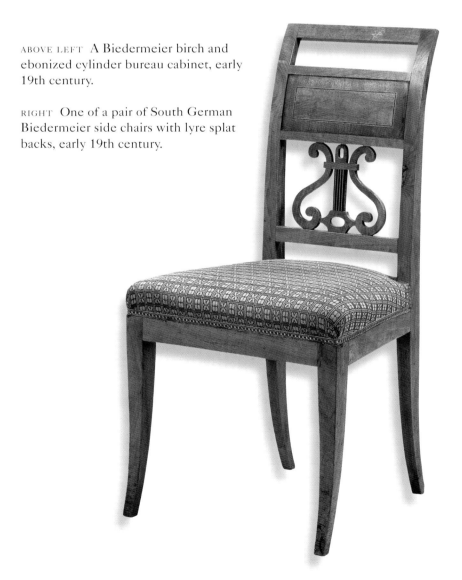

OPPOSITE A Biedermeier fruitwood and inlaid lit en bateau, early 19th century. The scrolled ends are typical of the style.

BELOW A long maple Shaker bench from the Enfield area of New Hampshire, mid-19th century. Many Shaker pieces were designed with communal living in mind.

OPPOSITE A recreated Shaker interior in the American Museum at Claverton Manor in Britain. The rocking chair is a typical feature, as is the row of pegs lining the walls on which chairs and utensils as well as clothes could be hung.

Shaker

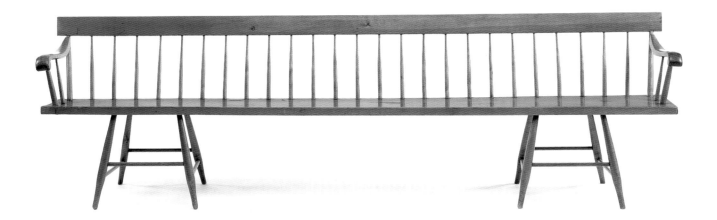

The Shakers, officially known as the United Society of Believers in Christ's Second Appearing, owed their origin to a group of Camisards, rebellious and visionary French Protestants who had come to England, and the Quakers. A congregation of what came to be known as 'Shaking Quakers' was formed in Bolton in 1747 by James and Jane Wardley, and they were joined by Ann Lee. She eventually became convinced that she was called to go to America, and arrived in New York in 1774. The first Shaker settlement was founded two years later at Niskayuna, or Watervliet, near Albany, New York. The first converts were mainly people working in agriculture, of Puritan-Protestant stock. Mother Ann died in 1784, but converts were numerous, and by 1800 the Shaker system had been firmly established.

The Shaker attitude to life and work was rooted in a distinct philosophy and culture. They found practical expression of their faith through doctrines of purity and celibacy and separation from the world. All was centred on the conviction that

devotion to Christ could not be complete without a common faith, common ownership of property and a common way of life. This ideal of oneness with Christ resulted in numerous 'orders' on uniformity in dress, speech and deportment, based on a desire for a united defence against the evils of worldliness.

Shakers had a high regard for cleanliness, order and simplicity, because they were seen as attributes of purity. Simplicity was not just an abstract notion: fabrics were woven in uncomplicated patterns and dyed in limited combinations of colour, houses were plain, and craftsmanship unpretentious. Whether at work, home or prayer, the doctrine of perfection was applied. The purpose of any object, whether a farm tool or a piece of furniture, was to fulfil its function with precision. Ostentation, whether in dress or craftsmanship, diverted the spirit from the idea of perfect oneness with Christ and so was frowned upon. The Shaker idea of beauty rested on the utility of an object: 'That which has in itself the highest use possesses the greatest beauty.' No matter how

humble, an object had to be 'without blemish'. Inferior or defective workmanship would not be tolerated, because it would be at odds with the community's high principles. Shaker furniture, dedicated to the use of the community as a whole, has a characteristically impersonal quality ('Possess these pieces as if you possess them not' is an old Shaker saying); but it reached standards of excellence that elevated provincial joiners to the level of fine craftsmen, with a guild-like pride in what they were producing.

The origins of the Shaker style in furniture lay in the craft traditions of colonial New England. The joiners welcomed into the early church were provincial workers, following techniques which had changed little over the preceding centuries. The first houses occupied by the Shakers contained an insignificant assortment of slat-back chairs, cottage beds and crude tables. Settlers had also arrived with the occasional stretcher table, inlaid chest-of-drawers or tallboy. Any piece of furniture was useful, so nothing was rejected in the early days because of its ornate appearance. However, within a few years, the Shakers had made the decision to supply their own needs as much as possible. A chair factory, tannery and smithy were in operation by 1789 at Niskayuna. The last decade of the century witnessed an increased activity in the making of furniture and

A beautiful simple Shaker pine cupboard over five
graduated drawers, thought to originate from the
New Lebanon area of Massachusetts, *c.* 1830–50.

other household goods, as communities were rapidly
established elsewhere in New England, and then in
Kentucky and Ohio. At various times, the Shakers
had eighteen major communities in eight states and
six smaller communities in Florida and Indiana.

It was not enough to replicate existing designs
in furniture. Many models were rejected because
they featured particular styles of leg or back, such as
cabriole or Windsor. Shaker furniture-makers sought to
produce pieces free from all semblance of ornament.
Carvings, extravagant turnings, veneering and inlay
did not fit with the ideal of purity. Instead, they used
light stains and varnishes, unadulterated treatments
that reflected the quiet joy at the centre of their
spiritual beliefs. The Shaker love of nature resulted
in beautiful wood left unspoiled and unconcealed.

In Shaker communities, 'brothers' and 'sisters'
sometimes lived in groups of as many as a hundred.
Shaker furniture, therefore, had to adapt to the needs
of groups rather than individuals. Desks were made
with tops facing both ways; long laundry tables
allowed two or more ironers to work together at any
one time; large cupboards and long benches and
dining tables were unexceptional.

With such emphasis on utility and simplicity,
Shaker furniture-makers developed certain distinctive
elements: legs, for example, were subtly tapered with
the foot omitted; neatly turned pegs served as drawer
pulls; and beds were placed on large wooden casters
so they could be moved for cleaning. There were no
escutcheons, brasses or mouldings, and dovetail joints
were often left exposed. The rows of pegs lining the
walls of almost every Shaker room form a unique
signature. From here everything could be suspended:
not just textiles, but such items as chairs and clocks,
keeping surfaces free from dirt and clutter. The
Shakers were innovators in chair-making, producing
a distinctive graceful three-slat chair and also many
rocking chairs. Intended originally for the elderly or
infirm, these were soon a feature of every dwelling.
Storage was well thought out, from case furniture
featuring cupboards and drawers to the distinctive
Shaker boxes made in many different sizes. Every
piece was expected to be as close to perfection as
the craftsman could achieve. Shaker craftsmanship
retained its distinctive simplicity as long as the
denomination survived, isolated from the vagaries
of domestic fashions in the wider world. It never
departed from its core philosophy either in character
or in the painstaking thoroughness with which it was
executed, until 1910, when the last Shaker
community went into the hands of the receiver.

Today, designers are well schooled in the idea
that the design of any object should be determined
by its practical use. The Shakers evolved this point
of view from a spiritual belief that soundness of
construction and perfection of workmanship were
proof of their intention to serve God. Their aim
was to eliminate what they perceived as superficial
beauty. In doing so, they achieved forms so pure,
simple and innocent that they created a whole new
aesthetic of beauty.

SHAKER: THE GOLDEN THREAD

Shaker-style furniture is still very much in evidence, but it is more interesting to look for the threads that bind it philosophically and spiritually with work being produced today. At the heart of Shaker style lie a love of and a commitment to raw and natural materials, worked by hand to express a feeling of purity, simplicity and connection with the natural world. In this, there is a direct link both to the Arts and Crafts Movement and to the later American Studio Movement.

Wales & Wales still use the finest craft techniques and materials to produce fine furniture, such as this deceptively simple dining table of solid rippled ash, 2007.

OPPOSITE The large dresser painted 'Dragon's Blood' red designed by Philip Webb *c.* 1860 for the dining room in Red House, the house he designed for William Morris.

Arts and Crafts

The Arts and Crafts Movement represents a reaction to the forces of industrialization. It was originally a British movement, but similar attitudes developed in other European countries and the USA as they too underwent a radical transformation. The discovery that technical progress did not necessarily coincide with an improvement in man's lot led to long campaigns for social, industrial and moral reform, much of which is still unresolved today. Those who drove the Arts and Crafts Movement forward were concerned not just with aesthetics, but with establishing a society where all would enjoy the freedom to be creative. It was a philosophy which embraced architecture and design and also the 'fine' arts of painting and sculpture.

This emphasis on design as something which should be seen within a social context was to have a significant influence on 20th-century thinking, as the Modern Movement was stimulated by the idea of an environment that would both serve and express people's needs. The British Arts and Crafts Movement was founded on the conviction that industrialization had brought with it the total destruction of a craftsman's dignity. Its proponents saw mechanical 'progress' in terms of human misery and degradation: poverty, overcrowded slums, grim factories and a dying countryside. William Morris (1834–96) wrote: 'Men living amidst such ugliness cannot conceive of beauty, and therefore, cannot express it.'

Behind the thinking of the Arts and Crafts Movement in England lay A. W. N. Pugin (1812–52), who believed that architecture should be an expression of moral integrity, rather than mere style. For him, the Gothic Revival that he spearheaded was an expression of faith: in his buildings he aimed at the restoration of the pre-Reformation spirit of the Middle Ages (this was the second Gothic Revival: the first was the Picturesque and Romantic style made famous by Horace Walpole at Strawberry Hill in the mid-18th century). He also loathed 'sham', laying emphasis on 'honest' – or revealed – furniture construction. Gothic was also praised by the art critic, writer and social critic John Ruskin (1819–1900), who rejected mechanization and standardization in favour of reverence for nature and natural forms. To Ruskin, Gothic embodied the values he sought in art: strength, solidity and aspiration. His attacks on capitalism and industrialization were a key inspiration for the Arts and Crafts Movement.

The towering figure of the Movement was William Morris. He and his friend Edward Burne-Jones (1833–98) met while at Oxford, where both were intended originally for holy orders. By the time they left, Burne-Jones had decided on a career as a painter, and Morris on one as an architect. Soon afterwards, Morris met someone else who was to be a lifelong friend, the architect Philip Webb (1831–1915).

By 1860, Morris, Burne-Jones and their friend the painter Dante Gabriel Rossetti (1828–82) were all married and Morris had moved into Red House in Kent, a landmark in 19th-century domestic architecture. Designed by Webb with contributions by Morris, the house, chiefly of red brick, was a vision of the ideal life that Morris and his friends had constructed for themselves first at Oxford and later in London. Red House featured ceiling paintings by Morris, wall-hangings both designed and worked by Morris and his wife Jane, furniture by Webb [167], some painted by Morris and Rossetti, and wall-paintings, stained glass and painted glass by Burne-Jones. The idea of an artists' collaborative crystallized when Morris and his friends were working together to furnish Red House. This led to the foundation in 1861 of Morris, Marshall, Faulkner & Co., later Morris & Co., affectionately christened 'The Firm', which brought together numerous craft skills, including carving, stained glass, embroidery,

OPPOSITE An oak dining-room suite designed by Frank Lloyd Wright for the Joseph W. Husser house in Chicago, Illinois, *c.* 1899 takes echoes of British Arts and Crafts over the Atlantic.

ABOVE A mahogany corner cabinet designed by C. F. A. Voysey in 1898 for the dining room of E. R. Hughes at 7 Lodge Place in London. The slatted top with pierced and shaped heart decoration was a favourite motif of the style.

textiles, mural decoration, woven and knitted carpets, glassware and of course furniture.

Morris believed that furniture fell into two distinct categories: 'necessary workaday furniture', which should be kept as simple as possible, and 'state' furniture, which he saw as 'the blossoms of the art of furniture' – an opportunity for carving, inlaying and painting. In the early years, 'the Firm' had produced variants of the modest Sussex rush-seated chair and the artisan green-stained furniture of the artist Ford Madox Brown (1821–93), but later there were also elaborate pieces produced by cabinetmakers such as George Jack (1855–1931) and W. A. S. Benson (1854–1924), which featured marquetry, inlay, and even silver mounts.

The successors of William Morris challenged the notion of 'state' furniture, preferring the understatement of so-called 'workaday' or 'cottage' furniture with its emphasis on straightforward construction and sympathetic use of native woods. Such honest, unpretentious furniture encapsulates the spirit of the Arts and Crafts, a democratic, domestic style that sits happily within many sizes and periods of home.

The Century Guild, probably the first of the important late 19th-century craft organizations, was founded in 1882 by the designer and architect Arthur Heygate Mackmurdo (1851–1942) together with his former pupil, Herbert Percy Horne (1864–1916). The production of its workshops included furniture and metalwork, wallpaper (entrusted to Jeffrey and Co. of Islington), enamelling and textiles. Artists associated with the Guild included the potter William de Morgan (1839–1917) and the enameller Clement Heaton (1861–1940). Fellow-travellers included the architect C. F. A. Voysey (1857–1941) [*181*].

In 1890 a group of young architects – William Lethaby (1857–1931), Ernest Gimson (1864–1919), Mervyn Macartney (1853–1932), Sidney Barnsley (1865–1926) and Reginald Blomfield (1856–1942) – set up Kenton & Co. For two years the group achieved a modest success, but in 1892 it folded owing to lack of capital. The younger members, Gimson, Barnsley, and Barnsley's brother Ernest (1863–1926), also an architect, decided to devote themselves to the craft of furniture-making, setting up workshops in the Cotswolds. While Sidney Barnsley, a purist, made all his own designs, Gimson's were executed by craftsmen working under his supervision. Native woods, such as oak, yew, elm and walnut, were generally used, with 'prestige' pieces occasionally inlaid with mother-of-pearl, silver, ivory and bone. Gimson was described by Nikolaus Pevsner as 'the greatest English artist-craftsman'.

The influence of Arts and Crafts as a philosophical movement spread through Europe and crossed the Atlantic. The architect C. R. Ashbee (1863–1942) visited the USA in 1900 and struck up an important friendship with the architect Frank Lloyd Wright (1867–1959), himself an admirer of both Ruskin and Morris. While in Chicago, Ashbee visited Wright's Husser House of 1899 [*180*], with its series of interconnecting rooms looking out over Lake Michigan – an architectural solution that was creatively individual, sympathetic to the site and artistically restrained. When Wright wrote that 'man is not made for architecture; architecture is made for man', he was of course speaking the language of Morris, Webb, Gimson, Voysey, and the other notables at the core of the British Arts and Crafts Movement.

BELOW A circular table by Albert-Armand Rateau, *c.* 1922. The top, of black marble, rests on a black-patinated bronze base with tapered legs, each topped with a stylized bird that projects slightly from under the table top.

Art Deco

The Art Deco period covers the years between the two World Wars, 1918–39. One of the legacies of the First World War was the sense of a break with the past. It was an era when public opinion – that of the mass consumer – became as important in forming tastes as the whims and preferences of the elite. It was also the age of huge and democratic technological advances: radio stations, the film industry, increased utilization of electrical power, manufacture of plastics, more accessible transport (both land and air), and advanced building techniques resulting in ever taller buildings. With increased communication on a global scale, the benefits were soon felt across the Western world.

However, it was the 'Exposition Internationale des Arts Décoratifs et Industriels Modernes', held in Paris in 1925, that is often seen as the defining moment of the aesthetic we recognize as Art Deco, and that gave the movement its name. The Exhibition was conceived as a stage on which to reassert France's authority as arbiter of taste and producer of luxury goods, and also to emphasize Paris's role as the world centre of fashion. In many ways it was a response to the way French goods were being copied or adapted for cheaper production elsewhere, particularly by France's old enemy, Germany. It was international, but post-war austerity and international relations ensured that only about two dozen countries participated, the majority of which were European. Germany and the United States were noticeable by their absence.

Within the main French section of the Exhibition, pavilions and galleries planned around courtyards and gardens were dedicated to leading designers, artistic groups and particular manufacturers. The goods on display were a poem to the lavish and the exotic, as the American critic Helen Appleton Read described in astonishment: 'sharkskin furniture, macabre bedroom schemes in violet blacks and blueish purples, jade and jeweled salons de bain, furniture representing negro sculpture, monkeyskin bedspreads and glass walls . . .' Sumptuousness was the common theme, whether it was the black and silver lacquered 'Fumoir' by Jean Dunand (1877–1942), featuring contemporary abstract art and screens inspired by African sculpture, or the 'Chambre de Madame' by André Groult (1884–1967), with its pastel hues and sinuous sharkskin-clad furniture [186].

To coincide with the Exhibition, the twelve-volume *Encyclopédie des arts décoratifs et industriels modernes* was issued. The illustrations that accompanied the text showed many of the diverse influences at work, including the ancient civilizations of Egypt, Greece and Mexico, primitive Africa, and exotic Asia. It was as if the designers of the period saw the whole history of the world and every culture within it as ripe for the picking. Among the range of French historical styles that Art Deco drew on was Louis XVI, with its Neoclassical forms and ornamentation (see pp. 150–54). Paul Follot (1877–1941), for example, frequently combined 18th-century shapes and traditional techniques with luxurious materials of the day. Other styles that were much favoured

because of their simple lines and warm wood veneers were the late 18th- and early 19th-century Directoire, Consulate, Empire and Restauration periods. Jacques-Emile Ruhlmann (1879–1933) was renowned for his reinterpretation of these earlier styles, stressing that while he found inspiration in Classical furniture, the art lay in reinterpreting it for modern tastes of comfort and style.

At the other end of the spectrum, the 1925 Exhibition embraced the avant-garde: Fauvism,

A richly conceived double-sided screen by Edgar Brandt (see p. 35), *c.* 1924. The five leaves, made of cast iron, wrought iron and brass, feature a lush tropical garden with a central fountain set against a background of rosettes.

This enfilade by Eugène Printz and Jean Dunand is veneered with kekwood and palm and has four doors of patinated brass and silver, the ones on the outside gently curved.

Cubism, Expressionism, Futurism, De Stijl and Constructivism had all made an impact on the decorative arts by the mid-1920s, affecting bookbinding and silversmithing, graphics and fashion, photography and film. Avant-garde artists and Deco designers often shared interests, patrons and friends. African art, for example, fascinated both the Cubists and the designers Eileen Gray (1878–1976), Pierre Legrain (1888–1929) and Maria Likarz (1893–1956).

Through Art Deco every aspect of modern living was given an exotic veneer, from the façades of cinemas to the packaging of perfume. Furniture featured tropical hardwoods and luxurious materials, such as ebony, sharkskin and lacquer, providing glamour and sensuousness. Forms were often inspired by African and other non-Western artefacts, such as Eileen Gray's extraordinary 'Pirogue' day bed in lacquered wood with silver leaf. Albert-Armand Rateau (1882–1938) combined highly skilled metalwork with exotic iconography [183], resulting, for example, in his patinated bronze chaise longue for the fashion designer Jeanne Lanvin. Rich, hedonistic effects were achieved with lacquer (used not just for furniture but often to clad ceilings and walls).

The 1925 Paris Exhibition took a movement that was already gathering speed internationally and put it firmly on the map. Art Deco began to travel, not just throughout Europe but to the United States, notably to New York, Chicago and Miami. Less well known is Shanghai Deco of the 1930s. Shanghai was

The pink and grey 'Chambre de Madame', designed by André Groult, at the 1925 Exposition Internationale des Arts Décoratifs et Industriels Modernes in Paris.

an extraordinary metropolis of foreign nationals, mainly French and British, and the sophisticated French community imported Art Deco for their architecture and interiors; more furniture was made by local craftsmen, using photographs, sketches, and rough drawings of the originals. The result was an interesting hybrid – furniture that is Deco in form, but which often features Chinese ornamentation, such as flowers, dragons, or stylized leaves and clouds. In essence, it is a sort of 20th-century Chinoiserie. Through the influence of the British, Bombay (now Mumbai) became the epicentre of Indo-Deco, of which the most significant patrons were the princes, who increasingly came to adopt Western lifestyles and tastes. When the Maharaja of Indore commissioned a new palace, Manik Bagh, in 1930, the furniture for his study was made by Ruhlmann in macassar ebony, the chairs for the

ballroom were by Wassili Luckhardt (1889–1972) and the chairs for the billiard room by Michel Dufet (1888–1985), while his bedroom featured Eileen Gray's 'Transat' armchair and Le Corbusier and Charlotte Perriand's chaise longue. The interior was decorated in high French style, including metal, glass and lacquered screens and canopied beds by Louis Sognot (1892–1970) and Charlotte Alix (1892–1987).

ART DECO:
THE GOLDEN THREAD

Like Regency, Art Deco drew on a myriad historic styles as well as embracing the avant-garde, but at its centre was the unapologetic celebration of luxury, particularly through the use of sumptuous and exotic materials. Luxury has been reinterpreted today by designers such as Ron Arad, who make use of materials that are not easily available and are difficult to work, such as woven stainless steel mesh, carbon fibre and cast silicon. Such work also means drawing on expensive and highly skilled craftsmanship. There is a strong link between the Art Deco aesthetic and that of the 1960s, when it was revived. The sexy and curvaceous work of Marc Newson, for example, which would not look out of place in the sets of *2001 A Space Odyssey* or *Barbarella*, at the same time looks back to Deco and designers such as André Groult.

The 'Pod of Drawers' by Marc Newson, of 1987, made of fibreglass and polished aluminium, echoes the curves of Groult's equally distinctive cabinet in the 1925 Exhibition [*opposite*].

American Studio Furniture

There is a tradition in America of highly expressive cabinetmaking that dates back to the Colonial period, as with the block-and-shell designs of Newport, Rhode Island [*141*].

In the second half of the 20th century, there was another wave of interest in individual design and craftsmanship, begun by studio artisans who rejected the mass production of the machine age. These innovative designer–makers hailed both from smalltown America and – for many were émigrés – from Europe. Their artistic and decorative approach to furniture was at odds with the Modern Movement, which was driven forward by mass-production designers and manufacturers, such as Charles and Ray Eames, George Nelson, Herman Miller and Knoll. Instead they belonged to the tradition of 'Americana', a term used to describe American folk decorative arts which go back to the earliest days of the pilgrim fathers. While Modernism originated in Europe, the tradition of small-scale production of high-end furniture by artist–craftsmen is one that is particularly strong in America, and also in Britain, where the Arts and Crafts movement first began (see pp. 178–82).

In recent years, Americana has become increasingly collectable, not only in the USA but also in Europe, where there is new appreciation of this highly individual and beautifully made furniture. Auction houses often include it in decorative art sales, while websites are also devoted to its charm.

Collectors appreciate it for its sculptural and artistic qualities, recognizing that it is an aesthetic that is not derivative from Europe – as so much in the States is – but that is uniquely and proudly in the American tradition.

The modern American Studio Movement started with Wharton Esherick (1887–1970), a woodworker craftsman, who began working at the tail end of the Arts and Crafts era. His asymmetrical forms and free-flowing organic style were the inspiration for later studio artisans, such as Wendell Castle (b. 1932), Michael Coffey (b. 1928), Sam Maloof (b. 1916), Arthur Espenet Carpenter (1920–2006) and Jack Rogers Hopkins (1920–2006) [*12*].

Esherick also inspired a number of designer–craftsmen who crossed the line into small studios, contract production, and even small factory manufacturing. These include George Nakashima (1905–90) [*189, 190*], Paul Evans (1931–87) and his long-time collaborator Phillip Lloyd Powell (1919–2008) [*191*], and Vladimir Kagan (b. 1927). For them, what began as individual handwork escalated into craft factories, some employing many workers – in the case of Evans, about a hundred. However, they never sacrificed their exacting standards or intense personal involvement with every piece that bore their name. Then as now, the distinction between designer and craftsman was blurred.

A third category comprises the furniture designers who also created fabulous interiors – names

A robust but elegant walnut chair with ottoman by George Nakashima, *c.* 1955. It would originally have been supplied with wool cushions.

such as Tommi Parzinger (1903–81), James Mont (1904–78) and Edward Wormley (1907–95). These designers worked primarily on private commissions at the very top end of the market. Many created complete interiors for their elite clientele, but what distinguishes them from designer–decorators is that they always recognized the individual piece of furniture to be the star of the show. Architects and designers such as Paul Laszlo (1900–1993) [*192*] and Samuel Marx (1885–1964) are also significant because of the way they embraced furniture as integral to their work.

It is hard to pick out particular names in a limited space, but this is an opportunity to pay tribute to four master craftsmen who are still working today. Wendell Castle first studied industrial design at the University of Kansas before switching to sculpture. Although highly regarded as a craftsman, woodworker and furniture designer [*31, 35, 191*], he still considers himself, first and foremost, to be a sculptor. The turning point in his early life was a 1958 road trip to rural Pennsylvania, where he dropped in unannounced on the famed Wharton Esherick. Castle was so struck by the old master's life

and work that back in Kansas he began to make furniture himself – at first derivative of the Scandinavian designs then so popular in America. Over the years, he progressed to increasingly sculptural forms, first exploring the possibilities of wood laminates and then venturing into plastics in the 1960s. It was a visit to Britain in the 1970s, when he met John Makepeace, founder of Parnham College (see p. 216), that inspired him to embrace the highest challenges of craftsmanship (in this period also, incidentally, he lectured to and inspired a young David Linley). This phase was characterized by fabulous trompe-l'oeil pieces, beautifully wrought still-lifes in various woods.

Castle was also drawn to the strong profiles of Art Deco and in particular the perfectly executed work of Jacques-Emile Ruhlmann. He embraced exotic woods, adding inlays of ivory and silver, striving for every detail and finish to be without flaw. By the 1990s, Castle's work was in museum collections across the USA. His most recent works include ones made primarily of polychromed fibreglass [*31*], often painted or gilded – as bold, confident and energetic as his earlier work.

Vladimir Kagan reached New Jersey in 1938 as a child – his family had fled the Nazis in Germany – and the young 'Vladi' adapted quickly to American life. After studying abroad and taking architecture courses at Columbia University, Kagan joined the family furniture-making business (his father was a Russian cabinetmaker). However, his true interest was in sculpture and painting. Kagan has always said that his mission was to 'interpret my century', and his furniture does indeed seem to capture certain defining moments, from the curves of the 1950s to the multifunctionalism of the 1970s. The latter inspired his 'Omnibus', a platform couch-bed-table-light-chair that could be reconfigured for any lifestyle.

As well as producing furniture, Kagan was commissioned to create 'personalized' interiors, the focus of which was often his sensual, sculptural furniture. He understood that furniture was about much more than function: it could be the conversation piece of a room. Kagan is considered by many to be a living legend; his 'originals' are limited editions available through Ralph Pucci International that replicate as closely as possible his classic pieces made in the 1950s and 1960s.

Michael Coffey majored in psychology, thinking of woodworking only as a hobby. However, the hobby took over – influenced by contemporaries such as George Nakashima, Wendell Castle and Sam Maloof. He finally took the plunge to embrace his passion full-time in 1973, moving to Vermont where he bought a house and workshop. His sculptural and monumental pieces are a blend of Art Nouveau curves and engineering precision. The organic shapes he is famous for were often inspired by the countryside of Vermont – meandering brooks, waving branches, the waves in water. Wood is his medium of choice, in particular

OPPOSITE A French olive, burr walnut and pandanus cloth sideboard by George Nakashima, 1978. Sliding doors open to reveal three central drawers and two adjustable shelves on each side.

LEFT The 'Transfigure' chair in mahogany by Wendell Castle, 2006, displays his signature organic shapes and love of natural forms.

BELOW This cabinet and wall sculpture were a collaboration between Paul Evans and Phillip Lloyd Powell, c. 1965.

Paul Laszlo's 'Dalí' console table, *c.* 1950, named after Laszlo's friend, the painter Salvador Dalí. Its adventurous, swirling shapes would not look out of place in a Dalí painting.

African Mozambique, which is similar to walnut. His organic and enigmatic forms often carry romantic and evocative names, such as the 'Aphrodite' rocker, 'Swahili' cabinet, and 'Lily Pad' table. He understands how the human senses connect emotionally with art, preferring clients to use his work rather than admire it from afar.

Born in California of Lebanese descent, Sam Maloof was originally a self-taught graphic artist. It is typical of his no-frills attitude that when he rented a one-room apartment after a stint in the army during World War II, he furnished it with pieces made from plywood and packing crates. During his long career, Maloof has remained committed to hand craftsmanship. He has always produced furniture that is simple and strong, with an underlying reverence for beautiful wood, and limits his output to what he can produce with his own hands – over five thousand individual designs during the past sixty years.

Virtually all Maloof's work is in black walnut, but he has also made use of oak, Brazilian rosewood and ebony. He never mixes timbers, and leaves his beautifully made joints on display. You won't find metal or man-made materials in a Maloof piece. Instead, each one is finished with several applications of a traditional turpentine and linseed-oil mix, applied with pints of elbow grease. Now in his nineties, Maloof is still producing furniture that is recognizably his – a signature that has remained unaltered through his long career. His graceful and comfortable chairs are still particularly in demand, especially the rocking chairs that he has been making since 1958. These are even represented in the official White House collection, having been owned by Presidents Reagan, Carter and Clinton.

In the 1990s many of the great names of the American Studio Movement found themselves fashionable once more. Designer Tom Ford, for example, when he was creative director at Gucci, singlehandedly revived the career of Vladimir Kagan by bringing him out of retirement to produce the 'Omnibus' for each of Gucci's 360 stores.

It is not possible to talk about the current escalation in interest in the decorative arts – such as design art – without recognizing that it was the American Studio Movement that largely paved the way for what we are seeing today.

AMERICAN STUDIO FURNITURE:
THE GOLDEN THREAD

The American Studio Movement was a direct descendant of the Arts and Crafts Movement, which had enormous influence on both sides of the Atlantic, both aesthetically and philosophically. It was a kickback against industrial processes, a way of re-engaging furniture with the hand of the maker. Highly individualistic and often unashamedly decorative, it makes a direct link to the design–art movement of today.

Danny Lane's glass and steel 'Little Wing', 2007, has an energetic movement at its centre that is reminiscent of the free-flowing organic shapes so loved by American Studio Movement makers.

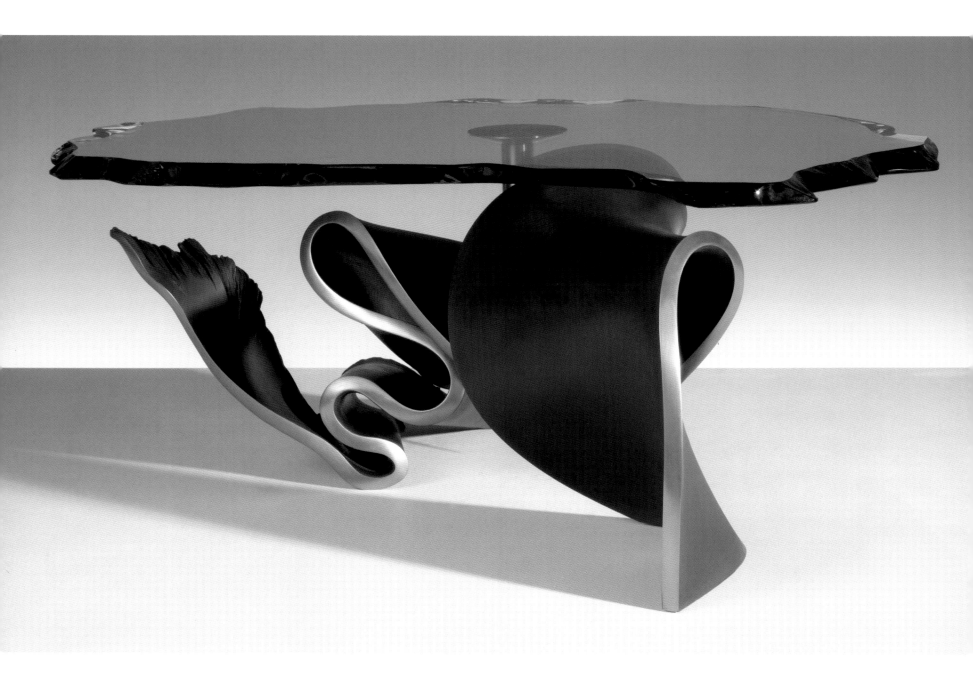

The New
Golden Age

Furniture as Art

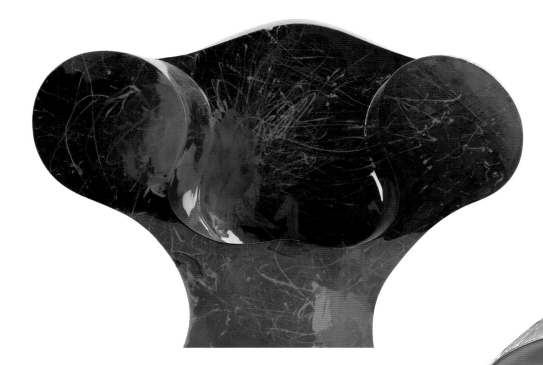

Where furniture is concerned, we live in interesting times. The first decade of the 21st century has seen an extraordinary shift in attitudes among the art establishment towards the idea of collectable contemporary limited-edition or one-off designs. Many major art galleries boast artist–designers on their list. For the Gagosian, in London with many branches abroad, it is Marc Newson; Ron Arad is represented by Timothy Taylor in London; while Moss in New York and Los Angeles has an exclusive relationship with Studio Job, Maarten Baas and the Campana brothers. Architects, such as Zaha Hadid and the American Frank Gehry (b. 1929), have also been persuaded to turn their vision to furniture.

Very few people could afford to own a building by either, but one of their extraordinary pieces of furniture, while costly, is within the grasp of a discerning and wealthy elite.

The terms 'design art' and 'art furniture' are often applied to this emerging movement, but in fact it heralds a return to the long neglected decorative arts. Just as *haute couture* represents the pinnacle of fashion, from which trends and innovations filter down to high street level, so this unashamedly luxurious and show-stopping furniture sets new standards from which we will all ultimately benefit.

PREVIOUS OPENING Pablo Reinoso's 'Spaghetti' double
bench, 2006.

OPPOSITE AND ABOVE Ron Arad's 'New Orleans' chair,
a limited-edition version of his 'Big Easy' design, 1999,
and two details of its surface, achieved by using pigmented
polyester (for a different colour scheme, see p. 49). Its
voluminous outline suggests an oversized armchair.

BELOW 'Blo Void 4' by Ron Arad, made of woven and
polished red aluminium, 2005.

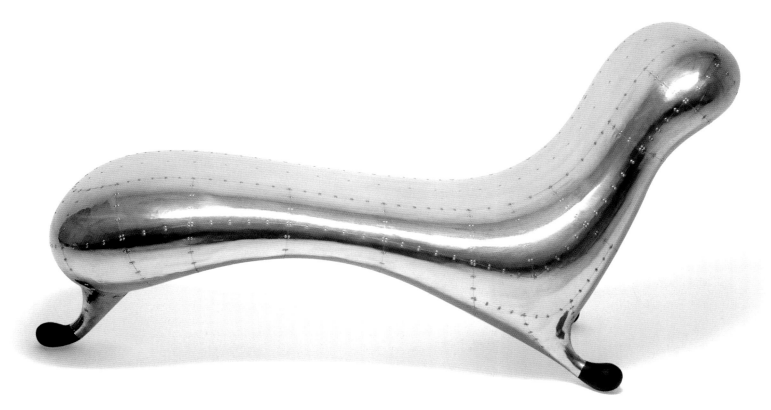

Limited-edition and one-off design

In October 2007, at Christie's auction house in London, a 1986 'Lockheed Lounge' [*above*] – one of only thirteen in existence – was sold for £748,000. Made by Marc Newson, the futuristic aluminium 'Lockheed' is now an icon of the burgeoning furniture limited-editions market. At the time of writing, the prototype (handmade by Newson in 1985) has been valued at about £1.25 million.

What took so many people by surprise was the fact that a piece of furniture – as opposed to fine art – could be so valuable. It would be wrong, however, to dismiss this development as a cynical and artificially created move by the art world. Limited editions and one-offs, by the very fact that they only comprise a handful of pieces, allow artist–designers the freedom to create something truly extraordinary. While mass-production furniture is constrained by questions of budget, the limits of available machinery, affordability of materials, and of course time, these special and spectacular creations need recognize no such constraints. If artist–designers wish to return to hand-crafted methods, they can do so. If they wish to use expensive materials or spend months at a computer exploring new digital forms, they can again do so. In effect, we all benefit from the limited-

Marc Newson's 'Lockheed Lounge' in aluminium and fibreglass was hand-crafted by him and first shown in a local gallery in his native Sydney in 1985. At the time of publishing, it has broken records for the highest price paid for a work by a living designer.

edition market, because it provides a stage on which artist–designers can really show what they are capable of and where their vision lies.

Design is important because it opens up new frontiers for mankind. It changes the way we think; it is linked to the way we evolve as people. There is a whole new generation of enthusiasts and collectors who appreciate how great design vision opens doors and possibilities. This is furniture that represents how intelligent, creative and ultimately optimistic human beings will continue to push out the boundaries and so transform the world we all live in.

Art or design?

It was the British designer Tom Dixon who once tongue-in-cheek said 'If a chair is too uncomfortable to sit on, it is sculpture. If not, it is design.'

OPPOSITE The 'Buisson' chair by French designer Vincent Dubourg, whose work is a fusion of furniture, architecture and sculpture. He uses techniques such as wood-bending and metal-casting to transform simple materials.

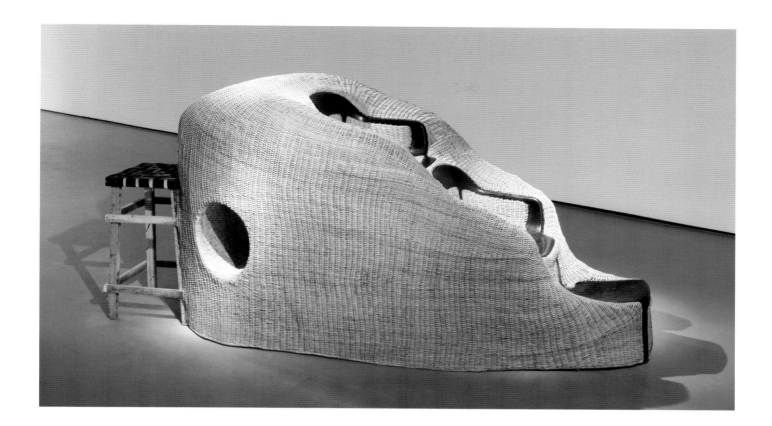

OPPOSITE The highly expressive 'Ram' chair by André Dubreuil, of 2005, is made of welded steel and suede. (The portrait above the fireplace is by the acclaimed German photographer Werner Pawlok.)

The three-tiered 'Siwa' chair, part of the 'Transplastic' collection by the Campana brothers, 2007. Sculpted from wicker, wood, leather and steel, it comments on the replacement of traditional wicker by modern plastic.

Certainly, in some circles there is resistance to the fact that 'design' should be produced for such an exclusive market. Shouldn't it be for the masses? Again, the fashion world provides a useful parallel. The international couture houses are expected continually to innovate, taking inspiration from many diverse sources to echo the world we live in culturally, politically, environmentally and aesthetically. If fashion were merely about clothes – something to keep us warm – there would be no couture, no trends and no progress.

The man who should be credited with pushing us to a new understanding of what art–design can be is Ron Arad. It was Arad who opened a gallery in London's Covent Garden back in 1983 called with prescience 'One Off'. Arad's own work has since acquired superstar status, lauded not just for its poetic forms [37, 196–97, 225], but for the way that he has in effect redefined notions of luxury through the use of radically different materials such as carbon fibre and cast resin.

It is no wonder that people are confused by trying to work out where design stops and art begins. Even the creatives at the heart of the movement are not in unison when it comes to defining the boundaries. People such as Tom Dixon [228, 230] and Philippe Starck [47, 223] almost certainly would describe themselves as designers, not artists. The Brazilian Campana brothers [45 and above] are less easy to label: Humberto (b. 1953) started out as a sculptor, but began producing more functional work when Fernando (b. 1961), an architect, became involved. The Chinese artist Shao Fan (b. 1964) produces furniture, but these are highly conceptual pieces. Zaha Hadid's furniture relates directly to the soaring organic shapes that can be seen in her buildings [21, 46].

What is important to stress is that this movement is about much more than owning a very expensive chair in a limited edition: it overlaps with the art world. When these makers create a chair, they are in fact commenting upon the chair. It is the philosophy behind the design that attracts serious collectors – the 'voice' of the maker. This is as true of a piece of furniture as it is of a painting or piece of sculpture.

THE DESIGN ACADEMY, EINDHOVEN

This remarkable school of industrial design in Holland deserves special mention, because so many excellent designers have emerged from its walls in recent years, including Marcel Wanders (b. 1963) [*25 and opposite*], Maarten Baas [*opposite, 208*], Jurgen Bey [*29, 59, opposite*], Studio Job collaborators Job Smeets (b. 1970) and Nynke Tynagel (b. 1977) [*51, 119, below, 206, 207*], and Demakersvan (see pp. 209–10) [*209*].

Under the direction of Li Edelkoort (b. 1950) – a renowned trend forecaster – it instils the idea that anything is possible. Students are encouraged to think for themselves and to go the distance in their quest to instigate change for the better. Not only do they graduate with a very broad design education, but the school's educational approach appears to give them confidence to produce astonishingly bold statement pieces.

Eindhoven also connects its students with the past – the notion that you can and should look backwards in order to leap forward.

In the 'Bavaria' table by Studio Job the age-old technique of marquetry is combined with modern laser technology to achieve the flawlessly executed design. 'Bavaria' is also the theme of a screen [*51*].

LEFT The 'Knotted' chair by
Marcel Wanders, Droog Design,
for Cappellini, 1996, is made from
'knotted' carbon and aramide fibre
cord with a resin finish.

BELOW 'Plastic Chair in Wood'
by Maarten Baas, of 2008, is inspired
by the paradoxes of modern China:
based on the ubiquitous plastic chair,
it is made from carved camphor wood.

LEFT The 'Pix' by Studio Makkink
& Bey, made out of short slats of wood
for a pixellated effect, created a new
'humble' take on the idea of a couture
show flat in the 'Witness Flat'
installation of 2008 (see also p. 59).

The Modern Movement

Furniture was historically a statement of taste, and a celebration of often remarkable craftsmanship. Wealthy collectors who commissioned pieces valued them no less highly than the art they hung on their walls. Then, in the second half of the 19th century, furniture became an industrialized product as well as a craft-made one. One of the most pioneering developments was the steam-bending of laminates and solid wood by Michael Thonet in Vienna: his company, Gebrüder Thonet, manufactured the first truly mass-produced designs. 'Bentwood' chairs [*cf. opposite*] were highly successful, owing mainly to the plethora of recently opened coffee houses in Vienna for which they were eminently suitable. Between 1859 and 1914 an astonishing forty million 'Model no. 14' chairs were produced, through the introduction of an assembly-line system of production.

The potential for true mass production of modern furniture was first explored at the Bauhaus School, founded in Weimar, Germany, in the early 20th century and later moved to Dessau under the direction of Walter Gropius (1883–1969). The 'Red and Blue Chair' [*right*] by the Dutch designer Gerrit Rietveld (1888–1964), first exhibited in 1923 about six years after he had conceived the design, is generally regarded as the first truly Modern chair: not only did it question the need for springing and upholstery, but it was constructed from roughly cut wood of standard sizes, making it viable for full-scale mass production. That never happened, probably because its aesthetics were too radical for popular appeal.

The Modern Movement resulted in many designs that have since acquired iconic status, such as the 'Barcelona Chair' of 1929, a collaboration between Ludwig Mies van der Rohe (1886–1969) and Lilly Reich (1885–1947); the 'Model B3' or 'Wassily' chair of 1925 by Marcel Breuer (1902–81); and the tubular steel and leather 'Model no. 2072' chaise longue, a collaboration between Le Corbusier (1887–1965),

Gerrit Rietveld's 'Red and Blue Chair' is an icon of the Modern Movement. Constructed from roughly cut and painted wood of standard sizes, it challenged the necessity of conventional springing and upholstery.

Pierre Jeanneret (1896–1967) and Charlotte Perriand (1903–99). These designs were brave and radical interpretations of industrial materials and processes.

It was not until after World War II had ended in 1945 that it was economically and technically feasible to mass-produce furniture on a large scale. In fact the war had an enormous impact on the furniture industry, particularly in the United States, because designers could apply the latest and most efficient technology developed in other manufacturing industries, such as aircraft. Cross-fertilization had benefits on both sides. During the war, the research of American brothers Charles (1907–78) and Ray (1912–88) Eames into the production of low-cost wood laminates had led to a commission from the US Navy to design and produce leg and arm splints in moulded plywood. The plywood and moulded polyester chairs they later produced were designed to mould around the seated body, achieving comfort without the need for lavish upholstery [*19*]. Their 'Plastic Shell' group of chairs

OPPOSITE The 'Spitting Image' chair by Rolf Sachs, of 2008, is made from clear-cut resin moulded from a traditional bentwood chair. It brings new relevance to a design that has been popular for over a hundred years. (The photograph on the wall is by Thomas Flechtner.)

with the magnificent furniture creations of the past. Historic forms were no longer considered desirable or relevant. Democracy, function, and industrialization were the ideals. Modernism as a concept did not allow much room for dissent.

The global recession of the 1970s resulted in a raft of utilitarian, rather bland, design. In Italy there was a reaction against this, with the emergence of several radical design groups which challenged the conservatism of the furniture industry. Best-known internationally is Memphis, founded in 1981 by a group including Ettore Sottsass. Memphis created furniture that used decoration for its own sake, borrowing ornamental references from previous historic and classical styles. It was labelled 'Post-Modern' (a term already current in architectural circles) in reference to its departure from the Modern Movement, and the fact that it was a reaction against Modernist principles.

was inspired by the Museum of Modern's Art 'Organic Design in Home Furnishings' competition of 1940, but it was not until 1950 that they could produce both the 'RAR 1' rocking chair [*above*] and 'DAR' dining chair.

With the economic boom after the war , many architect–designers concentrated on the development of innovative low-cost furniture. Enlightened companies such as Knoll and Herman Miller, both US-based, offered revolutionary design at an affordable price. With the emphasis on making design more accessible, the Modern Movement in effect cut its ties

ABOVE The 'RAR 1' rocking chair by Charles and Ray Eames, *c.* 1950, one of a group of plastic armchairs they developed in the early 1950s with Zenith Plastics of California.

RIGHT A screen and chest from the 'Perished' collection by Studio Job, 2006, decorated with inlays depicting animal skeletons. The objects are used as canvases on which to write in ancient hieroglyphics or modern graffiti. The dancing skeletons, violent and innocent, depict our times which are extravagant and violent.

Back to the future

It could be argued that what recent limited-edition and one-off design has done is to reconnect furniture with its pre-Modern Movement roots. These are pieces produced largely in modest-sized *ateliers*, not factories, just as the great *ébénistes* of Paris once worked. They harness age-old craft skills, such as marquetry and *pietra dura*, as well as the best of modern computer technology. They make use of rare and costly materials – both traditional (such as solid bronze and solid marble) and of today (such as hand-beaten aluminium and fibreglass) – but might also be created out of extraordinary choices, such as soft toys or whole cowhides. They are produced for serious collectors, not for the shopping mall. They pay lip service to function, but are far more relevant in terms of their extravagant forms and finishes.

To produce something beautiful or extraordinary is not enough. This is design that has to communicate an artist's vision of the world we live in. The age of superstar furniture is a far cry from the democratic but often ubiquitous designs of Modernism. For a while, it sent the whole idea of star pieces off course; but now artist–designers are leaping back over history to capture some of that 18th-century passion and excitement. The idea of luxury is no longer a dirty word either. Instead it has come to denote the best of what is produced creatively, just as it did in the Art Deco period (see pp. 183–86).

Of course, now as then, the market depends on having enough wealthy and interested patrons to support it. If nobody buys, nothing will be made. That is why the involvement of galleries and auction houses is such an important link in the chain.

It would be hasty to dismiss this as a flash-in-the-pan movement that could be all over in a couple of years. In fact it has been thirty years in the ripening when you look at the careers of Arad and his peers. Indeed, it could be argued that it is only now beginning to reach maturity, and that is why it makes column inches in the press. This is furniture that is absolutely of the moment, design at its most pure.

The 'Robber Baron' table by Studio Job, 2006–7, a patinated bronze 'factory' derived from interpretations of various early 20th-century works, including Peter Behrens's AEG factory and Battersea Power Station in London, mixed with Albert Speer's Neoclassicism.

The new star pieces

What makes some of these pieces such stars is the coupling of the ideas inherent in the designs with outstanding form, materials and ornamentation. The mix of traditional craftsmanship with computer technology also adds an interesting twist.

Content

Not all furniture has to sustain a narrative, but some makers use their designs to impart more than something purely aesthetic. The Campana brothers draw inspiration from their native Brazilian street life and carnival culture. The 'Transplastic' series, for example, uses the native Brazilian plant *apui*, which grows on and eventually chokes rainforest trees. The Campanas weave the rattan-like fibre around plastic furniture [45] and discarded man-made objects, such as dolls, flip-flops and tyres – a symbol of nature's triumph over the synthetic world.

Job Smeets and Nynke Tynagel, of Studio Job, are graduates of the Design Academy in Eindhoven (see p. 202), and narratives are at the heart of their work [*51, 202*]. In the 'Industry' series they represent capitalism as a deadly cocktail of helicopters, nuclear power plants, high-voltage pylons, guns, bullets, submarines, grenades and suchlike. The 'Robber Baron' series [*119, 207*] is described as 'tales of power, corruption, art and industry' – surreal and highly expressive pieces that reflect the excesses of the world's super-elite – while 'Perished' is ornamented with the dancing skeletons of wild animals [*206*].

Mozambique-born Gonçalo Mabunda (b. 1975) uses found objects, mainly armaments, to recreate African chieftain chairs, such as the 'Woman Throne'. These strong, uncompromising pieces are clearly sculptural, not functional – a way for the artist to comment on the violent politics of Africa.

Form

Marc Newson once said that the most perfect object he could imagine was an egg, and certainly much of his furniture is comfortingly ovoid in feel, from the curves of the 'Embryo' chair (1988) to the 'Pod of Drawers' (1987) [*187*] and 'Diode' lamp (2003). His work encapsulates a retro-futurist sensibility, with science-fiction names such as those of the 'Blackhole' and 'Event Horizon' tables.

The genius of Ron Arad is that he creates designs that are both functional and beautiful, while continually reinventing received notions of form and materials. Works such as 'Blo Void' [*197*] are graceful, elegant and highly crafted, the natural evolution from the masterpieces created by the *ébénistes* of 18th-century Paris.

Zaha Hadid takes her signature organic forms, reminiscent of Gaudí, and scales them up for momentous impact [*21, 46*]. This is furniture with real energy and movement. Fredrikson Stallard have produced outlandish shapes and monumental structures that catch and hold the attention [*111, 210*].

The American architects Benjamin Aranda (b. 1973) and Chris Lasch (b. 1972) have also produced wonderful tessellated furniture that challenges conventional forms. The 'Spaghetti Bale' bench by Pablo Reinoso is a romantic work that appears to be half bench and half woodland [*32; see also 194–95*], while 'Buisson' by French designer Vincent Dubourg (b. 1977) is entangled with branches [*199*]. Maarten Baas – another Eindhoven 'name' – has produced 'Transformations', a furniture installation that appears to have melted to the floor like chocolate.

LEFT 'Smoke' cabinet by Maarten Baas, 2004, part of a series of pieces made by artfully burning existing furniture and preserving the surface with clear epoxy.

OPPOSITE The limited-edition 'Cinderella' table in white Carrara marble by Demakersvan, 2008. Its sensuous organic form was achieved through the use of computer-aided graphics before being carved from a block of stone.

Materials

For the 'Robber Baron' series [*119*], Studio Job uses cast bronze with gilded reliefs, inspired by the work of André-Charles Boulle. The bronze commodes of Ingrid Donat (b. 1957) have a highly scarified surface texture that recalls the work of Gustav Klimt, while Elisabeth Garouste (b. 1949) has made use of such materials as white gold, silver leaf and bronze [*161*]. Marc Quinn created the 'Iceberg' desk, which appears as a frozen block of marble, until a hidden column section is pulled out to reveal a marble sculpted chair and footwell, transforming it from artwork into functional object. Ron Arad has made use of all kinds of materials, including polished stainless steel for the 'Cartier' table and 'D' sofa [*37, 225*], sprung steel for the 'Bad Tempered' chair, carbon fibre for the 'Oh Void' chair, and woven stainless steel for the 'Loop Loop' chair. Some designers add a touch of alchemy to existing materials: Maarten Baas preserves his 'Smoke' series of burnt furniture by covering it in epoxy resin and lacquer [*opposite*]. Others are exploring new uses for organic ones, such as the extraordinary cowhide benches of the German Julia Lohmann (b. 1977).

Ornamentation

Often it is the oldest craft techniques that are enjoying renewed popularity. Studio Job makes wonderful use of the traditional craftsmanship of marquetry, enhanced by modern laser technology to produce amazingly fine and intricate compositions. Marc Quinn has produced tables, chairs and desks of rough-hewn blocks of marble with mosaic images of flowers inlaid into the tops [*55*].

However, designers are also keen to explore new methods of ornamentation. At the time of writing Tom Dixon is experimenting with the electro-deposition of copper and the accretion of calcium on metal and stone structures immersed in large glass tanks filled with solutions. In this way he plans to 'grow' new furniture forms and surfaces underwater.

Technology

Computer technology allows designers to create increasingly wonderful forms. The 'Cinderella' table by Demakersvan [*below*] – the Dutch design house that brought together the talents of the twins Jeroen

'King Bonk' by Fredrikson Stallard, of painted fibreglass, 2008. The chairs may look as though they were designed with the assistance of a computer, but the shapes were derived from tying up upholstery foam with string; the resulting form was then carved with a chainsaw.

and Joep Verhoeven (b. 1976) and Judith De Grauw (b. 1976), all Eindhoven students – is a spectacular translation of sketches of 17th-century furniture that could only be created via the digital world. In the table and shelving she produced for displaying small sculptures [21], Zaha Hadid utilized the newest automative manufacturing technique to whittle solid blocks of aluminium into table legs and tops, which are then hand-polished, welded and polished again by expert craftsmen in Britain's Midlands area to create a single seamless piece. It is a clever combination of organic inspiration with mathematical intricacy and precision. Ron Arad too uses skilled craftsmen and expensive and ultra-sophisticated machines to create work that is essentially hand-made.

Craftsmanship

Meta (a branch of the British antiques company Mallett) was launched at Milan in 2008, with the intention of reinvigorating contemporary design by harnessing traditional craftsmanship [77–79]. 'Ivo 03' by Asymptote – the Egyptian Hani Rashid (b. 1958) and the Canadian Lise Anne Couture (b. 1959) – has a base of Tula steel, recreated from the analysis of a rare piece of Russian imperial Tula steel from 1780. In addition it draws on the skill of some of the craftsmen responsible for restoring the Kremlin Palace. The 'Quarry' series of Max Lamb brings together traditional stonemasonry skills with modern diamond-blade stonecutting equipment. Some quarries where he takes the stone are so isolated there is no electricity, so the only way to sculpt the stone is by hand, hammer and chisel.

When you start to see the connections between history and the amazing furniture of today, it becomes fascinating to interpret the influences and styles echoed in one from the other. This should not be confused with reproduction, which is at best a meticulous reworking of a period look and at worst a bad pastiche of the same. It is about finding the spirit of a golden age, still very much alive in the work of today's most creative, talented and skilled designers.

BELOW The 'George III' chest of drawers in oak by
Gareth Neal, 2008, appears to have an original Georgian
chest hidden within the timber. In fact it was produced
by using about 800 complex saw cuts.

Furniture as Craft

Germany has an excellent cabinetmaking tradition
and apprentice scheme, as does France, where
it is still possible to embark on the long and
demanding training that leads to being accepted
as an *ébéniste*. Britain is worth special mention,
however, because of the sheer number of crafts
workshops and the wealth of creative talent
that still flourishes there. This is largely thanks
to the British Craft Revival of the 1970s, which
is recognized as having re-ignited interest in
and appreciation of crafts skills that were in
danger of being lost for ever.

It is important to distinguish between these designer–makers and the artist–designers already mentioned. The latter are unlikely to make individual pieces by hand themselves, although often they do personally oversee the production of every piece that bears their name. Designer–makers are often involved

from sketchbook to workbench, a way of working supported by companies such as Linley and Litton [*opposite*]. Their way of working has changed little over the centuries. They are direct descendants of the Arts and Crafts tradition (see pp. 178–82).

Unlike artist–designers, who are driven to invent works, the designer–maker is more usually acting on a specific commission. But it is important to recognize that there is a huge gulf between master designer–makers and the majority of artisan craftsmen. The latter also produce work to commission, but do not necessarily have an eye for design. The 'man

The 'Umbrella Man' wardrobe by Andrew Varah, 1992, is an elaborate and witty design inlaid in various veneers. Umbrella handles act as door handles. Every piece is made on commission, so individual touches can be accommodated.

The 'Clin d'Oeil' dining table by French designer Andrée Putman, made by Litton of England in English walnut, silver, brass and leather, 2008. Putman enjoys an element of surprise in her work, such as concealed lift-up panels.

down the road' who can produce a bookcase or side table to order is doing a worthwhile job, but the result may lack an aesthetic signature; worse, it may be beautifully made but ugly to look at. The best designer–makers may also produce bookcases or side tables – or any other piece of furniture – to commission, but they will leave their signature on everything from the timber they choose to the form, proportion and finish they achieve. As with the American Studio Movement (pp. 188–92), these are craftspeople who use the medium of furniture to express their own philosophy and to show their appreciation of the materials they use, such as Gareth Neal, whose ingenuity creates the ghost of one piece of furniture within the framework of another [211, 215], and David Gates (b. 1966) who appears to defy the laws of balance with his three-legged table [236]. True designer–makers do not produce furniture that looks like everyone else's: the beauty of the work is in its personality, originality and quality.

The 'Trine' chair by John Makepeace, c. 1990, is made of layered and cut yew and oak, creating a striking veining. Makepeace was one of the first to champion the use of native and sustainable timbers in his designs.

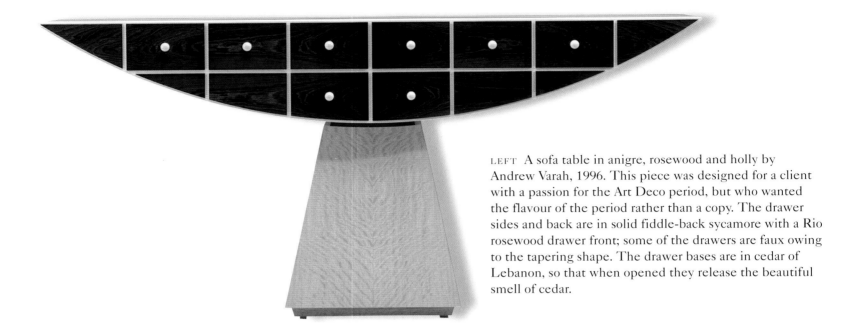

LEFT A sofa table in anigre, rosewood and holly by Andrew Varah, 1996. This piece was designed for a client with a passion for the Art Deco period, but who wanted the flavour of the period rather than a copy. The drawer sides and back are in solid fiddle-back sycamore with a Rio rosewood drawer front; some of the drawers are faux owing to the tapering shape. The drawer bases are in cedar of Lebanon, so that when opened they release the beautiful smell of cedar.

A continuing tradition

One of the joys of entrusting work to dedicated craftspeople comes from the knowledge that everyone involved is talented, skilled, and completely dedicated to their profession. Their absolute passion translates into the fine workmanship customers can enjoy.

Andrew Varah (b. 1944), for example, has been making bespoke furniture continually since 1968 [155, 212, above, opposite] and stays true to his belief that 'quality is remembered long after price is forgotten'. Using mainly English hardwoods, he has ensured that the sources from which he buys are environmentally sound and sustainable. In his workshop, he always tries to employ a newly qualified student from furniture college, ensuring that cabinetmaking skills learnt over decades are passed on to a new generation.

A piece of hand-made furniture has a character completely different from that of a manufactured one. It comes alive in some way. Bespoke pieces connect you to the hand and soul of the maker, and provide a continuing link to all those makers who have gone before. The best designer–makers invest a part of themselves in every piece they create. The world would be a poorer place without their skill and dedication. As Hilaire Belloc wrote, 'It is the business of the wealthy man to give employment to the artisan.'

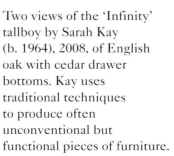

Two views of the 'Infinity' tallboy by Sarah Kay (b. 1964), 2008, of English oak with cedar drawer bottoms. Kay uses traditional techniques to produce often unconventional but functional pieces of furniture.

RIGHT One of the joys of bespoke furniture is that you can commission something that is very special functionally as well as aesthetically. On the 'Godchild's Cabinet' by Andrew Varah, 1991, each drawer represents one year of childhood treasures.

BELOW The limited-edition 'Anne' console table by Gareth Neal, 2007, of American walnut, ingeniously utilizes hundreds of individual saw cuts to create the ghost of a 1730 table within the framework of a modern one.

PARNHAM COLLEGE

Just as the Eindhoven Design Academy deserved a special mention (see pp. 202–3), so it is worth drawing attention to Parnham College in Dorset, which was founded by eminent furniture-maker John Makepeace (b. 1939) in 1977 and closed in 2000. It has a special place in David Linley's heart because it was here that he trained as a cabinetmaker himself. Parnham turned out many highly talented craftspeople, among them Wales & Wales, Konstantin Grcic, Mark Boddington, Rupert Senior and Charlie Carmichael of Senior & Carmichael, Andrea Stemmer, Sarah Kay, David Upfill-Brown, Nico Villeneuve, Stuart Padwick and Alastair Graham. The course tutor through much of its time was Robert Ingham, a highly respected designer–maker himself.

Makepeace first called his academy the School for Craftsmen in Wood. He had planned to open such a school in the United States with Wendell Castle (see pp. 189–90), but instead Castle became a regular tutor at Parnham.

The school offered an integrated education in making, design and business skills for those wishing to become professional furniture-makers. In effect it became the focus of the British Craft Revival in the 1970s, going on to inspire new generations of craftspeople.

By 1983, the sustainability of indigenous timbers had become a pressing issue. The Parnham Trust purchased Hooke Park, a 350-acre (some 140-hectare) mixed woodland, to research and demonstrate better forest management. To teach such issues, in 1987 Makepeace founded Hooke Park College, which is today amalgamated with London's Architectural Association. Makepeace must take much of the credit for the craft revival in Britain today, not least because of his entrepreneurial leadership that has encouraged continuing creativity and professionalism among furniture-makers.

OPPOSITE The 'Animal' console table with drawer by Wales & Wales, 2007, in solid ripple ash and olive ash, is an eloquent expression of the 'less is more' philosophy of design.

RIGHT Each of these chairs by Senior & Carmichael, first made in 1991, brings together a combination of at least four English woods collected after the 1987 hurricane in the south of England; they bear on the back the words 'Hurricane 1987'.

BELOW The 'Eighteen' cabinet by John Makepeace, 1996, crafted from a combination of English cherry, burr elm and cedar of Lebanon, features two sets of drawers with bronze handles, which elegantly taper in depth.

CLOCKWISE FROM ABOVE Details of the Linley 'Classic' games table, in walnut with a pedestal base of Macassar ebony and nickel, 1990; of the star-shaped bronze mechanism that expands the 'Jepu Balet' circular table by Senior & Carmichael to a ten-seater, 1992; and of the 'Flow' cabinet by

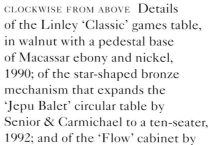

John Makepeace, 2006, which features a wave-like surface of shaped ash and holly with cedar of Lebanon drawer linings.

How To Treat a Star

PREVIOUS OPENING An ormolu-mounted amaranth, sycamore, kingwood and parquetry secrétaire à abattant, *c.* 1760, by Jean-François Oeben (see p. 131).

OPPOSITE A 1940s armoire in the style of André Arbus makes a magnificent focal point. In the foreground is a Gio Ponti chair of 1954; wall lights are by Felix Agostini, *c.* 1950s.

If you are fortunate enough to own a piece, or several pieces, of furniture that is truly special, you owe it to yourself to make sure it is displayed to full advantage. It does not matter whether your own star is of antique provenance, an inherited friend, an iconic design, or something very contemporary: it should be shown to best effect. Such designs are the axis around which the rest of an interior pivots. Star pieces are not about creating a room and then looking for an item of furniture that will fit. They are the opposite: pieces that demand a room be created to complement their own spectacular qualities.

Star pieces are the centrepiece of a room – those objects that hold the rest of a scheme together. You know you have found one when you develop tunnel vision on first encountering it. It is rather like falling in love: you can only see the object of your desire. The golden rule is always to follow your heart, because this is not the sort of furniture you easily find – far from it. If you are looking for a mirror and instead find the most wonderful table, forget the mirror and buy the table. You might never find one again that you love as much as this. Make it a rule in life never to regret anything and always to follow your instincts.

The first thing to analyse is why this piece of furniture has star quality. It could be due to scale: huge and imposing pieces are so attention-grabbing that they naturally make their presence felt in a room. Carry a tape measure with you at all times,

with a note not only of a room's dimensions but also that of its doorways. Something is only too big if you can't physically get it into the house. Great size is often an asset in terms of impact, so think big.

It might be more to do with form: a wonderfully sculptural quality that is at odds with pure function. The present vogue for design-art is pushing this idea to its limits, with one-off pieces and limited-edition series that are designed for maximum visual and tactile satisfaction, rather than to tick the box marked 'practicality'. Computer technology is allowing designers to invent new forms for furniture, feeding into this sculptural dimension. Before the advent of such software, it would have been too expensive to experiment with radical new forms on solid blocks of marble and timber, so designers and makers had to work within the perimeter of what they knew worked. Now all of that is changing, with exciting results.

It could be the material used or the surface decoration that makes this a piece that it is hard to ignore – matters of colour, pattern or texture. Again, innovative technologies are opening up new possibilities, from laser-cutting of marquetry to liquid metal patents. Antique pieces often appeal because of the rarity of the materials used and the lost craft skills that made their construction possible. A star piece of furniture often combines luxurious and beautiful materials with expert construction and ornamentation.

It could be the provenance – an entire history that has rendered it important and collectable. With so much attention now focused on 20th- and 21st-century makers, this is true both of antique furniture and of contemporary pieces. Furniture collectors today are as focused on the work being produced right now as on previous golden ages.

Star pieces can also be functional, of course, but it is important to distinguish between them and the furniture you own that is bought primarily for function. Everyone needs something to sit on, a surface to eat at, a bed to sleep in. Stars might well be chairs or tables or beds – but they bring something else into the room other than practicality. They are the extroverts of the design world, demanding attention and fully deserving admiration.

Consider what messages this furniture is conveying. Some is more masculine; some more feminine. Some is weighty and serious; some frivolous and witty. Some speaks of a simple, artisan life; some brings with it suggestions of palaces and grandeur. Some connects you to one individual; some to an entire political or social history. Once you begin to consider why this furniture is so important and appealing to you, it makes it easier to think about how you would like it set within a room.

There are two different approaches to designing around great furniture: one is to place an item within an existing scheme and make adjustments that will complement it. The other is to design a whole room around your chosen piece.

Take the former scenario first. The point about stars is that they have real attitude. They are not the shrinking violets of interior design, so you have to be prepared for the fact that when you place one in a room it may appear to fight with other things around it. It may at first seem too big, too brash, too bold for your home. Be patient. Wait a few days and allow your eye to settle. Once you have adjusted to the newcomer, you will be better able to judge how it has changed the dynamics of the scheme. One important thing about very sculptural furniture is that it needs space around it – room to breathe. It is a mistake to place two stars very close together, because neither of them will benefit from the other's presence. Each will be diminished, rather than complemented, by its neighbour. When you have assessed how well a room is working, you may find that you have to edit some furniture out in order to see such pieces at their best. Serious collectors of furniture often keep many pieces in storage for this very reason: they prefer to rotate their treasures, a few at a time, rather than risk killing their impact by crowding them in.

One thing that works very well is contrast. A room where all the furniture is of a similar period, style, colour and material may look tasteful, but it can also be very dull and bland. In Britain so-called 'brown' furniture – a term that encompasses workaday antique pieces from Georgian to Edwardian – fell out of favour with interior designers some years ago, on the grounds that it was boring. Happily, many are reintroducing these unpretentious, practical pieces into their schemes, as part of a whole mix of antique, vintage and contemporary. Brown furniture may not have much star quality, but it can be the perfect foil against which to place more

dynamic pieces. The secret is in looking for visual contrast, whether it is a change of texture, colour, scale, form, or age. By placing contrasting pieces near to each other, you create an interesting frisson, an unexpected note which brings a room alive. Interestingly, even quite ordinary furniture can start to resonate in a completely different way depending on the more spectacular objects around it. A room can become much more than a sum of its parts.

It is very much the same idea that has been popular in fashion for some time. Gone are the days when the truly stylish dressed head to toe in one designer label. Now those with fashion know-how mix high street bargains and vintage treasures with a few well chosen designer pieces. It is an inventive, confident approach, which is all about understanding how each garment works alongside the others; and it is also about dressing in a way that is not easily replicated by someone else. When we dress our homes we should be aiming for the same effect: an environment that is personal and individual to us, and which reflects our aesthetic judgment. Our choice of furniture is one of the most obvious ways to do this.

Exploring contrast

Once you open your eyes to the impact of strong contrasts, it becomes interesting to explore further. Take form, for example. You can play off an exuberantly curved and sculptural shape by placing it against one that is almost monastic in its simplicity. The qualities inherent in each will be magnified by their relationship. You can achieve a similar effect by playing with scale – placing over-scaled objects close to very diminutive ones. These varieties of scale and form introduce strong personality into a scheme.

Think too about contrasts accentuated by materials: velvet with glass, concrete with lacquer, steel with wood, to name but a few. Marry the matt with the shiny, the dense with the translucent, the rough with the smooth, the luxurious with the simple. Allow the eye to be inventive. In design, opposites often do attract, because they play against each other in unexpected ways. Surface ornamentation is another layer of texture. One of the joys of buying antique furniture is that materials it incorporates may be unavailable today owing to their rarity – not only

exotic animal skins, shell and horn, but also timbers that are seldom harvested or stones that are expensive to mine. This provides another rich seam to explore.

This ability to combine contrasting objects concerns not only furniture but also the art or other objects that you bring into the mix. Antique pieces can take on a new character and life when placed against bold contemporary art. Similarly, radically modern furniture can sit happily within classically grand interiors filled with fine collections of porcelain or silver. If you can train your eye to assess scale, form and texture, it is possible to marry all kinds of pieces together that neither history nor geography intended to meet. Antique Chinese furniture, for example, is a perennial favourite in the West because its clean lines makes it possible to use within many styles of home. The disciplined forms of Shaker furniture are equally adaptable, as are interrelated artisan pieces from the farmhouses of Europe. In fact star pieces are very often strong in form, but not so over-stylized that they would only suit one type of interior. The magic that allows so much diverse

A French kingwood and marquetry desk ornamented with gilt bronze, *c.* 1800, is juxtaposed with a Philippe Starck 'Rosy Angelis' lamp of 1994 and, on the wall, a work by Nikolai Sujetin.

furniture to live together happily under one roof is one reason why it is such an important tool within decorating and design.

Colour, texture and light

As well as considering space and juxtaposition when designing around furniture, you also need to think about the room as a backdrop to the things you love. If you are starting from scratch and designing with a particular piece in mind, you should choose a colour for the walls that will add to the drama and interest. Don't make the mistake of thinking you should keep to neutrals. Many timbers look rather grey and dull if placed against walls that are too pale. Often it is the rich shades so favoured in the past that provide a much more sympathetic canvas on which to display great furniture. Remember that colour changes according to light, so always test how colours look at different times of day by painting a panel of chipboard in your chosen shade and moving it around the room, so you can view it in different positions. Colour is more dramatic in big quantities, so if you find a shade you really like, you may want to order it a shade or two lighter to achieve the same effect in the entire room.

On the whole, it is best to go either for colour or for pattern on walls: you don't want too much confusion in the background taking the eye away from the furniture that is centre stage. Textural finishes, such as polished plaster, are a wonderful choice because they bring rich depth to walls, without demanding too much attention. Specialist plasterers mix traditional ingredients such as marble dust, gold and mother-of-pearl to achieve effects that range from earthy matt to shimmering gloss.

Flooring too should be chosen that will not distract the eye, so opt for natural floorcoverings, neutral carpet or traditional wood or stone. If your star piece has broken the budget to such an extent that you do not have money left to decorate at this point, don't worry. The fantastic thing about such furniture is that it looks wonderful no matter what the setting. Even if sanding the floorboards and painting the walls is all you can manage for now, you will still have created an interior with real style.

Lighting is also an essential consideration. Ideally, a room should be designed to look as good by night as by day. You may also need to protect furniture from direct sunlight, so it could be that it has to be placed in a slightly darker area of the room, or that you fit simple white roller blinds at windows that will block out very strong sunlight when necessary. It has never been easier to improve existing lighting schemes, by the use of additional lamps, or uplighters at floor or skirting-board height placed to cast a beam of light up onto key pieces of furniture. Generally speaking, light from the side or below is more effective than that from above. A central pendant produces light so diffused that it makes a room look dull and uncomfortable, while ceiling spotlights are often too bright and unforgiving. A beam of light directed onto your own star piece will make it appear as if it really is in the spotlight,

ABOVE This elegant secretaire cabinet is by René Prou and dates from the 1940s. On it stands a sculpture by Orlandini for Sèvres. The chairs are by Maxim Old, while the bronze lights are by Arlus, *c.* 1950s.

OPPOSITE A Ron Arad 'D' sofa, 1994, made of mirror-polished stainless steel, takes pride of place in front of floor-to-ceiling windows. The lights, by Jules Leleu, date from the 1940s.

bringing out the beauty of surface, ornamentation and upholstery. If the surface is reflective – such as glass or lacquer – you can use it to bounce light back into the room, adding to the magic and glamour. Another effective idea is to place small tubes of LCD light horizontally on top of a piece of furniture, such as a bookcase, where they are concealed by the pediment. When turned on, these cast a soft glow up to the ceiling, enhancing the atmosphere of a room. If you are commissioning a special piece of furniture, remember that improved fibre optics make it possible for lighting to be easily integrated into the design, not only for practical purposes, such as lighting the inside of a cupboard, but also as part of the beauty and interest of the piece.

BELOW The 'Lanceolate Tallboy' by Linley, 2008, of Macassar ebony and ripple sycamore, is a contemporary play on the concept of a collector's cabinet: the bottom half has the suggestion of legs veneered onto a lightbox.

OPPOSITE A Shiro Kuramata chair, 'How High The Moon', 1986, with a Rolf Sachs 'Switch Stool', 1995, and a Martin Maloney lamp. The painting is by Walter Dahn (1981).

Arranging the furniture

When it comes to how furniture is arranged within a room, be sympathetic to the architecture. If you are lucky enough to have a home with excellent proportions, then use furniture to accentuate this through symmetry. Pairs – of chairs, cabinets, tables – have a long history in the art of decorating, because the impact of two identical pieces is so much greater than just one. If the room is not architecturally special, you can make it appear more so by placing furniture so that pieces balance each other, without

being identical – tables or cabinets of similar dimensions and materials, for example. One of the most effective ways of decorating a room, a classic approach still embraced by designers today, is to create an interior that is correct in its proportions, complemented by symmetrical groups of furniture, and then to shake it all up with the addition of one unexpected object – a slightly challenging note that brings the rest of the scheme alive.

Don't be afraid of scale. It stands to reason that large rooms need magnificent pieces of furniture, otherwise you can feel engulfed by the space. But so long as a piece of furniture can be physically manoeuvred into a room, it will not be too large for it. Even in rooms of modest proportions, an overscaled piece can be an asset, actually making the dimensions appear bigger than they are. If you furnish a small room with small pieces of furniture, you are only accentuating how poky it is.

Use furniture to create zones within a room, particularly a living room which might need to fulfil many functions. Rather than having just one seating area, consider whether you can create an additional one or two – somewhere to read a book by the window, perhaps, or to enjoy a game for two or a light supper tête-à-tête. In huge open-plan spaces, you can use large freestanding pieces of furniture to create 'walls' between one zone and another. In a small space, consider commissioning a bespoke piece of furniture that will not only fit a space perfectly, but correspond exactly to your wishes.

Finally, be prepared to move furniture around, trying out new positions and combinations until you find the one that works best for you. Don't stay static. Often if you have the urge to redecorate, it is not so much that the room is tired, but that it is time to rearrange furniture, art and objects and breathe some life into the scheme once again. The only thing you are never likely to become bored of, if you choose well in the first place, is the star of the show.

The hall

The hall is like a decongestion chamber. It allows you or your guests to make the adjustment from outside to inside – a punctuation point where you can take off wet coats, leave umbrellas, tidy hair and

A Tom Dixon 'Crown' chair, 1994, makes an intriguing punctuation point in a hall filled with contemporary artworks.

OPPOSITE A 'Pearl' coffee table by Mattia Bonetti, 2007, is teamed here with chairs by Charles and Ray Eames ('La Chaise', 1948, in front of the screen), Marco Zanuso (right), and Gio Ponti. The Cubist-inspired screens were commissioned by Definitive in 1989; lights by Pierre Desderot, 1970s.

generally prepare yourself for being sociable and amusing. A feeling of safety and comfort should be palpable the moment you walk through the door. The hall is where you can leave the stresses of the day and savour the warmth and comfort of arriving at your destination.

The wonderful thing about furnishing a hall is that there are few practical points to consider. You need a place for outdoor clothing, shoes, dog leads, umbrellas and so forth, but other than that you have a space that is perfect as a sort of private gallery. Much is said about the importance of first impressions, and certainly the hall is a place where you can give a very firm indication of your own passions and priorities. Star pieces here can be anything from wonderful carved gilt tables and elaborately overscaled mirrors to limited-edition chairs and family heirlooms. Because it is a transition space, it lends itself particularly well to furniture, objects and art that are perhaps bolder and quirkier than you might present in the rest of the house. You won't tire of anything, because you simply don't stop long enough for that to happen.

Theatre and drama are the key words here. You want to create a feeling of welcome, both for your guests and for yourself, but you also want to excite and inspire – to engender a feeling that this is the beginning of an interesting journey through a house. Because halls are relatively small areas, it might be that you could push the budget by using materials or finishes that would be too expensive in larger reception rooms, and create a feeling of instant glamour and luxury. Lighting is an essential part of the hall's success, so if you do create a space that is like a gallery, remember that it is crucial to light the objects you wish to display. Smell is the source of much sensory delight, so make sure your hall always smells wonderful too. Scented candles and flowers are the obvious ways to do this, but there are few better smells than that of beeswax polish, so polish furniture here on a regular basis.

The hall is all about anticipation of what is to follow, so make yours as exciting and visually interesting as you can. It is the natural home for a star piece: choose one to display here that is the signature of your home.

The living room

If space permits, most people today like to have two living areas: a relaxed family snug for watching television, and a more elegant space in which to entertain guests. If that is not an option, you are faced with the dilemma of whether to hide the TV or leave it on proud display. Televisions tend to become the focus of a room, detracting from the impact of a star piece: if you cannot banish such technology, commission a bespoke television and home leisure cabinet, which will hide the ugliness of cables and suchlike while also providing a beautiful focal point. Star pieces in living rooms should grab the attention from the moment you step through the door. They are the sort of furniture that deserves respect and admiration.

OPPOSITE This show-stopping steel rod chandelier was made by Tom Dixon as a bespoke commission in the 1990s, as were the steel-and-wood dining chairs. The table is French and dates from the 1930s.

RIGHT A Tommi Parzinger design for a dining room, reproduced in his East 57th Street showroom, New York, in the 1950s.

Living rooms are often a challenge to design well, because so many different zones are needed within them, often ones with conflicting purposes – space both for family comfort and for entertaining friends and business associates; for displaying prized possessions and for concealing the flotsam and jetsam of everyday life; for reading a book quietly and for hosting a cocktail party. Every piece of furniture chosen is likely, therefore, to have a purpose. Unless you have a great deal of space available, the chances are that a star piece will also be used. It could be anything from a magnificent bookcase or handsome chest-on-stand to a fabulously crafted one-off coffee table or iconic day bed. The art of mixing such pieces in the living room is to choose other essential and functional furniture – such as robust sofas or occasional tables – that is quiet enough to blend in happily, rather than shrieking for attention. Remember the idea of allowing stars to breathe. Juxtaposition is also important, so introduce contrast of form, scale or texture for an additional layer of interest and beauty.

When it comes to the arrangement of furniture, try to avoid doing the obvious. While it may be necessary to have seating grouped around the fireplace or the ubiquitous television, it is more interesting to have one or two additional sitting areas, so that the room can be enjoyed from more than one angle. A sculptural chair or day bed, which is also fully functional, can be the ideal way of creating this – perhaps placed in front of a window for reading.

In many contemporary homes, traditional living rooms have been almost entirely replaced by huge kitchens that also incorporate zones for living and dining. There is no reason why such spaces would not also benefit from the introduction of a star piece, such as an oversized armoire

or dresser, huge refectory table, or fantastic apothecary's cabinet.

The dining room

As with the hall, a dedicated dining room offers the perfect environment in which to display the furniture, objects and art that speak of your own interests. Guests will enjoy the conversation pieces you surround them with, an intriguing insight into your life and that of your family. Of course the star piece here may well be a hand-crafted table or set of limited-edition chairs, but it may also be something not quite so obvious. The table and chairs may have been chosen more for comfort, size and function, while a star piece – such as a bespoke sideboard or magnificent contemporary chandelier – has more than a purely practical purpose. It is a way of bringing another element of beauty and character into a room.

It seems a shame that so many people have sacrificed the dining room for a home office or TV room, so that every meal is taken in the kitchen. There is something special about having somewhere in the house that is used only for eating together – even if it be only Sunday lunch, birthday celebrations, or formal dinners. If you can, now is the time to reclaim the dining room. Because dining rooms are used for relatively small amounts of time, you can go a notch braver in terms of decoration than you might do in the living room or kitchen. You might opt for a bolder colour scheme, for example, or introduce a note of luxury or glamour through wonderful combinations of texture, such as velvet and silk, or taffeta and linen. Think of this as a stage set on which you and your guests are going to take part in some witty and thought-provoking play. Try to create an atmosphere that gives them a treat as they walk through the door.

While this may be a room that is also used by day, you should really decorate it with night-time in mind. Walls with a slightly glossy finish are perfect for reflecting candlelight, as of course are mirrors. Don't ignore the ceiling, either: paint it the same shade as the walls, or add some unexpected touch, such as reams of pleated silk, creating a tent-like feeling. Make sure that lighting is subtle and unobtrusive – strong enough for guests to see what they are eating, but low enough to engender a feeling of intimacy and comfort.

The star piece or pieces that you choose for the dining room are central to the success of the scheme. Colours, textures and lighting should all be deployed to show them to best advantage.

The bedroom

If there is one room where the star piece should be the dominant feature, it is the bedroom. Beds themselves are natural stars, so choose one for yourself which is not only comfortable to sleep in, but which makes you feel immediately relaxed when you walk into the bedroom after a long and tiring day. Dress it beautifully with sumptuous linen, throws

and cushions. Bedrooms should be all about pleasing the senses, particularly that of touch.

It is hard to beat the romance and grandeur of a four-poster bed, whether it is a lavishly hung antique treasure or a contemporary interpretation with no drapes at all. Beds that stretch up towards the ceiling not only have visual impact, but make us feel protected and comforted. Antique half-testers, with their canopies of faded silks, are also highly evocative not only of the past but of childhood fairytales and other fantasies. Beds should always have headboards, not just for comfort, but because without they look so stark and unfinished. Headboards are also a canvas on which to introduce more textural interest, such as faux ostrich skin, buttoned chintz or unbleached linen. If a low headboard is your taste, choose a bed that has textural interest – such as the carved variety so popular once in provincial Europe – or search for one that you love for its colour or ornamentation. You can buy beds today covered in every surface material imaginable, from leather or metallic varnish to silk or suede.

The bed need not be the only star piece in the room. If space permits, you may also have an imposing wardrobe, a handsome dressing table or a curvaceous day bed. Bedrooms should be places of personal pleasure, so introduce objects here that you really treasure and which make your heart lift. If there are two of you to consider, you need to step lightly around each other's taste and feelings. Star pieces should bond you together, rather than push you apart.

If you do have furniture that has real impact in the bedroom, create a setting that is calming and quiet. You don't want to overload the senses here. Walls, floors and ceiling should be texturally pleasing, but keep colours more muted. Use pattern sparingly. Don't overdo lavish window dressings and other soft furnishings, which might distract the eye from the beauty of the furniture and objects on show. Remember that you will need lighting that works on two levels: the functional sort for applying make-up, reading, and so on; and the atmospheric type, which calms your mind at the end of a frantic day. Throw light onto your much-loved star pieces.

Guest rooms also benefit from the addition of star beds. They might not be quite so spectacular and special as your own, but it is inhospitable to offer those staying a tatty old thing, long past its prime. At the very least give it the star treatment with a new headboard and some wonderfully sensuous bedlinen. In doing so, you will make friends and family feel cherished and welcome.

A concept sketch in watercolour, 2007, showing the design for an Art Deco-inspired Linley suite at Claridge's Hotel in London, in tones of silver and soft lilac. The bed, dressing table and mirror are original Deco pieces which were carefully restored. To complement these, a Deco-influenced carpet and tub chairs were commissioned.

COMMISSIONING YOUR OWN STAR PIECE

Furniture-making is not just a way of earning a living, but a way of life. It is not a highly paid profession, but it demands immense commitment, passion and love for the subject. When you order a bespoke piece of furniture, you are supporting a whole tier of craftsmanship that is part of our history and heritage.

If you have the desire to create something which is truly personal to you – unique, enduring and beautifully crafted – then commissioning a piece of furniture allows you to fulfil that dream. A bespoke piece is not only made to your specifications but tailored to your needs. The creative journey you embark upon when you decide to commission a one-off design is as rewarding, enriching and exciting a process as the furniture that results from it. You can be involved with the design of an eye-catching and elegant piece literally from the drawing board onwards, giving you a chance to add in special touches and heartfelt references that mean something very personal to you and your family.

ABOVE AND OPPOSITE In the 'Butterfly' table and benches by Based Upon, 2007, real butterflies are preserved within the surface, a contemporary metaphor for the way life is trapped within layers of the earth and revealed as fossils.

Why commission?

People commission special pieces of furniture for a number of reasons. It might be by default: you see something you love, but the dimensions are wrong for your own home. Perhaps you find what you consider to be the perfect dining table or desk, but then realize it would have to be slimmer or shorter to fit comfortably into the room you have in mind. Sometimes people commission something because they have been looking for an antique piece for months, but can't find exactly what they want. Also, antiques are obviously limited to the types of furniture that existed at a particular time: the coffee table, for example, is a relatively recent innovation. People may commission dining tables to suit their preferred number of people, often with leaves so that more can be accommodated if necessary.

However, a more common reason to go down the bespoke path is that you can have exactly what you want and create something that is unique to you. Bespoke is by its nature highly personal and individual. Your piece will be a limited edition of one. You can include motifs that mean something to you or your family, have your initials integrated into the design, or make a reference to a pastime you love. Pieces of truly special furniture are ideal ways of marking special occasions. For a wedding, for example, you might like to have a table made with your favourite quotation inscribed around the edge.

For a silver wedding, you could commission a desk inset with a silver plaque commemorating the date. A new generation of furniture designers is recognizing memories and emotions as important vocabularies within the creative process, a means to invest a piece with more than monetary value. The only limit to what is possible is your own imagination.

Where to start

People are often unaware of all that a bespoke piece of furniture can offer. Start by collecting as many visual references as possible to help demonstrate your taste and inspirations: use magazines, books, brochures, even photographs of museum pieces. Think about whether you fall into the classic or the contemporary camp, or somewhere between the two. Decide what you want in terms of function, and whether you would like some clever touch such as secret drawers or ingenious mechanics. At the very least, decide whether you favour light or dark wood, metal, glass, or combinations of different materials. If you are commissioning as one half of a couple, it is important you both envisage the same sort of result.

You then have to find a craftsperson with whom to work. This will usually be by word of

mouth, and may be someone local to you. Visit their workshop, look at photographs of previous work, and if possible arrange to visit previous customers and see examples of the furniture they have made *in situ*. The main problem you may encounter is that there is a difference between designing a piece of furniture and making it. Some makers are brilliant at the latter, but not so good at the former. That means a lot of the designing is going to depend on you, unless you also employ a designer to help you through that process.

You can judge how good a maker is at the design process by the quantity and quality of the

questions that he or she asks you. These should not all revolve around shape and finish, but should also relate to you as an individual: where is the piece to go? Who will use it? How often will it be used? Are children also likely to use it? What do you want from it other than the obvious? A desk, for example, may need to provide accommodation for a laptop computer as well as a writing surface. A bedside table could include special compartments for watches or drinking water.

Of course there are aesthetic questions to answer too: do you like legs, or a pedestal? Square or round? Rectangular or kidney-shaped? How many drawers? A top that lifts? Your maker cannot be expected to be a mindreader. If you know you want a certain shape of leg, or that you love oak and hate walnut, it is up to you to communicate these facts. Invite the maker to visit your home and see

OPPOSITE This elegantly balanced three-legged side table in English oak, brown oak and black steel by David Gates, 2003, is a clever take on the traditional hall table.

A detail of Danny Lane's 'Burr Elm' table, 2005, which incorporates glass and steel as well as elm. The contours of the timber make a pleasing contrast to the smoothness of the glass.

where the piece is to go: he or she may spot the need to take into account skirting height, or possible sun damage from south-facing windows. The more time that you invest in the commissioning process, the more chance there is that you will truly love the finished item.

The reason why people use specialist bespoke companies is that many offer an in-house design service, which ensures that customers end up with precisely the piece of furniture they want. At the initial consultation, you may be invited to look through the maker's library of furniture books and previously commissioned designs, and you should be encouraged to ask lots of questions. You may also be shown a whole palette of finishes in your chosen material, so that with the designer you can begin to select the combinations you want.

By the second consultation, your maker will probably have produced a series of line drawings to establish that he or she is going in the right direction. After further consultation, it is usual to produce a computer-generated three-dimensional colour design, which allows you to see precisely what the piece will look like. It is also possible to show the design in different colours and finishes at the press of a button. Once you have approved the design, a technical drawing is produced. This is the blueprint from which the workshop will make the piece – an immensely detailed document, which communicates the requirements down to millimetres. This intensive design process means that you should never have any unwanted surprises: the piece of furniture you receive will be the one you are expecting.

Generally speaking, there are two stages to the design process. The first concerns the form of the furniture – its size, shape and profile. You will also have to decide whether or not you want drawers in a table, for example, as this will influence the construction of the carcass. If there are to be any ingenious mechanical touches, they too will have to be agreed at this stage, as will technical gadgetry such as integrated lighting.

The second concerns surface decoration. On timber, this may involve carving, inlay, marquetry, gilding, integrating another material such as silver or leather, or using the grain of a fine timber as the main decoration. Once you have found a craftsperson you are happy to work with, trust their eye. He or she is going to be more expert than you at choosing the appropriate timber or selecting the veneers needed for a piece of marquetry. Allow the individual maker to decide on such things, because that is their professional field and you should give them a degree of artistic licence.

BELOW AND BELOW RIGHT Details of the 'Helix' dining table and 'Helix' sideboard, both by Linley, 2004, in Santos rosewood and walnut. Note the double helix marquetry on the sideboard.

Each bespoke piece will be priced individually to reflect the craftsmanship involved, the time taken, the materials used, and the size. Great care is taken to understand the nuances of each design before production begins, so that a piece is priced accurately. If the price quoted is too high, a good designer should be able to suggest ways of bringing it into budget. A cupboard with drawers, for example, is bound to be more expensive than one without (it can take over a day to make one drawer if you are using traditional cabinetmaking skills to exacting standards). Similarly, a table with expanding leaves will be more expensive than one without, because of the runners and mechanics concealed within the frieze. The more complicated the decoration and the more skills it involves, the higher the price. It is not that bespoke pieces are charged at a premium: it is simply that by their very nature they are unique and often more complex, and therefore take longer to make.

Local craftspeople may not be able to offer this kind of sophisticated design service, so it is crucial that you communicate effectively exactly what your requirements are. Rather than relying on the traditional drawing on the back of an envelope, make sure you at least commission a drawing to scale, showing as much detail as is possible. You will, however, have to expect a degree of artistic licence in the absence of a highly detailed technical drawing, so there may have to be compromises once the making begins.

Timbers

For many makers, wood is the primary material. It is enduring, practical, robust and beautiful. Other materials go in and out of fashion, but wood is timeless and has the advantage of improving with

Watercolour sketches of bespoke commissions for a wardrobe and a desk, from the archives of Linley. Different views are shown of each piece, and dimensions and timbers are indicated.

age. Timbers offer a whole palette of colours with which to work, so one of the first things you need to do is familiarize yourself with the many types and hues. There is a distinction between timbers used to construct a piece of furniture and those used for veneers and the like.

Most furniture-makers in Britain favour timbers such as oak, walnut and sycamore for construction. It is best to avoid Brazilian mahogany because there are ethical issues surrounding its logging: instead you could consider utile, which looks very like mahogany. Makers are usually careful about where they source timbers from, and try to use ones that are sustainable as far as possible. All timbers should be second-seasoned – dried once in a kiln and once in the workshop – which reduces the moisture content to a point where the wood is less likely to move.

A vintage watercolour sketch showing the design for a bespoke drinks cabinet by Linley. Computer graphics now give an even more accurate picture of how a finished piece will look.

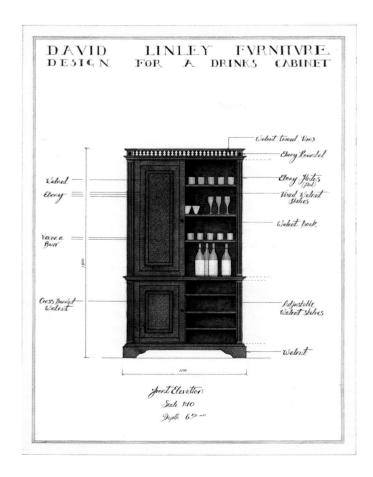

When it comes to veneers, there are many beautiful varieties to choose from, including burr oak, burr walnut, burr ash, ripple sycamore, rosewood, satinwood, ebony and Macassar ebony. Veneers are a way of really personalizing a piece, perhaps through the use of a marquetry or parquetry pattern. It helps to carry out the selection process with a bespoke designer, because she or he knows which timbers go with which, just as an interior designer would know which fabrics to use with which wallpaper.

Special touches

It is enormous fun to incorporate special magical touches, such as hidden compartments, in a bespoke design [*cf. 76–79*]. They add an element of wit and intrigue, a link to a previous age when furniture was valued not just for function but for the pleasure such craftsmanship brought. People are fascinated by the way you can operate a device, such as turning a handle in one part that causes a drawer to spring open in another. However, it takes a great deal of skill to invent such mechanisms and then make them, so that does affect the price. If you can afford to include special mechanics in your own piece, you won't regret it: challenge your friends to work out how it is done, and enjoy the amazement on their faces.

If you don't want to include something too complicated, there are other ways of introducing unexpected and personal touches. For example, drawers can be lined in flamboyant materials such as pony skin, velvet or gold leaf. It is also possible to marry high-tech solutions with very classic pieces of furniture, such as media cabinets with plasma screens that rise up at the touch of a button, cocktail cabinets with pop-out trays for integrated iPod holders, and fibre-optic lighting effects within a cabinet door.

The workshop

The remarkable thing about making furniture is that you create something extraordinary from nothing more than raw materials. A craftsperson begins with a technical drawing and nothing else. The finished item is down to his or her eye and skill.

ABOVE AND ABOVE RIGHT The making of the 'Bronze Poly Chair' by Max Lamb, 2007: it is hand-carved from a block of polystyrene and then cast in solid bronze. Only one chair can be cast from each mould, so each is unique.

If you are having a bespoke piece of furniture made, then you want it to be the work of one person from beginning to end. There is a big difference between a production-line workshop and a craft workshop. The former may have lots of identical pieces going through, where one person makes a particular part over and over again but does not have the opportunity to take responsibility for the finished whole. The second system means that an individual is allotted one design to produce from beginning to end, from selecting the correct timbers to handing over the finished piece. This results in a far better piece of furniture and one that has a little bit of that person's essence in its very making.

Nobody goes into furniture-making expecting to acquire a fortune, so whoever you commission has spent years acquiring a skill they are passionate about. There is a real love for what they are doing. Craftspeople are rightly proud of their work, and that pride and love and passion are going to be in your piece of furniture. It is usual to study furniture-making at college or university and then enter a workshop as an apprentice or 'improver'. Improvers begin by making something fairly simple and then take on more complex pieces as their skill and experience widen. By the time an individual is good enough to create a one-off, you can be certain they have many years of solid experience behind them.

Bespoke commissions keep alive a whole heritage of craft skills. It is not just cabinetmakers who benefit, but specialists such as carvers, gilders, upholsterers, jewellers, lighting experts, metal-workers and marquetry cutters. One-off furniture is a complex business, which explains why it takes five to six months from the first design consultation to delivery of the finished item.

A common misconception is that handmade means low-tech. In fact the use of technology means that marquetry, for example, can be cut to great precision with a computer-driven laser. However, this does not take any skill out of the work. It is still down to the marquetry cutter to select the timbers in the first place, which demands a true artist's eye because the veneers have to be chosen and shaded to achieve the required effect. And the elements, once cut, will be hand-assembled in the piece of furniture – a highly skilled and fascinating process, rather like constructing a hugely complicated jigsaw puzzle.

The star at home

By the time a special piece of furniture arrives, you will be looking forward to it with excitement. Even with the best computer-generated images, there is nothing to beat the vibrancy and lustre of the finished item in real life, so you can be sure of a thrilling moment. There is often quite a lot of emotion too, particularly when something has been commissioned to mark a special occasion. Your craftsperson should make sure that they help you site the piece in the right place and show you how to operate any special touches, such as concealed drawers. They will want to know you are as happy with it as they are, so don't hold back on your enthusiasm. Give yourself a pat on the back too: you have stepped out of the crowd and used your own imagination and enthusiasm to help create something that is totally unique and therefore quite wonderful.

OPPOSITE The 'Crack' coffee table by Based Upon in platinum finish, 2007, takes pride of place in a sumptuous country house by Sir John Soane, finding a natural affinity with the antique furniture and art that surrounds it.

BUYING ANTIQUE FURNITURE

For the novice furniture collector, buying antiques can seem rather a daunting prospect. Nobody wants to feel that they may not make a wise choice and that ultimately they could be throwing their money away. The first thing to say is that you should always buy something first and foremost because you like it. Do not try to second-guess the market: even the greatest experts fall foul at times doing that. Furniture is part of your home and something that should give you enjoyment every day. The sensible thing is to listen to your heart, but then use your head as well: check the condition and character of a piece before buying it. The second thing to stress is that there is a great deal of help and advice available – not only the expertise of auction houses and reputable antique dealers, but also books, websites, specialist magazines and collectors' societies. Visit museums to see collections of furniture. Try to familiarize yourself with the subject as much as you are able. If you have a will to find out more, you can. Every minute you can spend doing some research of your own will be time well spent.

If you do not know where to start, then buy things you can actually use: side tables, desks, chests-of-drawers and chairs are all good choices. British 'brown' furniture has had a bad press in recent years, but in fact it will never be out of favour for long because there is so much in this category that is elegant, timeless, practical and likeable. If you do not know where to start when collecting, then Regency furniture [*167–69*] is always a good choice, because it is classic and versatile enough to fit into many styles and sizes of home. It may date from two hundred years ago, but much of it has such mastery of line and richness of timber that it looks as good now as it did then.

When you buy an antique, you are joining a whole line of people and homes that it has been a part of – a romantic notion, but a cheering one. If you care for the piece you buy, it will almost certainly retain a resale value should you want to sell it at a later date to buy something else. As you acquire more knowledge about particular periods, makers and styles, you will enjoy the discovering and buying process even more. You can then build up a relationship with dealers or auction houses that you trust, and they in turn will alert you to pieces in which they think you might be interested. You will be on the road to being an expert collector. If you are buying from a reputable source, you have a wealth of knowledge at your disposal, so use it. If it is an auction house, go to viewing days and ask lots of questions. Furniture is understandably affected by its journey through life, so a few knocks or repairs are permissible. Some antiques have been around for centuries and have seen every kind of disaster, from wars to floods, so they are unlikely to be in perfectly pristine condition. If one is, you should perhaps be suspicious. The important thing is to be aware of what may have been replaced, when, and why.

You can learn a lot about a piece of furniture from reading the description in an auction catalogue. Most auction houses try to give a fair and frank view of what they are selling, so an entry may well draw your attention to possible flaws, such as 'drawer handles missing, one flap detached' on a table, 'previously with castors' on a chair, or 're-gilt' on a gilded sofa.

The condition report

You can also ask to see a condition report on your chosen piece. This is rather like a house survey and will go into much greater detail about the condition an object is in. Unlike a survey, it is free of charge. You can also, again free of charge, ask an auction-house representative to go through the report with you, explaining the various statements. This is often worth doing, because to the untrained eye a condition report can seem full of rather worrying dramas. You need a certain amount of experience and sophistication to understand the difference between a repair that is perfectly respectable and one that may have decreased the value of a piece. There is, for example, a subtle difference between a repair which is in keeping with the original and an 'improvement' that runs contrary to the maker's

original intention. It is also important to understand when a repair may have been made: a late 18th-century repair to a late 17th-century piece may not affect the value at all, whereas an early 20th-century repair to such a piece might well do. This is difficult to understand unless you have the help of an expert to guide and advise you.

Things to consider

When viewing, do not be shy. Pick things up, look underneath, study the back and sides, try to get a sense of whether a piece 'feels' right to you. Your eyes and instinct can tell you an awful lot. It may be, for example, that two pieces have been brought together and married into one, such as a bureau and a cabinet that were never intended to meet, or a table top and pedestal that are at odds. If you take the time to look, you may notice how unbalanced a piece seems or that there appears to be the work of two hands here, not one. On the other hand, not every cabinetmaker was a genius, and there may be nothing untoward at all. If in doubt, ask for advice from someone who is more expert in the field than you. The oddity might be just part of the quirkiness of the design, and nothing to worry about at all. The more you look at furniture, the more you can train your eye to become a better judge of balance, proportion, colour and decoration.

You should be on the lookout for signs of intervention. If something looks disturbed in some way, you have to ask why: unexplained cuts or screws in the underside of timber, for example, may point to a major repair or even a change to the original structure. It would also be rather suspicious if the underframe had been polished, as it would imply something had been covered up: why else polish something that is not on display? The underside of the feet of an old piece of furniture should show signs of considerable wear.

An early George III mahogany worktable, neatly executed in the finest timber by a leading cabinetmaker for the 4th Earl of Shaftesbury for St Giles's House in Dorset [*cf. 97*] and later in the Samuel Messer collection, so it combines quality and provenance.

OPPOSITE A George III mahogany clothes press attributed to Thomas Chippendale. It does not take a very practised eye to appreciate the fluency and mastery of such workmanship.

RIGHT A George III mahogany hexagonal tripod table attributed to Thomas Chippendale, illustrating the importance of balance, proportion and timber. Pieces attributed to prominent cabinetmakers like Chippendale will always have a strong appeal.

In carved furniture, fluency is a key word. If pieces have been cut down at some point in their life, the carving will not fit properly together. Before 1850, most furniture would have been hand-carved, so the fact that it is not precisely uniform is a good sign. If it is uniform, that points to the use of industrial processes.

Look too at the internal frame of the carcass. Most antique frames in Britain and France are made of oak (in northern Europe and Italy they tend to be of a soft wood such as pine). Oak changes colour when exposed to air, so if you take a drawer out, it should be paler on the inside than on the underside, where it will have been exposed to the air. Generally speaking, if the grain on the baseboard of the drawer lining runs sideways it implies a greater age than where the grain runs from front to back.

Reflect on the timber. With woods such as mahogany or rosewood, colour is of the essence and adds to the value accordingly. The figuring – the way a timber is displayed for maximum decorative effect – also points to the skill of the maker. Rather than buying something that has been stripped and restored, you should value the natural patina – the build-up over centuries of wax and dirt which actually makes the richness of wood sing out. Again you do have to do some homework, though: French furniture, for example, tends to be far more highly polished than English, so a French piece that has spent its life in England will have a far richer patina of age than one from France. Do not be put off by scars and blemishes on the surface: they often add to the history and character of a piece.

Woodworm is something that people worry about perhaps more than is necessary. Undue staining might indicate a woodworm problem that someone has attempted to cover up, so you should investigate. Small holes may indicate that a piece has had worm, but that does not mean it is still live. Because of possible litigation, no auction house or dealer is likely to guarantee that a piece is definitely free of worm, but the chances are that it is not a problem. Tap the woodworm holes and if dust comes out of them, the worms are alive. The problem is very treatable, so do not let a few holes put you off buying something – but do make sure you tackle the problem quickly.

Provenance

Provenance is not just about knowing when a piece of furniture was made, by whom, or for whom. In fact you may know none of those things for certain and still have a piece of furniture with interesting provenance, because it is a question of building up knowledge of its entire life. If it was ever owned by someone notable, for example, then its worth is likely to go up accordingly; and it gives you a direct link to that person, which is in itself fascinating.

In Britain, we are lucky that so much documentation has survived from the great country

One of a pair of giltwood sofas supplied by Thomas Chippendale *c.* 1773 to Sir Penistone Lamb, 1st Viscount Melbourne, for the Saloon of Brocket Hall in Hertfordshire.

houses of the aristocracy, so it is often possible to trace back exactly when a piece of furniture was ordered, who commissioned it, and who made it. It is also rather fun to look through vintage copies of magazines, such as *Country Life*, see a piece in context decades ago, and note that it is unchanged. If you have an inherited piece of your own, that too has the added value of provenance connecting you to previous generations – something that makes it unique and of more than monetary value. Remember too that often there are lots of discoveries still to be made about an item of furniture. You may be buying something that will unravel its mysteries as in the best sort of detective story, as future generations' research may well fill in gaps. It is worth remembering that an interesting provenance also helps a piece keep its resale value.

Upholstery

Ideally, you should try to buy upholstered items that have retained their original webbing and fillings of horsehair, wool or down, because they provide the clue to the shape of the original upholstery. Leather-lined cushions are usually a sign that the upholstery is truly old. If you have a Regency sofa with its original shaped and tailored cushions, it is so much more satisfying than one where the cushions have been replaced with ubiquitous foam rubber or similar. The fact is that they did things better then – which is precisely why antiques never really fall from fashion. (For upholstery, see pp. 62–67.)

Newer webbing means that the chair has been renovated or may even be a reproduction. On close-nailed furniture, study the nails carefully. If they are identical, they have been manufactured industrially, which implies a date after 1850. Nails should not overlap, but have a small breathing space between them. This indicates the skill of the upholsterer; sloppy work often indicates a later restoration job.

It stands to reason that you should never buy something with its original upholstery intact and restore it with contemporary equivalents. Seek the help of a recommended specialist restorer who will be able to strengthen the upholstery without removing and replacing it.

BUYING AT AUCTION

First of all, make sure you fully understand the premium that will be payable if your bid is successful, and work out your budget accordingly. It makes sense to set a figure in your head that you will not go above: be warned that once the adrenaline starts rushing, it can be difficult to stop.

Premiums vary from auction house to auction house, but are usually in the region of 20 per cent on the price. There is normally a sliding scale: the greater the bid price of the lot in question, the lower the percentage of the premium. In Britain, VAT is payable on the premium, but not on the price of the lot, unless that has been imported from outside the EU.

The catalogue will give an estimate of the price that a lot is likely to reach, based on prices paid recently at auction for items of a comparable type, in similar condition, of similar rarity and provenance. Estimates do not include the buyer's premium or taxes. The reserve price is the confidential minimum price that the seller will accept. If a lot does not have a reserve price, this will usually be indicated in the catalogue.

To bid at auction, you will first have to register: this entitles you to a 'paddle', which you hold up when bidding, so that the auctioneer can identify you. Registration is the way that auction houses protect themselves and their clients from rogue bidders. They need to be sure you are who you say you are, so typically a new buyer will be asked to supply a bank reference and two forms of identification. Allow at least half an hour before the auction starts to complete the registration process. You can usually pay by credit card if you wish, and you are given roughly one week to settle your bill. If you renege on a bid, the auction house will pursue you through legal means.

If you can't attend the auction in person, you can ask the auction house to bid on your behalf. To do this, you write to the auction house stating the maximum price you are prepared to bid; the auction house will then bid for you at the lowest possible price (taking into account the reserve price). Telephone bidding is also possible in some instances.

Once you have paid for your lot, you will have a certain amount of free storage time (typically about twenty-eight days) before you must either remove your furniture or begin to pay storage costs. It makes sense, therefore, to plan any transport needed well in advance.

To restore or not?

There is a fine line to tread between conservation and restoration. In general terms, it is better to keep as much of the original as you can and to repair and conserve. Over-restoration can lower the value of a piece by destroying, for example, the surface patina of wood, traces of old gilding, or original upholstery materials.

It is usually better to buy something that may appear distressed, but has not been restored in any way, than to buy something that has been obviously repaired. You can restore an antique now with the best available knowledge of the 21st century, rather than first having to undo a bad restoration from the 19th or 20th century.

Beware of new products that promise miraculous results. Even museums have made errors of judgment, such as trying out on upholstery new much-lauded glues that have turned out to be fugitive, destroying the original fibres, or using 'wonder' oils on furniture that have seeped into the patina, ruining its beauty. On the whole, traditional tried-and-tested remedies are the safest and most effective. Beeswax is always preferable to chemical polishes, for example, because it does not destroy the natural surface of wood.

A George III fustic, wenge, mahogany and ebonized commode, supplied *c.* 1773–75 to the 9th Earl of Winchelsea and 4th Earl of Nottingham for Burley-on-the-Hill, Rutland, attributed to Mayhew and Ince.

There is an enormous wealth of knowledge available in the restoration and conservation world – people have made it their life's work – so make use of that information and do not do anything hasty.

★ ★ ★ ★ ★

AUTHORS' ACKNOWLEDGMENTS

We would like to thank all those who have given support to this book at Christie's, Linley, and Thames & Hudson, in particular the following.

At Christie's, John Hardy for his patience, wit, generosity of time and breadth of understanding; Amin Jaffer, Philippe Garner, John Hays, Joy McCall, Orlando Rock, Theow H. Tow and Charmian Baynham for sharing their special expertise; Charlotte Grant and her team at Christie's picture library, but most especially Margarita Crutchley and Laura Nixey for determinedly tracking down the archive images requested; Andrew Spira for checking the text with such painstaking care; Catherine Manson for her support, even while on maternity leave; all those in the furniture department who helped source reference material, especially Desiree Woehler for the heroic amount of photocopying she undertook on our behalf; and Jean Earley, Olivia Hague, Olivia Stewart and Anne Wakely for their constant efficiency and goodwill.

At Linley, Craig Allen, Christina Macmillan, Sarah Rose and John Wilsher for their time, knowledge and enthusiasm; also the Linley Marketing team for being such a support.

We would also like to thank Caroline Michel and Robert Caskie at PFD for their encouragement and persistence; Theo Theodorou, Alastair Graham and Gareth Williams for sharing their knowledge, enthusiasm and passion for the subject; Mr and Mrs Rolf Sachs and Mr and Mrs Julian Treger for generously allowing us access to their own furniture collections; Todd Merrill for his generosity in sharing his expertise; Andreas von Einsiedel for the original photography he undertook on our behalf (and the book's designer, Niki Medlik, who guided him); Lucy Macmillan for her invaluable help with picture research – and of course all the artists and designers who have allowed us to include examples of their work within these pages.

In addition, we would like to express the following individual thanks.

To my darling wife, Serena, and my wonderful children, Charles and Margarita, for their huge love and support. My mother, who throughout her life opened my eyes to beauty. My grandmother, Queen Elizabeth, who taught me to appreciate fine workmanship and who was a constant source of inspiration. My father for encouraging me to be observant and questioning, and also for his wicked sense of humour. Ruth Kennedy for her endless enthusiasm and everything she has done over many years. Philippe Lizop without whom so many things in my life would not have happened. And finally, my co-authors, Charles Cator and Helen Chislett, who have been an honour to work with and from whom I have learnt so much.

David Linley

To my parents, Peter and Katharine Cator, for their constant support, interest and encouragement throughout my working life at Christie's. My friends and colleagues (past and present) in the furniture and collections department at Christie's, many of whom are mentioned above, for the constant exchange of ideas and information. And of course my co-authors, David Linley and Helen Chislett.

Charles Cator

To John, Rosie and Florence for being so patient through the many 'lost' weekends spent on bringing this book to fruition: I could not have done it without you. To my parents for passing on a love of books and a love of writing. And to David and Charles for giving me the opportunity to work on such a fascinating project.

Helen Chislett

DESIGNERS

DAVID ADJAYE adjaye.com
AL-SABAH alsabahcollection.com
RON ARAD ronarad.com
ARANDA/LASCH arandalasch.com
ASYMPTOTE asymptote.net
AVL ateliervanlieshout.com
MAARTEN BAAS maartenbaas.com
BARBEROSGERBY barberosgerby.com
BASED UPON basedupon.co.uk
BISAZZA bisazza.com
TORD BOONTJE tordboontje.com
SEBASTIAN BRAJKOVIC sebastianbrajkovic.com
CAMPANA BROTHERS campanas.com
WENDELL CASTLE wendellcastle.com
AIVEEN DALY aiveendaly.com
DEMAKERSVAN demakersvan.com
TOM DIXON tomdixon.net
JULIENNE DOLPHIN-WILDING dolphinwilding.com
INGRID DONAT ingriddonat.com
DRIFT designdrift.nl
FREDRIKSON STALLARD fredriksonstallard.com
DAVID GATES davidgatesfurniture.co.uk
ALASTAIR GRAHAM alastairgraham.com
ZAHA HADID zahahadid.com
SARAH KAY kay-stemmer.com
THOMAS KENNEDY kennedy-scagliola.com
MAX LAMB maxlamb.org
DANNY LANE dannylane.co.uk
LITTON littonfurniture.com
JULIA LOHMANN julialohmann.co.uk
GONÇALO MABUNDA goncalomabunda.net
JOHN MAKEPEACE johnmakepeacefurniture.com
JULIAN MAYOR julianmayor.com
HELEN AMY MURRAY helenamymurray.com
GARETH NEAL garethnealfurniture.co.uk
MARC NEWSON marc-newson.com
POTTINGER & COLE pottingerandcole.co.uk
ANDRÉE PUTMAN andreeputman.com
CAROLYN QUARTERMAINE carolynquartermaine.com
MARC QUINN marcquinn.com
PABLO REINOSO pabloreinoso.com
ROLF SACHS rolfsachs.com
SENIOR & CARMICHAEL seniorcarmichael.co.uk
SPINA spinadesign.co.uk
SQUINT squintlimited.com
PHILIPPE STARCK starck.com
STUDIO JOB studiojob.nl
STUDIO MAKKINK & BEY jurgenbey.nl
ANDREW VARAH varah.co.uk
WALES & WALES walesandwales.com
MARCEL WANDERS marcelwanders.com
RICHARD WOODS richardwoodsstudio.com

GALLERIES

ALBION GALLERY
albion-gallery.com
CARPENTERS WORKSHOP GALLERY
3 Albemarle Street, London W1S 4HE
0044 203 051 5933
cwgdesign.com
CHRISTIE'S
salerooms in Amsterdam, Dubai, Geneva, Hong Kong,
London, Los Angeles, Milan, New York, Paris and Zurich
christies.com
CONTRASTS GALLERY
181 Middle Jiangxi Road, G/F, Shanghai 200002
0086 21 6323 1989
133 Middle Sichuan Road, B/F, Shanghai 200002
0086 21 6321 9606
798 Art District, 4 Jiu Xianqiao Road, Chao Yang District,
Beijing 100015
0086 10 6432 1369
contrastsgallery.com
DESIGN MIAMI/BASEL
designmiami.com
ESTABLISHED & SONS
5–7 Wenlock Road, London N1 7SL
0044 207 608 0990
2–3 Duke Street, St James's, London SW1Y 6BJ
0044 207 968 2040
establishedandsons.com
FRIEDMAN BENDA
515 West 26th Street, New York, NY 10001
001 212 239 8700
friedmanbenda.com
GAGOSIAN GALLERY
branches in Beverly Hills, Hong Kong, London, New York
and Rome
gagosian.com
DAVID GILL GALLERIES
3 Loughborough Street, London SE11 5RB
0044 207 793 1100
60 Fulham Road, London SW3 6HH
0044 207 589 5946
davidgillgalleries.com
CRISTINA GRAJALES
10 Greene Street, 4th floor, New York, NY 10013
001 212 219 9941
cristinagrajalesinc.com
JOHNSON TRADING GALLERY
490 Greenwich Street, New York, NY 10013
001 212 925 1110
johnsontradinggallery.com
LINLEY
60 Pimlico Road, London SW1W 8LP
0044 207 730 7300
46 Albemarle Street, London W1S 4JN
0044 207 290 1410
davidlinley.com

TODD MERRILL ANTIQUES
65 Bleecker Street, New York, NY 10012
001 212 673 0531
merrillantiques.com
META (at Mallett)
141 New Bond Street, London W1S 2BS
0044 207 495 5375
929 Madison Avenue, New York, NY 10021
001 212 249 8664
madebymeta.com
MOSS
152 Greene Street, New York, NY 10012
001 212 204 7100
8444 Melrose Avenue, Los Angeles, CA 90069
001 323 866 5260
mossonline.com
PERIMETER
47 rue Saint-André des Arts, 75006 Paris
0033 155 420122
perimeter-editions.com

KENNY SCHACHTER / ROVE
Lincoln House, 33–34 Hoxton Square, London N1 6NN
0044 7979 408 914
rovetv.net
SEBASTIAN & BARQUET
601 West 26th Street, Suite 300, New York, NY 100001
001 212 488 2245
19 Bruton Place, London W1J 61Z
0044 207 495 8988
sebastianbarquet.com
GALERIE PATRICK SEGUIN
5 rue des Taillandiers, 75011 Paris
00331 4700 3235
patrickseguin.com
TIMOTHY TAYLOR GALLERY
15 Carlos Place, London W1K 2EX
21 Dering Street, London W1S 1AL
0044 207 409 3344
timothytaylorgallery.com

SELECT BIBLIOGRAPHY

Nancy Aakre and Joanna Ekman, eds, *Courts and Colonies, the William and Mary Style in Holland, England and America*, University of Washington Press, New York, 1988

Göran Alm, *Great Royal Palaces of Sweden*, M.T. Train/Scala, Milan, 1997

Edward Deming Andrews and Faith Andrews, *Shaker Furniture, The Craftsmanship of an American Communal Sect*, Dover Publications, New York, 1937, 1964

Geoffrey Beard, *Upholsterers and Interior Furnishing in England, 1530–1840*, Yale University Press, New Haven and London, 1997

Charlotte Benton, Tim Benton and Ghislaine Wood, *Art Deco, 1910–1939*, V&A Publications, London, 2003

Adam Bowett, *English Furniture 1660–1714, from Charles II to Queen Anne*, Antique Collectors Club, Woodbridge, 2002

Antoine Chenevière, *Russian Furniture, The Golden Age 1780–1840*, Weidenfeld & Nicholson, London, 1988

Craig Clunas, *Chinese Furniture*, V&A Publications, Westerham, 1987

Frances Collard, *Regency Furniture*, Antique Collectors' Club, Woodbridge, 1985

Clive Edwards, *Encyclopaedia of Furniture Materials, Trades and Techniques*, Ashgate, Cambridge, 2000

Svend Eriksen, *Early Neo-Classicism in France*, Faber & Faber, London, 1974

Charlotte and Peter Fiell, *Modern Chairs*, Taschen, Cologne, 1993

John Fowler and John Cornforth, *English Decoration in the 18th Century*, Barrie & Jenkins, London, 1974

Christopher Gilbert, *The Life and Work of Thomas Chippendale*, Studio Vista for Cassell with Christie's, London, 1978

John Gloag, rev. Clive D. Edwards, *John Gloag's Dictionary of Furniture*, Unwin Paperbacks, London, 1990

Håkan Groth, *Neoclassicism in the North*, Thames & Hudson, London, 1990

Helen Hayward, ed., *World Furniture*, Hamlyn, London, 1965

Morrison H. Heckscher, *American Rococo*, Metropolitan Museum of Art, New York, 1992

Georg Himmelheber, *Biedermeier 1815–1835*, Prestel, Munich, 1989

Dawn Jacobsen, *Chinoiserie*, Phaidon, London, 1993

Amin Jaffer, *Furniture From British India and Ceylon*, V&A Publications, London, 2001

Edward Lennox-Boyd, ed., *Masterpieces of English Furniture, The Gerstenfield Collection*, Christie's, London, 1998

David Linley *Extraordinary Furniture*, Mitchell Beazley, London, 1996

Todd Merrill and Julie V. Iovine, *Modern Americana, Studio Furniture from High Craft to High Glam*, Rizzoli, New York, 2008

John Morley, *Regency Design, 1790–1840*, Zwemmer, London, 1993

— *The History of Furniture*, Thames & Hudson, London, and Bulfinch Press, Boston and New York, 1999

Gillian Naylor, *The Arts and Crafts Movement*, Studio Vista, London, 1971

Bill Pallot, *L'Art du siège au XVIIIe siècle en France*, A.C.R.-Gismondi Editions, Paris, 1987

Steven Parissien, *Regency Style*, Phaidon, London, 1992

Alexandre Pradere, *French Furniture Makers*, Sotheby's, London, 1989

Monique Riccardi-Cubitt, *The Art of the Cabinet*, Thames & Hudson, London, 1992

Peter Thornton, *Seventeenth-Century Interior Decoration in England, France and Holland*, Yale University Press, New Haven and London, 1978

Francis Watson et al., *The History of Furniture*, Orbis, London, 1976

PICTURE CREDITS

Where not otherwise stated, images are courtesy of Christie's Images Ltd.

frontispiece: top row, left With the kind permission of The Great Steward of Scotland's Dumfries House Trust, © Christie's Images 2007; *middle row, centre* Luke Hayes Photography; *middle row, right* Peter Wood; *bottom row, left* Severine van Wersch, courtesy of FAT Galerie; *bottom row, centre* Mark Henderson; *bottom row, right* Lee Mawdsley – 5 *top* Wayne Pottinger for Pottinger & Cole; *bottom* Peter Wood – 6 Alun Callender – 7, 8 courtesy of Linley – 9 Archives Galerie Aveline, Paris – 12 J. Cernius, courtesy of Todd Merrill Antiques – 14 Lee Funnell – 15 *left* courtesy of Galerie Patrick Seguin; *right* Marcos Bevilacqua – 16 Mark Henderson – 17 Byron Slater – 18 *above* courtesy of Marc Newson Ltd – 19 Andreas von Einsiedel, Use of 'La Chaise' courtesy of Eames Office, LLC (www.eamesoffice.com) – 20 © RMN/Daniel Arnaudet – 21 Luke Hayes Photography – 22, 23 Andreas von Einsiedel (*p. 23* © DACS 2009) – 25 courtesy of Friedman Benda – 29 Daria Scagliola en Stijn Brakkee – 30 *left* David Brook; *right* courtesy of Marc Newson Ltd – 31 *top* courtesy of Marc Newson Ltd; *centre* courtesy of Squint; *bottom* courtesy of Carpenters Workshop Gallery – 32 courtesy of Carpenters Workshop Gallery – 33 *above and below left* Severine van Wersch, courtesy of FAT Galerie; *below right* courtesy of Wales & Wales – 34 Peter Wood – 35 *above left* courtesy of Friedman Benda; *above right and below* courtesy of Carpenters Workshop Gallery – 36 Mark Henderson – 37 Andreas von Einsiedel – 38 *above and below* The Royal Collection © 2009 Her Majesty Queen Elizabeth II – 39 *above* Ed Reeve, courtesy of Albion Gallery; *below* courtesy of Marc Newson Ltd and Gagosian Gallery – 41 *above left* Mark Henderson; *below* courtesy of Alastair Graham – 42 Marcos Bevilacqua – 43 *above* Marcos Bevilacqua; *below* courtesy of Linley – 44 *above* Ed Reeve, courtesy of Albion Gallery; *below* courtesy of Marc Newson Ltd – 45 Ed Reeve, courtesy of Albion Gallery – 46 Luke Hayes Photography – 47 *above* courtesy of Philippe Starck; *below* courtesy of Ralph Nauta and Lonneke Gordijn – 49 *above* courtesy of Carpenters Workshop Gallery; *below* Philip Karlberg, courtesy of Established & Son – 51 R. Kot, courtesy of Moss, N.Y. – 55 *below* courtesy of Carpenters Workshop Gallery – 58 *above* Tom Foxall – 59 Alain Speltdoorn – 65 V&A Images/Victoria & Albert Museum – 68 courtesy of Carolyn Quartermaine and Château de Beloeil (chateaudebeloeil.com) – 69 courtesy of Aiveen Daly – 70 *top* courtesy of Robbie Spina and Joe Zito; *centre and bottom* courtesy of Aiveen Daly – 71 *above left and right* Marcos Bevilacqua; *below* courtesy of Linley – 72 *above* courtesy of Mattia Bonetti and Contrasts Gallery; *below* courtesy of Sheikh Majed J. Al Sabah – 73 courtesy of Squint – 76 courtesy of Linley – 77–79 Lee Mawdsley, courtesy of Meta – 82 Andreas von Einsiedel – 84 British Museum, London – 86 Wright and Brian Franczynk, courtesy of Todd Merrill Antiques – 87 *above* Museo dei Conservatori, Rome; *below* Museo Archeologico Nazionale, Naples – 98 With the kind permission of The Great Steward of Scotland's Dumfries House Trust, © Christie's Images 2007 – 99–102 copyright National Trust Picture Library/Andreas von Einsiedel – 103 Julian de Hauteclocque Howe, courtesy of Contrasts Gallery – 111 *left* Thomas Brown, courtesy of David Gill Galleries; *right* Federico Cedrone, courtesy of Bisazza – 119 *left* R. Kot, courtesy of Moss, N.Y.; *right* courtesy of Alastair Graham – 125 The Royal Collection © Her Majesty Queen Elizabeth II – 133 courtesy of Carpenters Workshop Gallery – 135 With the kind permission of The Great Steward of Scotland's Dumfries House Trust, © Christie's Images Ltd 2007 – 138 *above left* With the kind permission of The Great Steward of Scotland's Dumfries House Trust, © Christie's Images Ltd 2007 – 155 *left* courtesy of Linley; *right* Paul Lapsley – 161 Thomas Brown, courtesy of Mattia Bonetti and David Gill Galleries – 175 Reproduced courtesy of The American Museum in Britain (Bath U.K.) – 177 courtesy of Wales & Wales – 179 copyright National Trust Picture Library/Nadia Mackenzie – 186 Bibliothèque des Arts Décoratifs, Paris, Collection Maciet/ © ADAGP, Paris and DACS, London 2009 – 187 courtesy of Marc Newson Ltd – 191 *above* courtesy of Friedman Benda; *below* Dorsey Reading, courtesy of Todd Merrill Antiques – 192 courtesy of Eric Philippe Gallery, Todd Merrill Antiques – 193 Peter Wood – 194–95 courtesy of Carpenters Workshop Gallery – 196 courtesy of Carpenters Workshop Gallery – 198 Carin Katt, courtesy of Marc Newson Ltd – 199 courtesy of Carpenters Workshop Gallery – 200 Andreas von Einsiedel – 201 Ed Reeve, courtesy of Albion Gallery – 202 R. Kot, courtesy of Moss, N.Y. – 203 *top* courtesy of Marcel Wanders Studio/Cappellini; *centre* courtesy of Contrasts Gallery; *bottom* Alain Speltdoorn – 204, 205 Andreas von Einsiedel (*p. 205* © DACS 2009) – 206 *above* Andreas von Einsiedel, Use of Eames Rocking Chair (RAR) courtesy of Eames Office, LLC (www.eamesoffice.com); *below* R. Kot, courtesy of Moss, N.Y. – 207 R. Kot, courtesy of Moss, N.Y. – 208, 209 courtesy of Carpenters Workshop Gallery – 210 Thomas Brown, courtesy of David Gill Galleries – 211 James Champion – 212 Paul Lapsley – 213 *above* courtesy of Litton Furniture; *below* courtesy of John Makepeace – 214 *above* Paul Lapsley; *below* Peter Davey, courtesy of Kay & Stemmer – 215 *above* Paul Lapsley; *below* Damian Chapman – 216 courtesy of Wales & Wales – 217 *above* courtesy of Senior & Carmichael; *below left and far right, below* courtesy of John Makepeace; *below centre* courtesy of Linley; *far right, centre* Stuart Brown – 221–225 Andreas von Einsiedel – 226 courtesy of Linley – 227–230 Andreas von Einsiedel (*p. 229* coffee table courtesy of Mattia Bonetti; Use of 'La Chaise' courtesy of Eames Office, LLC (www.eamesoffice.com)– 231 courtesy of Donald Cameron, Todd Merrill Antiques – 233 Marianne Topham for Linley – 234, 235 Mark Henderson – 236 Edward Barber – 237 Peter Wood – 238–240 courtesy of Linley – 241 courtesy of Max Lamb – 243 Mark Henderson and Mr James Perkins

INDEX

Page numbers in *italic* refer to illustrations and related captions